PRAYERS
&
PRESIDENTS

INSPIRING FAITH
FROM LEADERS OF THE PAST

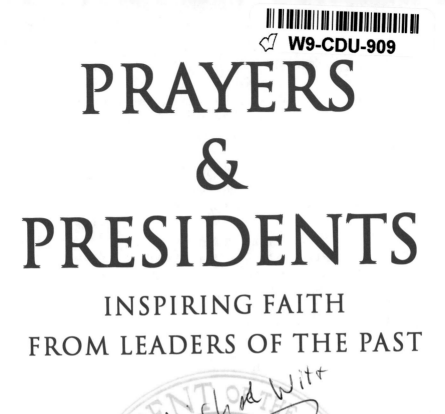

Fr. Michael Witt

America Needs You!

William Federer

WILLIAM J. FEDERER

PRAYERS and PRESIDENTS
-Inspiring Faith from Leaders of the Past
by William J. Federer

For other, contact: Amerisearch, Inc.
P.O. Box 20163 St. Louis, MO 63123
314-487-4395, 314-487-4489 fax 1-888-USA-WORD
www.amerisearch.net   wjfederer@gmail.com

HISTORY / EDUCATION   ISBN 978-0-9827101-1-1

Cover design by Dustin Myers,
DustinMyersDesign.com 573-308-6060

FREE EBOOK

As owner of this book, you have a limited-time
opportunity to receive a free pdf *ebook* of this title.
Simply email **wjfederer@gmail.com** with subject line

SEND FREE EBOOK "PRAYERS & PRESIDENTS"

Amerisearch, Inc., P.O. Box 20163, St. Louis, MO 63123
1-888-USA-WORD, 314-487-4395 voice/fax
www.amerisearch.net, wjfederer@gmail.com

TABLE OF CONTENTS

INTRODUCTION

Days of Prayer have a long history in America. Colonists declared Days of Prayer during droughts, Indian attacks and threats from other nations. Edward Winslow's record of the Pilgrims' experiences, reprinted in *Alexander Young's Chronicles of the Pilgrims* (Boston, 1841), stated:

"Drought and the like considerations moved not only every good man privately to enter into examination with his own estate between God and his conscience, and so to humiliation before Him, but also to humble ourselves together before the Lord by Fasting and Prayer."

In colonial Connecticut, settlers proclaimed by legal authority a day in early spring for Fasting and Prayer. The governor customarily selected Good Friday as the annual spring fast. In 1668, the Virginia House of Burgesses in Jamestown passed an ordinance stating:

"The 27th of August appointed for a Day of Humiliation, Fasting and Prayer, to implore God's mercy: if any person be found upon that day gaming, drinking, or working (works of necessity excepted), upon presentment by church-wardens and proof, he shall be fined one hundred pounds of tobacco."

A notable Day of Prayer was in 1746, when French Admiral d'Anville sailed for New England, commanding the most powerful fleet of the time - 70 ships with 13,000 troops. He intended to recapture Louisburg, Nova Scotia, and destroy from Boston to New York, all the way to Georgia. Massachusetts Governor William Shirley declared a Day of Prayer and Fasting, October 16, 1746, to pray for deliverance.

In Boston's Old South Meeting House, Rev. Thomas Prince prayed "Send Thy tempest, Lord, upon the water...scatter the ships of our tormentors!" Historian Catherine Drinker Bowen related that as he finished praying, the sky darkened, winds shrieked and church bells rang "a wild, uneven sound...though no man was in the steeple." A hurricane subsequently sank and scattered the entire French fleet.

With 4,000 sick and 2,000 dead, including Admiral d'Anville, French Vice-Admiral d'Estournelle threw himself on his sword. Henry Wadsworth Longfellow wrote in his *Ballad of the French Fleet*:

"Admiral d'Anville had sworn by cross and crown, to ravage with fire and steel our helpless Boston Town...From mouth to mouth spread tidings of dismay, I stood in the Old South saying humbly: 'Let us pray!'...Like a potter's vessel broke, the great ships of the line, were carried away as smoke or sank in the brine."

As raids from France and Spain increased, Ben Franklin proposed a General Fast, which was approved by Pennsylvania's President and Council, and published in the Pennsylvania Gazette, December 12, 1747:

"We have...thought fit...to appoint...a Day of Fasting & Prayer, exhorting all, both Ministers & People...to join with one accord in the most humble & fervent supplications that Almighty God would mercifully interpose and still the rage of war among the nations & put a stop to the effusion of Christian blood."

On May 24, 1774, Thomas Jefferson drafted a Resolution for a Day of Fasting, Humiliation and Prayer to be observed as the British blockaded Boston's Harbor. Robert Carter Nicholas, Treasurer, introduced the Resolution in the Virginia House of Burgesses, and, with support of Patrick Henry, Richard Henry Lee and George Mason, it passed unanimously:

"This House, being deeply impressed with apprehension of the great dangers, to be derived to British America, from the hostile invasion of the City of Boston, in our sister Colony of Massachusetts... deem it highly necessary that the said first day of June be set apart, by the members of this House as a Day of Fasting, Humiliation and Prayer, devoutly to implore the Divine interposition, for averting the heavy calamity which threatens destruction to our civil rights...Ordered, therefore that the Members of this House do attend...with the Speaker, and the Mace, to the Church in this City, for the purposes aforesaid; and that the Reverend Mr. Price be appointed to read prayers, and the Reverend Mr. Gwatkin, to preach a sermon."

George Washington wrote in his diary, June 1, 1774: "Went to church, fasted all day." Virginia's Royal Governor, Lord Dunmore, interpreted this Resolution as a veiled protest against King George III, and dissolved the House of Burgesses, resulting in legislators meeting in Raleigh Tavern where they conspired to form the first Continental Congress.

On April 15, 1775, just four days before the Battle of Lexington, the Massachusetts Provincial Congress, led by John Hancock, declared:

"In circumstances dark as these, it becomes us, as men and Christians, to reflect that, whilst every prudent measure should be taken to ward off the impending judgments...the 11th of May next be set apart as a Day of Public Humiliation, Fasting and Prayer...to confess the sins...to implore the Forgiveness of all our Transgression."

On April 19, 1775, in a Proclamation of a Day of Fasting and Prayer, Connecticut Governor Jonathan Trumbull beseeched that:

"God would graciously pour out His Holy Spirit on us to bring us to a thorough repentance and effectual reformation that our iniquities may not be our ruin; that He would restore, preserve and secure the liberties of this and all the other British American colonies, and make the land a mountain of Holiness, and habitation of righteousness forever."

On June 12, 1775, less than two months after the Battles of Lexington and Concord, where was fired "the shot heard 'round the world," the Continental Congress, under President John Hancock, declared:

"Congress...considering the present critical, alarming and calamitous state...do earnestly recommend, that Thursday, the 12th of July next, be observed by the inhabitants of all the English Colonies on this Continent, as a Day of Public Humiliation, Fasting and Prayer, that we may with united hearts and voices, unfeignedly confess and deplore our many sins and offer up our joint supplications to the All-wise, Omnipotent and merciful Disposer of all Events, humbly beseeching Him to forgive our iniquities...It is recommended to Christians of all denominations to assemble for public worship and to abstain from servile labor and recreations of said day."

On July 5, 1775, the Georgia Provincial Congress passed:

"A motion...that this Congress apply to his Excellency the Governor...requesting him to appoint a Day of Fasting and Prayer throughout this Province, on account of the disputes subsisting between America and the Parent State."

On July 7, 1775, Georgia's Provincial Governor replied:

"Gentlemen: I have taken the...request made by...a Provincial Congress, and must premise, that I cannot consider that meeting as constitutional; but as the request is expressed in such loyal and dutiful terms, and the ends proposed being such as every good man must most ardently wish for, I will certainly appoint a Day of Fasting and Prayer to be observed throughout this Province. Jas. Wright."

On July 12, 1775, in a letter to his wife explaining the

Continental Congress' decision to declare a Day of Public Humiliation, Fasting and Prayer, John Adams wrote:

"We have appointed a Continental fast. Millions will be upon their knees at once before their great Creator, imploring His forgiveness and blessing; His smiles on American Council and arms."

On July 19, 1775, the Continental Congress' Journals recorded:

"Agreed, The Congress meet here to morrow morning, at half after 9 o'clock, in order to attend divine service at Mr. Duche's' Church; and that in the afternoon they meet here to go from this place and attend divine service at Doctor Allison's church."

In his Cambridge headquarters, Washington ordered, March 6, 1776:

"Thursday, the 7th...being set apart...as a Day of Fasting, Prayer and Humiliation, 'to implore the Lord and Giver of all victory to pardon our manifold sins and wickedness, and that it would please Him to bless the Continental army with His divine favor and protection,' all officers and soldiers are strictly enjoined to pay all due reverence and attention on that day to the sacred duties to the Lord of hosts for His mercies already received, and for those blessings which our holiness and uprightness of life can alone encourage us to hope through His mercy obtain."

On March 16, 1776, the Continental Congress passed without dissent a resolution presented by General William Livingston declaring:

"Congress....desirous...to have people of all ranks and degrees duly impressed with a solemn sense of God's superintending providence, and of their duty, devoutly to rely...on his aid and direction...do earnestly recommend Friday, the 17th day of May be observed by the colonies as a Day of Humiliation, Fasting and Prayer; that we may, with united hearts, confess and bewail our manifold sins and transgressions, and, by sincere repentance and amendment of life, appease God's righteous displeasure, and, through the merits and mediation of Jesus Christ, obtain this pardon and forgiveness."

On May 15, 1776, General George Washington ordered:

"The Continental Congress having ordered Friday the 17th instant to be observed as a Day of Fasting, Humiliation and Prayer, humbly to supplicate the mercy of Almighty God, that it would please Him to pardon all our manifold sins and transgressions, and to prosper the arms of the United Colonies, and finally establish the peace and freedom of America upon a solid and lasting foundation; the General commands all officers and soldiers to pay strict obedience to the orders of the Continental Congress; that, by their unfeigned and pious observance of their religious duties, they may incline the Lord and Giver of victory to prosper our arms."

On April 12, 1778, at Valley Forge, General Washington ordered:

"The Honorable Congress having thought proper to recommend to the United States of America to set apart Wednesday, the 22nd inst., to be observed as a day of Fasting, Humiliation and Prayer, that at one time, and with one voice, the righteous dispensations of Providence may be acknowledged, and His goodness and mercy towards our arms supplicated and implored: The General directs that the day shall be most religiously observed in the Army; that no work shall be done thereon, and that the several chaplains do prepare discourses."

On April 6, 1780, at Morristown, General Washington ordered:

"Congress having been pleased by their Proclamation of the 11th of last month to appoint Wednesday the 22nd instant to be set apart and observed as a day of Fasting, Humiliation and Prayer...there should be no labor or recreations on that day."

On October 11, 1782, the Congress of the Confederation passed:

"It being the indispensable duty of all nations...to offer up their supplications to Almighty God...the United States in Congress assembled...do hereby recommend it to the inhabitants of these states in general, to observe...the last Thursday, in the 28th day of November next, as a Day of Solemn Thanksgiving to God for all his mercies."

On November 8, 1783, at the conclusion of the Revolutionary War, Massachusetts Governor John Hancock issued:

"The Citizens of these United States have every Reason for Praise and Gratitude to the God of their salvation...I do...appoint...the 11th day of December next (the day recommended by the Congress to all the States) to be religiously observed as a Day of Thanksgiving and Prayer, that all the people may then assemble to celebrate...that he hath been pleased to continue to us the Light of the Blessed Gospel...That we also offer up fervent supplications...to cause pure Religion and Virtue to flourish...and to fill the world with his glory.

On February 21, 1786, New Hampshire Governor John Langdon proclaimed: a Day of Public Fasting and Prayer:

"It having been the laudable practice of this State, at the opening of the Spring, to set apart a day...to...penitently confess their manifold sins and transgressions, and fervently implore the divine benediction, that a true spirit of repentance and humiliation may be poured out upon all...that he would be pleased to bless the great Council of the United States of America and direct their deliberations...that he would rain down righteousness upon the earth, revive religion, and spread abroad the knowledge of the true God, the Saviour of man, throughout the world. And all servile labor and recreations are forbidden on said day."

At the Constitutional Convention, 1787, Ben Franklin stated:

"In the beginning of the Contest with Great Britain, when we were sensible of danger, we had daily prayer in this room for Divine protection."

Proclaiming a Day of Prayer, Ronald Reagan said January 27, 1983:

"In 1775, the Continental Congress proclaimed the first National Day of Prayer...In 1783, the Treaty of Paris officially ended the long, weary Revolutionary War during which a National Day of Prayer had been proclaimed every spring for eight years."

On October 31, 1785, James Madison introduced a bill in the Virginia Legislature titled, "For Appointing Days of Public Fasting and Thanksgiving," which included: "Forfeiting fifty pounds for every failure, not having a reasonable excuse."

Yale College had as its requirement, 1787:

"All the scholars are obliged to attend Divine worship in the College Chapel on the Lord's Day and on Days of Fasting and Thanksgiving appointed by public authority."

The same week Congress passed the Bill of Rights, President George Washington declared, October 3, 1789:

"It is the duty of all nations to acknowledge the Providence of Almighty God, to obey His will...and humbly to implore His protection and favor; and Whereas both Houses of Congress have by their joint Committee requested me 'to recommend to the People of the United States a Day of Public Thanksgiving and Prayer to be observed by acknowledging with grateful hearts the many signal favors of Almighty God, especially by affording them an opportunity peaceably to establish a form of government for their safety and happiness'...

"I do recommend...the 26th day of November next, to be devoted by the People of these United States to the service of that great and glorious Being, who is the beneficent Author of all the good that was, that is, or that will be; That we may then all unite in rendering unto Him our sincere and humble thanks...for the peaceable and rational manner in which we have been enabled to establish constitutions of government for our safety and happiness, and particularly the national one now lately instituted, for the civil and religious liberty with which we are blessed...Humbly offering our prayers...to the great Lord and Ruler of Nations, and beseech Him to pardon our national and other transgressions."

After the Whiskey Rebellion in western Pennsylvania, President Washington proclaimed a Day of Prayer, January 1, 1796:

"All persons within the United States, to...render sincere and hearty thanks to the great Ruler of nations...particularly for the possession of constitutions of government...and fervently beseech the kind Author of these blessings...to establish habits of sobriety, order, and morality and piety."

During a threatened war with France, President John Adams declared a Day of Fasting, March 23, 1798, then again on March 6, 1799:

"As...the people of the United States are still held in jeopardy by...insidious acts of a foreign nation, as well as by the dissemination among them of those principles subversive to the foundations of all religious, moral, and social obligations...I hereby recommend...a Day of Solemn Humiliation, Fasting and Prayer; That the citizens...call to mind our numerous offenses against the Most High God, confess them before Him with the sincerest penitence, implore His pardoning mercy, through the Great Mediator and Redeemer, for our past transgressions, and that through the grace of His Holy Spirit, we may be disposed and enabled to yield a more suitable obedience to His righteous requisitions... 'Righteousness exalteth a nation but sin is a reproach to any people.'"

James Madison, known as the "Chief Architect of the Constitution," wrote many of the Federalist Papers, convincing the States to ratify the Constitution, and introduced the First Amendment in the first session of Congress. During the War of 1812, President James Madison proclaimed a Day of Prayer, July 9, 1812, stating:

"I do therefore recommend...rendering the Sovereign of the Universe...public homage...acknowledging the transgressions which might justly provoke His divine displeasure...seeking His merciful forgiveness...and with a reverence for the unerring precept of our holy religion, to do to others as they would require that others should do to them."

On July 23, 1813, Madison issued another Day of Prayer, referring to: "religion, that gift of Heaven for the good of man." When the British marched on Washington, D.C., citizens evacuated, along with President and Dolly Madison. The British burned the White House, Capitol and public buildings on August 25, 1814.

Suddenly dark clouds rolled in and a tornado touched down sending debris flying, blowing off roofs and knocking down chimneys on British troops. Two cannons were lifted off the ground and dropped yards away. A British historian wrote: "More British soldiers were killed by this stroke of nature than from all the firearms the American troops had mustered." British forces then fled and rains extinguished the fires.

James Madison responded by proclaiming, November 16, 1814:

"In the present time of public calamity and war a day may be...observed by the people of the United States as a Day of Public Humiliation and Fasting and of Prayer to Almighty God for the safety and welfare of these States...of confessing their sins and transgressions, and of strengthening their vows of repentance...that He would be graciously pleased to pardon all their offenses."

In 1832, as an Asiatic Cholera outbreak gripped New York, Henry Clay asked for a Joint Resolution of Congress to request the President set:

"A Day of Public Humiliation, Prayer and Fasting to be observed by the people of the United States with religious solemnity."

On April 13, 1841, when 9th President William Harrison died, President John Tyler issued a Day of Prayer and Fasting:

"When a Christian people feel themselves to be overtaken by a great public calamity, it becomes them to humble themselves under the dispensation of Divine Providence."

On July 3, 1849, during a cholera epidemic, President Zachary Taylor proclaimed:

"The providence of God has manifested itself in the visitation of a fearful pestilence which is spreading itself throughout the land, it is fitting that a people whose reliance has ever been in His protection should humble themselves before His throne...acknowledging past transgressions, ask a continuance of the Divine mercy. It is earnestly recommended that the first Friday in August be observed throughout the United States as a Day of Fasting, Humiliation and Prayer."

On December 14, 1860, President James Buchanan issued a Proclamation of a National Day of Humiliation, Fasting and Prayer:

"In this the hour of our calamity and peril to whom shall we resort for relief but to the God of our fathers? His omnipotent arm only can save us from the awful effects of our own crimes and follies...Let us...unite in humbling ourselves before the Most High, in confessing our individual and national sins...Let me invoke every individual, in whatever sphere of life he may be placed, to feel a personal responsibility to God and his country for keeping this day holy."

On August 12, 1861, after the Union lost the Battle of Bull Run, President Abraham Lincoln proclaimed:

"It is fit...to acknowledge and revere the Supreme Government of God; to bow in humble submission to His chastisement; to confess and deplore their sins and transgressions in the full conviction that the fear of the Lord is the beginning of wisdom...Therefore I, Abraham Lincoln...do appoint the last Thursday in September next as a Day of Humiliation, Prayer and Fasting for all the people of the nation."

On March 30, 1863, President Abraham Lincoln proclaimed a National Day of Humiliation, Fasting and Prayer:

"The awful calamity of civil war...may be but a punishment inflicted upon us for our presumptuous sins to the needful end of our national reformation as a whole people...We have forgotten God...We have vainly imagined, in the deceitfulness of our hearts, that all these blessings were produced by some superior wisdom and virtue of our own. Intoxicated with unbroken success, we have become...too proud to pray to the God that made us! It behooves us then to humble ourselves before the offended Power, to confess our national sins."

After Lincoln was shot, President Johnson issued, April 29, 1865:

"The 25th day of next month was recommended as a Day for Special Humiliation and Prayer in consequence of the assassination of Abraham Lincoln...but Whereas my attention has since been called to the fact that the day aforesaid is sacred to large numbers of Christians as one of rejoicing for the ascension of the Savior: Now...I, Andrew

Johnson, President of the United States, do suggest that the religious services recommended as aforesaid should be postponed until...the 1st day of June."

During World War I, President Wilson proclaimed May 11, 1918:

"'It being the duty peculiarly incumbent in a time of war humbly and devoutly to acknowledge our dependence on Almighty God and to implore His aid and protection...I, Woodrow Wilson...proclaim...a Day of Public Humiliation, Prayer and Fasting, and do exhort my fellow-citizens...to pray Almighty God that He may forgive our sins."

During World War II, Franklin D. Roosevelt prayed during the D-Day invasion of Normandy, June 6, 1944:

"Almighty God, our sons, pride of our nation, this day have set upon a mighty endeavor, a struggle to preserve our Republic, our Religion and our Civilization, and to set free a suffering humanity...Help us, Almighty God, to rededicate ourselves in renewed faith in Thee in this hour of great sacrifice."

When WWII ended, President Truman declared in a Day of Prayer, August 16, 1945:

"The warlords of Japan...have surrendered unconditionally... This is the end of the...schemes of dictators to enslave the peoples of the world...Our global victory...has come with the help of God...Let us...dedicate ourselves to follow in His ways."

In 1952, President Truman made the National Day of Prayer an annual observance, stating:

"In times of national crisis when we are striving to strengthen the foundations of peace...we stand in special need of Divine support."

In April of 1970, President Richard Nixon had the nation observe a Day of Prayer for Apollo 13 astronauts.

On May 5, 1988, President Reagan made the National Day of Prayer the first Thursday in May, saying:

"Americans in every generation have turned to their Maker in prayer...We have acknowledged...our dependence on Almighty God."

President George W. Bush declared Days of Prayer after the Islamic terrorist attacks of September 11, 2001, and after Hurricane Katrina.

As America faces challenges in the economy, from terrorism and natural disasters, one can gain inspiring faith from leaders of the past.

᷈

GEORGE WASHINGTON

GEORGE WASHINGTON, JUN. 1, 1774, DIARY ENTRY ON DAY BRITISH BLOCKADED BOSTON'S HARBOR:

Went to church and fasted all day.

❦

GEORGE WASHINGTON, JUL. 4, 1775, ORDER FROM CAMBRIDGE HEADQUARTERS TO ARMY:

The General most earnestly requires, and expects due observance of those articles of war...which forbid profane cursing, swearing and drunkenness; And in like manner requires and expects, of all Officers, and Soldiers, not engaged on actual duty, a punctual attendance of Divine Services, to implore the blessings of Heaven upon the means used for our safety and defense.

❦

GEORGE WASHINGTON, SEP. 14, 1775, TO COLONEL ARNOLD ON ADVANCING INTO CANADA:

I also give it in charge to you to avoid all disrespect of the religion of the country, and its ceremonies. Prudence, policy, and a true Christian spirit will lead us to look with compassion upon their errors without insulting them. While we are contending for our own liberty, we should be very cautious not to violate the rights of conscience of others, ever considering that God alone is the Judge of the hearts of men, and to Him only in this case they are answerable.

≪

GEORGE WASHINGTON, JUL. 2, 1776, ORDER FROM NEW YORK HEADQUARTERS:

The time is now near at hand which must probably determine whether Americans are to be freemen or slaves; whether they are to have any property they can call their own; whether their houses and farms are to be pillaged and destroyed, and themselves consigned to a state of wretchedness from which no human efforts will deliver them.

The fate of unborn millions will now depend, under God, on the courage and conduct of this army. Our cruel and unrelenting enemy leaves us no choice but a brave resistance, or the most abject submission. We have, therefore to resolve to conquer or die. Our own country's honor calls upon us for a vigorous and manly exertion, and if we now shamefully fail, we shall become infamous to the whole world.

Let us rely upon the goodness of the cause, and the aid of the Supreme Being in whose hands victory is, to animate and encourage us to great and noble actions.

≪

GEORGE WASHINGTON, JUL. 9, 1776, ORDER FROM NEW YORK HEADQUARTERS UPON RECEIVING DECLARATION:

The Colonels or commanding officers of each regiment are directed to procure Chaplains...to see that all inferior officers and soldiers pay them a suitable respect and attend carefully upon religious exercises.

The blessing and protection of Heaven are at all times necessary but especially so in times of public distress and danger -The General hopes and trusts, that every officer and man, will endeavour so to live, and act, as becomes a Christian Soldier, defending the dearest Rights and Liberties of his country.

≪

GEORGE WASHINGTON, AUG. 3, 1776, ORDER TO ARMY, PAROLE UXBRIDGE, COUNTERSIGN VIRGINIA:

Troops may have an opportunity of attending public worship,

as well as take some rest after the great fatigue they have come through; The General in future excuses them from fatigue duty on Sundays...

The General is sorry to be informed that the foolish, and wicked practice, of profane cursing and swearing (a Vice heretofore little known in an American Army) is growing into fashion; he hopes the officers will, by example, as well as influence, endeavour to check it, and that both they, and the men will reflect, that we can have little hopes of the blessing of Heaven on our Arms, if we insult it by our impiety, and folly; added to this, it is a vice so mean and low, without any temptation, that every man of sense, and character, detests and despises it.

∾

GEORGE WASHINGTON, APR. 21, 1778, LETTER FROM VALLEY FORGE TO JOHN BANISTER ON PAST WINTER:

No history, now extant, can furnish an instance of an Army's suffering such uncommon hardships as ours has done and bearing them with the same patience and fortitude. To see men without clothes to cover their nakedness, without blankets to lay on, without shoes, by which their marches might be traced by the blood from their feet, and almost as often without provisions as with; marching through frost and snow, and at Christmas taking up their winter quarters within a day's march of the enemy, without a house or hut to cover them till they could be built and submitting without a murmur, is a mark of patience and obedience which in my opinion can scarce be paralleled.

∾

GEORGE WASHINGTON, MAY 2, 1778, TO TROOPS AT VALLEY FORGE:

The Commander-in-Chief directs that Divine service be performed every Sunday at 11 o'clock, in each Brigade which has a Chaplain. Those Brigades which have none will attend the places of worship nearest to them. It is expected that officers of all ranks will, by their attendance, set an example for their men. While we are zealously performing the duties of good citizens and soldiers, we certainly ought not to be inattentive to the higher duties of religion. To the distinguished character of Patriot, it should be our highest Glory to laud the more distinguished Character of Christian.

∾

GEORGE WASHINGTON, MAY 12, 1779, MIDDLE BROOK ENCAMPMENT ADDRESS TO DELAWARE CHIEFS ON INDIAN YOUTHS TO BE TRAINED IN AMERICAN SCHOOLS:

Brothers: I am glad you have brought three of the Children of your principal Chiefs to be educated with us. I am sure Congress will open the Arms of love to them, and will look upon them as their own Children, and will have them educated accordingly. This is a great mark of your confidence and of your desire to preserve the friendship between the Two Nations to the end of time, and to become One people with your Brethren of the United States...

You do well to wish to learn our arts and ways of life, and above all, the religion of Jesus Christ. These will make you a greater and happier people than you are. Congress will do everything they can to assist you in this wise intention; and to tie the knot of friendship and union so fast, that nothing shall ever be able to loose it...And I pray God He may make your Nation wise and strong.

∽

GEORGE WASHINGTON, JUN. 14, 1783, TO GOVERNORS ON DISBANDING ARMY, ON PLAQUE IN ST. PAUL'S CHAPEL, NY, AND POHICK CHURCH, FAIRFAX COUNTY, VA, WHERE WASHINGTON WAS VERSTRYMAN 1762-84:

Almighty God; We make our earnest prayer that Thou wilt keep the United States in Thy Holy protection; and Thou wilt incline the hearts of the Citizens to cultivate a spirit of subordination and obedience to Government; and entertain a brotherly affection and love for one another and for their fellow Citizens of the United States at large, and particularly for their brethren who have served in the Field.

And finally that Thou wilt most graciously be pleased to dispose us all to do justice, to love mercy, and to demean ourselves with that Charity, humility, and pacific temper of mind which were the Characteristics of the Divine Author of our blessed Religion, and without a humble imitation of whose example in these things we can never hope to be a happy nation. Grant our supplication, we beseech Thee, through Jesus Christ our Lord. Amen.

∽

GEORGE WASHINGTON, FEB. 8, 1785, FROM MOUNT VERNON TO CONTINENTAL CONGRESS PRESIDENT:

Toward the latter part of the year 1783, I was honored with a letter from the Countess of Huntington, briefly reciting her benevolent intention of spreading Christianity among the Tribes of Indians inhabiting our Western Territory; and expressing a desire of my advice and assistance to carry this charitable design into execution. I wrote her Ladyship...that I would give every aid in my power, consistent with the ease and tranquility, to which I meant to devote the remainder of my life, to carry her plan into effect...Her Ladyship has spoken so feelingly and sensibly, on the religious and benevolent purposes of the plan, that no language of which I am possessed, can add aught to enforce her observations.

ॐ

GEORGE WASHINGTON, MAY 25, 1787, OPENING REMARKS TO DELEGATES OF CONSTITUTIONAL CONVENTION, INDEPENDENCE HALL, PHILADELPHIA:

The event is in the Hand of God!

ॐ

GEORGE WASHINGTON, AUG. 15, 1787, LETTER FROM PHILADELPHIA TO MARQUIS DE LAFAYETTE:

I am not less ardent in my wish that you may succeed in your plan of toleration in religious matters. Being no bigot myself to any mode of worship, I am disposed to indulge the professors of Christianity in the church with that road to Heaven which to them shall seem the most direct, plainest and easiest, and the least liable to exception.

ॐ

GEORGE WASHINGTON, APR. 30, 1789, FIRST INAUGURAL:

It would be peculiarly improper to omit, in this first official act, my fervent supplications to that Almighty Being who rules over the universe, who presides in the councils of nations and whose providential aids can supply every human defect...

In tendering this homage to the Great Author of every public and private good, I assure myself that it expresses your sentiments not less than my own...

We ought to be no less persuaded that the propitious smiles of Heaven can never be expected on a nation that disregards the eternal rules of order and right which Heaven itself has ordained.

❧

GEORGE WASHINGTON, MAY 10, 1789, TO UNITED BAPTIST CHURCHES OF VIRGINIA:

If I could have entertained the slightest apprehension that the Constitution framed by the Convention, where I had the honor to preside, might possibly endanger the religious rights of any ecclesiastical Society, certainly I would never have placed my signature to it;...for you doubtless remember I have often expressed my sentiments, that any man, conducting himself as a good citizen, and being accountable to God alone for his religious opinions, ought to be protected in worshipping the Deity according to the dictates of his own conscience.

❧

GEORGE WASHINGTON, MAY 1789, TO GENERAL ASSEMBLY OF PRESBYTERIAN CHURCHES IN THE US:

It is not necessary for me to conceal the satisfaction I have felt upon finding that my compliance with the call of my country and my dependence on the assistance of Heaven to support me in my arduous undertakings have, so far as I can learn, met the universal approbation of my countrymen. While I reiterate the professions of my dependence upon Heaven as the source of all public and private blessings; I will observe that the general prevalence of piety, philanthropy, honesty, industry, and economy seems, in the ordinary course of human affairs, particularly necessary for advancing and conforming the happiness of our country.

While all men within our territories are protected in worshipping the Deity according to the dictates of their consciences; it is rationally to be expected from them in return, that they will be emulous of evincing the sanctity of their professions by the innocence of their lives and the beneficence of their actions; for no man who is profligate in his morals, or a bad member of the civil community, can possibly be a true Christian, or a credit to his own religious society.

I desire you to accept my acknowledgments for your laudable endeavors to render men sober, honest, and good citizens, and the obedient subjects of a lawful government, as well as for your prayers to Almighty God for His blessings on our common country, and the humble instrument which He has been pleased to make use of in the administration of its government.

∽

GEORGE WASHINGTON, REPLY TO MAY 6, 1789 LETTER FROM HEBREW CONGREGATION, SAVANNAH, GEORGIA:

Happily the people of the United States have in many instances exhibited examples worthy of imitation, the salutary influence of which will doubtless extend much farther if gratefully enjoying those blessings of peace which (under the favor of Heaven) have been attained by fortitude in war, they shall conduct themselves with reverence to the Deity and charity toward their fellow-creatures.

May the same wonder-working Deity, who long since delivering the Hebrews from their Egyptian Oppressors planted them in the promised land - whose Providential Agency has lately been conspicuous in establishing these United States as an independent Nation - still continue to water them with the dews of Heaven and to make the inhabitants of every denomination participate in the temporal and spiritual blessings of that people whose God is Jehovah.

∽

GEORGE WASHINGTON, JUL. 1789, TO DIRECTORS OF THE SOCIETY OF UNITED BRETHREN:

You will also be pleased to accept my thanks for the treatise you presented, (An account of the manner in which the Protestant Church of the Unitas Fratrum, or United Brethren, preach the Gospel and carry on their mission among the Heathen,) and be assured of my patronage in your laudable undertakings...It will be a desirable thing, for the protection of the Union, to co-operate...with the disinterested endeavors of your Society to civilize and Christianize the Savages of the Wilderness. Under these impressions, I pray Almighty God to have you always in His Holy keeping.

∽

GEORGE WASHINGTON, AUG. 1789, TO EPISCOPAL CHURCH OF NEW YORK, NEW JERSEY, PENNSYLVANIA, DELAWARE, MARYLAND, VIRGINIA & NORTH CAROLINA:

Gentlemen: I sincerely thank you for your affectionate congratulations on my election to the chief magistracy of the United States...On this occasion it would ill become me to conceal the joy I have felt in perceiving the fraternal affection, which appears to increase every day among friends of genuine religion.

It affords edifying prospects, indeed, to see Christians of different denominations dwell together in more charity, and conduct themselves in respect to each other with a more Christian-like spirit than every they have done in any former age, or in any other nation.

I receive with the greater satisfaction your congratulations on the establishment of the new constitution of government...The moderation, patriotism, and wisdom of the present federal Legislature seem to promise the restoration of order and our ancient virtues, the extension of genuine religion, and the consequent advancement of our respectability abroad, and of our substantial happiness at home. I request, most reverend and respected Gentlemen, that you will accept my cordial thanks for your devout supplications to the Supreme Ruler of the Universe in behalf of me. May you, and the people whom you represent, be the happy subjects of the divine benedictions both here and hereafter.

❦

GEORGE WASHINGTON, OCT. 3, 1789, NATIONAL DAY OF THANKSGIVING PROCLAMATION:

Whereas it is the duty of all nations to acknowledge the Providence of Almighty God, to obey His will, to be grateful for his benefits, and humbly to implore His protection and favor...we may then unite in most humbly offering our prayers and supplications to the great Lord and Ruler of Nations, and beseech Him to pardon our national and other transgressions, to enable us all...to render our national government a blessing to all the People...to promote the knowledge and practice of true religion and virtue.

❦

GEORGE WASHINGTON, JAN. 1790, TO HEBREW CONGREGATIONS OF PHILADELPHIA, NEWPORT, CHARLESTOWN & RICHMOND:

The liberal sentiment towards each other which marks every

political and religious denomination of men in this country stands unrivaled in the history of nations...The power and goodness of the Almighty were strongly manifested in the events of our late glorious revolution and His kind interpositions in our behalf has been no less visible in the establishment on our present equal government.

In war He directed the sword and in peace He has ruled in our councils. My agency in both has been guided by the best intentions, and a sense of the duty which I owe my country...May the same temporal and eternal blessings which you implore for me, rest upon your congregations.

✍

GEORGE WASHINGTON, MAR. 15, 1790, TO BISHOP JOHN CARROLL & ROMAN CATHOLICS OF AMERICA:

I feel that my conduct, in war and in peace, has met with more general approbation than could reasonably have been expected and I find myself disposed to consider that fortunate circumstance, in a great degree, resulting from the able support and extraordinary candour of my fellow-citizens of all denominations...

America, under the smiles of a Divine Providence, the protection of a good government, and the cultivation of manners, morals, and piety, cannot fail of attaining an uncommon degree of eminence, in literature, commerce, agriculture, improvements at home and respectability abroad...I presume that your fellow-citizens will not forget the patriotic part which you took in the accomplishment of their Revolution, and the establishment of their government; or the important assistance which they received from a nation in which the Roman Catholic faith is professed...

May the members of your society in America, animated alone by the pure spirit of Christianity, and still conducting themselves as the faithful subjects of our free government, enjoy every temporal and spiritual felicity.

✍

GEORGE WASHINGTON, AUG. 17, 1790, TO HEBREW CONGREGATION, NEWPORT, RHODE ISLAND:

It is now no more that toleration is spoken of as if it were the indulgence of one class of people that another enjoyed the exercise of their inherent natural rights, for, happily, the Government of the United States, which gives to bigotry no sanction, to persecution no assistance, requires only that they who live under its protection should demean themselves as good citizens in giving it on all occasions their effectual support...

May the children of the stock of Abraham who dwell in this land continue to merit and enjoy the good will of the other inhabitants - while every one shall sit in safety under his own vine and fig tree and there shall be none to make him afraid. May the Father of all mercies scatter light, and not darkness, upon our paths, and make us all in our several vocations useful here, and in His own due time and way everlastingly happy.

∽

GEORGE WASHINGTON, 1790, TO OVERSEER OF HIS ESTATE, WRITING FROM NEW YORK:

I shall not close this letter without exhorting you to refrain from spirituous liquors; they will prove your ruin if you do not. Consider how little a drunken man differs from a beast; the latter is not endowed with reason, the former deprives himself of it; and when that is the case, acts like a brute, annoying and disturbing every one around him; nor is this all, nor, as it respects himself, the worst of it. By degrees it renders a person feeble, and not only unable to serve others but to help himself; and being an act of his own, he falls from a state of usefulness into contempt, and at length suffers, if not perishes, in penury and want. Don't let this be your case.

Show yourself more of a man and a Christian than to yield to so intolerable a vice, which cannot, I am certain (to the greatest lover of liquor), give more pleasure to sip in the poison (for it is no better) than the consequence of it in bad behavior at the moment, and the more serious evils produced by it afterwards, must give pain. I am your Friend, George Washington.

∽

JOHN ADAMS

JOHN ADAMS, FEB. 22, 1756, DIARY ENTRY

Suppose a nation in some distant Region should take the Bible for their only law Book, and every member should regulate his conduct by the precepts there exhibited! Every member would be obliged in conscience, to temperance, frugality, and industry; to justice, kindness, and charity towards his fellow men; and to piety, love, and reverence toward Almighty God...What a Eutopia, what a Paradise would this region be.

JOHN ADAMS, FEB. 1765, NOTES ON A DISSERTATION ON THE CANON AND FEUDAL LAW:

I always consider the settlement of America with reverence and wonder, as the opening of a grand scene and design in Providence for the illumination of the ignorant, and the emancipation of the slavish part of mankind all over the earth.

JOHN ADAMS, SEP. 7, TO WIFE ABIGAIL REGARDING FIRST SESSION OF CONTINENTAL CONGRESS:

When the Congress met, Mr. Cushing made a motion that it should be opened with Prayer... Accordingly, next morning [Rev. Duche'] appeared...and read several prayers in the established form, and read the collect for the seventh day of September, which was the 35th Psalm. You must remember, this was the next morning after we heard the horrible rumor of the cannonade of Boston. I never saw a greater effect upon an audience. It seemed as if heaven had ordained that Psalm to be read on that morning. After this, Mr. Duche', unexpectedly to every body, struck out into an extemporary prayer, which filled the bosom of every man present. I must confess, I never heard a better prayer, or one so well pronounced...with such fervor, such ardor, such earnestness and pathos, and in language so elegant and sublime, for America, for the Congress, for the province of Massachusetts Bay, and especially the town of Boston. It has had an excellent effect upon everybody here. I must beg you to read that Psalm.

∽

JOHN ADAMS, JUN. 21, 1776, STATEMENT

Statesmen, my dear Sir, may plan and speculate for liberty, but it is Religion and Morality alone, which can establish the Principles upon which Freedom can securely stand. The only foundation of a free Constitution is pure Virtue, and if this cannot be inspired into our People in a greater Measure, than they have it now, they may change their Rulers and the forms of Government, but they will not obtain a lasting liberty.

∽

JOHN ADAMS, JOHN JAY & BENJAMIN FRANKLIN, SEP. 3, 1783, SIGNED TREATY OF PARIS ENDING THE WAR:

In the name of the Most Holy and Undivided Trinity. It having pleased the Divine Providence to dispose the hearts of the most serene and most potent Prince George the Third, by the Grace of God, King of Great Britain, France, and Ireland, Defender of the Faith,...and of the United States of America, to forget all past misunderstandings and differences...Done at Paris, this third day of September, in the year of our Lord one thousand seven hundred and eighty-three.

∽

JOHN ADAMS, JUL. 26, 1796, DIARY ENTRY MADE WHILE VICE-PRESIDENT ON THOMAS PAINE'S AGE OF REASON:

The Christian religion is, above all the Religions that ever prevailed or existed in ancient or modern times, the religion of Wisdom, Virtue, Equity, and Humanity. Let the Blackguard Paine say what he will; it is Resignation to God, it is Goodness itself to Man.

∾

JOHN ADAMS, MAR. 4, 1797, INAUGURAL:

With humble reverence, I feel it to be my duty to add, if a veneration for the religion of a people who profess and call themselves Christians, and a fixed resolution to consider a decent respect for Christianity among the best recommendations for the public service, can enable me in any degree to comply with your wishes, it shall be my strenuous endeavor that this sagacious injunction of the two Houses shall not be without effect...May that Being who is supreme over all, the Patron of Order, the Fountain of Justice, and the Protector in all ages of the world of virtuous liberty, continue His blessings upon this nation.

∾

JOHN ADAMS, MAR. 23, 1798, NATIONAL DAY OF HUMILIATION, FASTING & PRAYER PROCLAMATION:

That the citizens of these States, abstaining on that day from their customary worldly occupations, offer their devout addresses to the Father of Mercies...with the deepest humility, acknowledge before God the manifold sins and transgressions with which we are justly chargeable as individuals and as a nation, beseeching Him at the same time, of His infinite grace, through the Redeemer of the World, freely to remit all our offenses, and to incline us by His Holy Spirit to that sincere repentance and reformation which may afford us reason to hope for His inestimable favor and heavenly benediction.

∾

JOHN ADAMS, OCT. 11, 1798, TO OFFICERS OF 1ST BRIGADE, 3RD DIVISION OF MILITIA OF MASSACHUSETTS:

We have no government armed with power capable of contending with human passions unbridled by morality and religion. Avarice, ambition, revenge, or gallantry, would break the strongest cords of our Constitution as a whale goes through a net. Our Constitution was made only for a moral and religious people. It is wholly inadequate to the government of any other.

JOHN ADAMS, MAR. 6, 1799, NATIONAL DAY OF HUMILIATION, FASTING & PRAYER PROCLAMATION:

That they call to mind our numerous offenses against the Most High God, confess them before Him with the sincerest penitence, implore His pardoning mercy, through the Great Mediator and Redeemer, for our past transgressions, and that through the grace of His Holy Spirit, we may be disposed and enabled to yield a more suitable obedience to His righteous requisitions...That He would interpose to arrest the progress of that impiety and licentiousness in principle and practice so offensive to Himself and so ruinous to mankind; That He would make us deeply sensible that "Righteousness exalteth a nation."

∽

JOHN ADAMS, NOV. 22, 1800, 4TH ANNUAL ADDRESS, BEGINNING 1ST SESSION IN NEW CAPITOL:

It would be unbecoming the representatives of this nation to assemble for the first time in this solemn temple without looking up to the Supreme Ruler of the Universe and imploring His blessing. May this territory be the residence of virtue and happiness! In this city may that piety and virtue, that wisdom and magnanimity, that constancy and self-government, which adorned the great character whose name it bears be forever held in veneration! Here and throughout our country may simple manners, pure morals, and true religion flourish forever!

∽

JOHN ADAMS, JAN. 21, 1810, TO DR. BENJAMIN RUSH:

The Christian Religion...is the brightest of the glory and the express portrait of the eternal, self-evident, independent, benevolent, all-powerful and all-merciful Creator, Preserver and Father of the Universe, the first good, first perfect, and first fair. It will last as long as the world. Neither savage nor civilized man could ever have discovered or invented it. Ask me not then whether I am a Catholic or Protestant, Calvinist or Arminian. As far as they are Christians, I wish to be a fellow disciple of them all.

∽

JOHN ADAMS, DEC. 25, 1813, TO THOMAS JEFFERSON:

I have examined all religions, as well as my narrow sphere, my straightened means, and my busy life, would allow; and the result is that the Bible is the best Book in the world. It contains more philosophy than all the libraries I have seen.

THOMAS JEFFERSON

THOMAS JEFFERSON, MAY 24, 1774, PRAYER RESOLUTION, DRAFTED AS BRITISH PLANNED TO BLOCKADE BOSTON'S HARBOR; INTRODUCED BY ROBERT CARTER NICHOLAS, SUPPORTED BY PATRICK HENRY, RICHARD HENRY LEE & GEORGE MASON; PASSED UNANIMOUSLY:

This House, being deeply impressed with apprehension of the great dangers, to be derived to British America, from the hostile invasion of the City of Boston, in our Sister Colony of Massachusetts Bay, whose commerce and harbour are, on the first Day of June next, to be stopped by an Armed force, deem it highly necessary that the said first day of June be set apart, by the Members of this house, as a day of Fasting, Humiliation, and Prayer,

Devoutly to implore the divine interposition, for averting the heavy Calamity which threatens destruction to our Civil Rights, and the Evils of civil War; to give us one heart and one Mind firmly to oppose, by all just and proper means, every injury to American Rights; and that the Minds of his Majesty and his Parliament, may be inspired from above with Wisdom, Moderation, and Justice, to remove from the loyal People of America all cause of danger, from a continued pursuit of Measures, pregnant with their ruin.

❦

THOMAS JEFFERSON, JUL. 6, 1775, IN THE DECLARATION OF THE CAUSES AND NECESSITY FOR TAKING UP ARMS:

With a humble confidence in the mercies of the Supreme and impartial God and Ruler of the Universe, we most devoutly implore His divine goodness to protect us.

❦

THOMAS JEFFERSON, 1776, ORIGINAL ROUGH DRAFT OF THE DECLARATION OF INDEPENDENCE:

He has waged cruel war against human nature itself, violating it's most sacred rights of life and liberty in the persons of a distant people who never offended him, captivating & carrying them into slavery in another hemisphere, or to incur miserable death in their transportation thither. This piratical warfare, the opprobium of INFIDEL Powers, is the warfare of the...king of Great Britain. Determined to keep open a market where MEN should be bought & sold, he has prostituted his negative for suppressing every legislative attempt to prohibit or to restrain this execrable commerce.

❦

THOMAS JEFFERSON, JUL. 4TH, 1776, DECLARATION OF INDEPENDENCE:

Laws of Nature and of Nature's God...We hold these truths to be self-evident, that all men are created equal. That they are endowed by their Creator with certain inalienable rights...The Representatives of the United States of America, in General Congress, Assembled, appealing to the Supreme Judge of the world for the rectitude of our intentions...with a firm reliance on the protection of Divine Providence, we mutually pledge to each other our Lives, our Fortunes, and our sacred Honor.

❦

THOMAS JEFFERSON, 1781, NOTES ON STATE OF VIRGINIA, QUERY 18, ENGRAVED ON JEFFERSON MEMORIAL:

God who gave us life gave us liberty. And can the liberties of a nation be thought secure when we have removed their only firm basis, a conviction in the minds of the people that these liberties are of the Gift of God? That they are not to be violated but with His wrath? Indeed, I tremble for my country when I reflect that God is just; that His justice cannot sleep forever.

❧

THOMAS JEFFERSON, JAN. 16, 1786, VIRGINIA STATUTE OF RELIGIOUS FREEDOM:

Almighty God hath created the mind free;...all attempts to influence it by temporal punishments, or burdens, or by civil incapacitations, tend only to begat habits of hypocrisy and meanness, and are a departure from the plan of the Holy Author of religion, who being Lord both of body and mind, yet chose not to propagate it by coercions on either, as was in His Almighty power to do, but to extend it by its influence on reason alone.

❧

THOMAS JEFFERSON, MAR. 4, 1801, FIRST INAUGURAL:

Enlightened by a benign religion, professed, indeed, and practiced in various forms, yet all of them inculcating honesty, truth, temperance, gratitude, and the love of man; acknowledging and adoring an overruling Providence, which by all its dispensations proves that it delights in the happiness of man here and his greater happiness hereafter. With all these blessings, what more is necessary to make us a happy and prosperous people? Still one thing more...a wise and frugal Government, which shall restrain men from injuring one another, shall leave them otherwise free to regulate their own pursuits of industry and improvement, and shall not take from the mouth of labor the bread it has earned.

❧

THOMAS JEFFERSON, DEC. 8, 1801, 1ST ANNUAL MESSAGE:

Whilst we devoutly return our thanks to the beneficent Being who has been pleased to breathe into them the spirit of consolation and forgiveness, we are bound with peculiar gratitude to be thankful to Him that our own peace has been preserved through a perilous season...I can not omit recommending a revisal of the laws on the subject of naturalization...Shall we refuse to the unhappy fugitives from distress that hospitality which the savages of the wilderness extended to our fathers arriving in this land? Shall the oppressed humanity find no asylum of this globe?

∽

THOMAS JEFFERSON, JAN. 1, 1802, TO NEHEMIAH DODGE & DANBURY BAPTIST ASSOCIATION, CT:

Gentleman, The affectionate sentiments of esteem and approbation which you are so good as to express towards me, on behalf of the Danbury Baptist Association, give me the highest satisfaction. My duties dictate a faithful and zealous pursuit of the interests of my constituents, and in proportion as they are persuaded of my fidelity to those duties, the discharge of them becomes more and more pleasing.

Believing with you that religion is a matter which lies solely between man and his God, that he owes account to none other for his faith or his worship, that the legislative powers of government reach actions only, and not opinions, I contemplate with sovereign reverence that act of the whole American people which declared that their legislature should "make no law respecting an establishment of religion, or prohibiting the free exercise thereof," thus building a wall of separation between church and State.

Adhering to this expression of the supreme will of the nation in behalf of the rights of conscience, I shall see with sincere satisfaction the progress of those sentiments which tend to restore to man all his natural rights, convinced he has no natural right in opposition to his social duties. I reciprocate your kind prayers for the protection and blessing of the common Father and Creator of man, and tender you for yourselves and your religious association, assurances of my high respect and esteem. Thomas Jefferson.

∽

THOMAS JEFFERSON, APR. 21, 1803, TO DR. BENJAMIN RUSH:

My views...are the result of a life of inquiry and reflection, and very different from the anti-christian system imputed to me by those who know nothing of my opinions. To the corruptions of Christianity I am, indeed, opposed; but not to the genuine precepts of Jesus himself. I am a Christian in the only sense in which he wished any one to be; sincerely attached to his doctrines in preference to all others.

∽

THOMAS JEFFERSON, MAR. 4, 1805, SECOND INAUGURAL:

I know that the acquisition of Louisiana has been disapproved by some from a candid apprehension that the enlargement of our territory would endanger the union, but who can limit the extent to which the federative principle may operate effectively?...In matters of religion I have considered that its free exercise is placed by the Constitution independent of the powers of the General Government. I have therefore undertaken, on no occasion, to prescribe the religious exercise suited to it; but have left them, as the Constitution found them, under the direction and discipline of state and church authorities by the several religious societies.

∽

THOMAS JEFFERSON, MAR. 4, 1805, SECOND INAUGURAL:

I shall need, too, the favor of that Being in whose hands we are, who led our forefathers, as Israel of old, from their native land and planted them in a country flowing with all the necessities and comforts of life, who has covered our infancy with His Providence and our riper years with His wisdom and power, and to whose goodness I ask you to join with me in supplications that He will so enlighten the minds of your servants, guide their councils and prosper their measures, that whatever they do shall result in your good, and shall secure to you the peace, friendship and approbation of all nations.

∽

THOMAS JEFFERSON, JAN. 23, 1808, TO SAMUEL MILLER:

I consider the government of the United States as interdicted by the Constitution from intermeddling with religious institutions, their doctrines, discipline, or exercises. This results not only from the provision that no law shall be made respecting the establishment or free exercise of religion, but from that also which reserves to the states the powers not delegated to the United States [10th Amendment].

Certainly no power to prescribe any religious exercise, or to assume authority in religious discipline, has been delegated to the General government. It must then rest with the States as far as it can be in any human authority...I do not believe it is for the interest of religion to invite the civil magistrate to direct its exercises, its discipline, or its doctrines...Every religious society has a right to determine for itself the times for these exercises, and the objects proper for them, according to their own particular tenets.

✎

THOMAS JEFFERSON, SEP 18, 1813, TO WILLIAM CANBY:

Of all the systems of morality, ancient and modern, which have come under my observation, none appear to me so pure as that of Jesus.

✎

THOMAS JEFFERSON, SEP. 26, 1814, TO MILES KING:

We have heard it said that there is not a Quaker or a Baptist, a Presbyterian or an Episcopalian, a Catholic or a Protestant in heaven; that on entering that gate, we leave those badges of schism behind...Let us not be uneasy about the different roads we may pursue, as believing them the shortest, to that our last abode; but following the guidance of a good conscience, let us be happy in the hope that by these different paths we shall all meet in the end. And that you and I may meet and embrace, is my earnest prayer.

✎

THOMAS JEFFERSON, JAN. 9, 1816, TO CHARLES THOMSON ON HIS BOOK, *THE LIFE & MORALS OF JESUS OF NAZARETH:*

I am a real Christian, that is to say, a disciple of the doctrines of Jesus.

✎

THOMAS JEFFERSON, NOV. 4, 1820, TO JARED SPARKS:

I hold the precepts of Jesus as delivered by Himself, to be the most pure, benevolent and sublime which have ever been preached to man.

✎

THOMAS JEFFERSON, APR. 11, 1823, TO JOHN ADAMS:

We see, too, evident proofs of the necessity of a Superintending Power to maintain the Universe in its course and order...So irresistible are these evidences of an Intelligent and Powerful Agent that, of the infinite numbers of men who have existed thro' all time, they have believed, in the proportion of a million at least to Unit, in the hypothesis of an eternal pre-existence of a Creator, rather than in that of self-existent Universe.

✎

JAMES MADISON

JAMES MADISON, NOV. 9, 1772,
TO HIS COLLEGE FRIEND, WILLIAM BRADFORD:

A watchful eye must be kept on ourselves lest while we are building ideal monuments of Renown and Bliss here we neglect to have our names enrolled in the Annals of Heaven.

✥

JAMES MADISON, JUN. 20, 1785, RELIGIOUS FREEDOM-A MEMORIAL AND REMONSTRANCE, VIRGINIA ASSEMBLY:

Before any man can be considered as a member of Civil Society, he must be considered as a subject of the Governor of the Universe...Much more must every man who becomes a member of any particular Civil Society, do it with a saving of his allegiance to the Universal Sovereign.

We maintain therefore that in matters of Religion, no man's right is abridged by the institution of Civil Society, and that Religion is wholly exempt from its cognizance.

✥

JAMES MADISON, JUN. 20, 1785, RELIGIOUS FREEDOM-A MEMORIAL & REMONSTRANCE, VIRGINIA ASSEMBLY:

The policy of the bill is adverse to the diffusion of the light of Christianity. The first wish of those who ought to enjoy this precious gift, ought to be, that it may be imparted to the whole race of mankind. Compare the number of those who have as yet received it, with the number still remaining under the dominions of false religions, and how small is the former! Does the policy of the bill tend to lessen the disproportion? No; it at once discourages those who are strangers to the Light of Truth, from coming into the regions of it.

∽

JAMES MADISON, 1787, UNITED STATES CONSTITUTIONAL CONVENTION, PHILADELPHIA, PENNSYLVANIA:

All men having power ought to be distrusted.

∽

JAMES MADISON, 1788, FEDERALIST PAPER #39:

That honourable determination which animates every votary of freedom, to rest all our political experiments on the capacity of mankind for self-government.

∽

JAMES MADISON, JUN. 12, 1788, JOURNAL ENTRY:

There is not a shadow of right in the General Government to intermeddle with religion...The subject is, for the honor of America, perfectly free and unshackled. The government has no jurisdiction over it.

∽

JAMES MADISON, MAR. 4, 1809, FIRST INAUGURAL:

In these my confidence will under every difficulty be best placed, next to that which we have all been encouraged to feel in the guardianship and guidance of that Almighty Being whose power regulates the destiny of nations, whose blessings have been so conspicuously dispensed to this rising Republic, and to whom we are bound to address our devout gratitude for the past, as well as our fervent supplications and best hopes for the future.

∽

JAMES MADISON, JUL. 9, 1812, NATIONAL DAY OF PUBLIC HUMILIATION & PRAYER PROCLAMATION:

I do therefore recommend...rendering the Sovereign of the Universe and the Benefactor of mankind the public homage due to His holy attributes; of acknowledging the transgressions which might justly provoke the manifestations of His divine displeasure; of seeking His merciful forgiveness;...that in the present season of calamity and war He would take the American people under His peculiar care;...that He would inspire all nations with a love of justice and of concord, and with a reverence for the unerring precept of our holy religion, to do to others as they would require that others should do to them.

∽

JAMES MADISON, MAR. 4, 1813, SECOND INAUGURAL:

I should be compelled to shrink if I had less reliance on the support of an enlightened and generous people, and felt less deeply a conviction that the war with a powerful nation, which forms so prominent a feature in our situation, is stamped with that justice which invites the smiles of Heaven on the means of conducting it to a successful termination.

∽

JAMES MADISON, JUL. 23, 1813, NATIONAL DAY OF PUBLIC HUMILIATION & PRAYER PROCLAMATION:

If the public homage of a people can ever be worthy of the favorable regard of the Holy and Omniscient Being to whom it is addressed, it must be...guided only by their free choice, by the impulse of their hearts and the dictates of their consciences; and such a spectacle must be interesting to all Christian nations as proving that religion, that gift of Heaven for the good of man, freed from all coercive edicts, from that unhallowed connection with the powers of this world which corrupts religion...and making no appeal but to reason, to the heart, and to the conscience, can spread its benign influence everywhere and can attract to the divine altar those freewill offerings of humble supplication, thanksgiving, and praise which alone can be acceptable to Him whom no hypocrisy can deceive and no forced sacrifices propitiate.

∽

JAMES MADISON, NOV. 16, 1814, NATIONAL DAY OF PUBLIC FASTING & PRAYER PROCLAMATION:

The National Legislature having by a Joint Resolution expressed their desire that in the present time of public calamity and war a day may be recommended to be observed by the people of the United States as a day of public humiliation and fasting and of prayer to Almighty God for the safety and welfare of these States, His blessing on their arms, and a speedy restoration of peace...

I...recommend...offering...humble adoration to the Great Sovereign of the Universe, of confessing their sins and transgressions, and of strengthening their vows of repentance...that He would be graciously pleased to pardon all their offenses against Him...that He would in a special manner preside over the nation...giving success to its arms."

❧

JAMES MADISON, MAR. 4, 1815, NATIONAL DAY OF THANKSGIVING PROCLAMATION:

No people ought to feel greater obligations to celebrate the goodness of the Great Disposer of Events and of the Destiny of Nations than the people of the United States...To the same Divine Author of Every Good and Perfect Gift we are indebted for all those priviledges and advantages, religious as well as civil, which are so richly enjoyed in this favored land...I now recommend...a day on which the people of every religious denomination may in their solemn assemblies unite their hearts and their voices in a freewill offering to their Heavenly Benefactor of their homage of thanksgiving and of their songs of praise.

❧

JAMES MADISON, NOV. 20, 1825, LETTER TO FREDERICK BEASLEY:

The belief in a God All Powerful wise and good, is so essential to the moral order of the World and to the happiness of man, that arguments which enforce it cannot be drawn from too many sources nor adapted with too much solicitude to the different characters and capacities to be impressed with it.

❧

JAMES MONROE

JAMES MONROE, MAR. 4, 1817, FIRST INAUGURAL:

Under this Constitution...the States, respectively protected by the National Government under a mild, parental system against foreign dangers, and enjoying within their separate spheres, by a wise partition of power, a just proportion of the sovereignty...are the best proofs of wholesome laws well administered....

And if we look to the condition of individuals what a proud spectacle does it exhibit! On whom has oppression fallen in any quarter of our Union? Who has been deprived of any right of person or property? Who restrained from offering his vows in the mode which he prefers to the Divine Author of his being? It is well known that all these blessings have been enjoyed in their fullest extent...

Such, then, is the happy Government under which we live...a government which protects every citizen in the full enjoyment of his rights, and is able to protect the nation against injustice from foreign powers...

∽

JAMES MONROE, MAR. 4, 1817, FIRST INAUGURAL:

What raised us to the present happy state?...The Government has been in the hands of the people. To the people, therefore, and to the faithful and able depositaries of their trust is the credit due...

It is only when the people become ignorant and corrupt, when they degenerate into a populace, that they are incapable of exercising the sovereignty.

Usurpation is then an easy attainment, and an usuper soon found. The people themselves become the willing instruments of their own debasement and ruin...

If we persevere in the career in which we have advanced so far and in the path already traced, we can not fail, under the favor of a gracious Providence, to attain the high destiny which seems to await us....

I enter on the trust to which I have been called by the suffrages of my fellow-citizens with my fervent prayers to the Almighty that He will be graciously pleased to continue to us that protection which He has already so conspicuously displayed in our favor.

∽

JAMES MONROE, DEC. 2, 1817, 1ST ANNUAL MESSAGE:

For advantages so numerous and highly important it is our duty to unite in grateful acknowledgments to that Omnipotent Being from whom they are derived, and in unceasing prayer that He will endow us with virtue and strength to maintain and hand them down in their utmost purity to our latest posterity.

∽

JAMES MONROE, NOV. 16, 1818, 2ND ANNUAL MESSAGE:

For these inestimable blessings we can not but be grateful to that Providence which watches over the destiny of nations...

When we view the blessings with which our country has been favored, those which we now enjoy, and the means which we possess of handing them down unimpaired to our latest posterity, our attention is irresistibly drawn to the source from whence they flow. Let us then, unite in offering our most grateful acknowledgments for these blessings to the Divine Author of All Good.

∽

JAMES MONROE, NOV. 14, 1820, 4TH ANNUAL MESSAGE:

When, then, we take into view the prosperous and happy condition of our country...it is impossible to behold so gratifying, so glorious a spectacle without being penetrated with the most profound and grateful acknowledgments to the Supreme Author of All Good for such manifold and inestimable blessings...

And more especially by the multiplied proofs which it has accumulated of the great perfection of our most excellent system of government, the powerful instrument in the hands of our All-merciful Creator in securing to us these blessings.

∽

JAMES MONROE, MAR. 5, 1821, SECOND INAUGURAL:

That these powerful causes exist, and that they are permanent, is my fixed opinion; that they may produce a like accord in all questions touching, however remotely, the liberty, prosperity, and happiness of our country will always be the object of my most fervent prayers to the Supreme Author of All Good...

With full confidence in the continuance of that candor and generous indulgence from my fellow-citizens at large which I have heretofore experienced, and with a firm reliance on the protection of Almighty God, I shall forthwith commence the duties of the high trust to which you have called me.

∽

JAMES MONROE, DEC. 3, 1821, 5TH ANNUAL MESSAGE:

Deeply impressed with the blessings which we enjoy, and of which we have such manifold proofs, my mind is irresistibly drawn to that Almighty Being, the great source from whence they proceed and to whom our most grateful acknowledgments are due.

∽

JAMES MONROE, DEC. 7, 1824, 8TH ANNUAL MESSAGE:

The view which I have now to present to you of our affairs, foreign and domestic, realizes the most sanguine anticipations which have been entertained of the public prosperity...For these blessings we owe to Almighty God, from whom we derive them, and with profound reverence, our most grateful and unceasing acknowledgments.

∽

JAMES MONROE, DEC. 7, 1824, 8TH ANNUAL MESSAGE:

Having commenced my service in early youth, and continued it since with few and short intervals, I have witnessed the great difficulties to which our Union has been exposed, and admired the virtue and intelligence with which they have been surmounted. From the present prosperous and happy state I derive a gratification which I can not express. That these blessings may be preserved and perpetuated will be the object of my fervent and unceasing prayers to the Supreme Ruler of the Universe.

∾

JAMES MONROE, STATEMENT:

The establishment of our institutions forms the most important epoch that history hath recorded...To preserve and hand them down in their utmost purity to the remotest ages will require the existence and practice of the virtues and talents equal to those which were displayed in acquiring them.

∾

JAMES MONROE, STATEMENT:

Of the liberty of conscience in matters of religious faith, of speech and of the press; of the trial by jury of the vicinage in civil and criminal cases; of the benefit of the writ of habeas corpus; of the right to keep and bear arms...If these rights are well defined, and secured against encroachments, it is impossible that government should ever degenerate into tyranny.

∾

JOHN QUINCY ADAMS

JOHN QUINCY ADAMS, SEP. 26, 1810, DAIRY ENTRY:
I have made it a practice for several years to read the Bible through in the course of every year.

ᕯ

JOHN QUINCY ADAMS, SEP. 1811, LETTER TO HIS SON, WRITTEN AS U.S. MINISTER, ST. PETERSBURG, RUSSIA:
So great is my veneration for the Bible, and so strong my belief, that when duly read and meditated on, it is of all books in the world, that which contributes most to make men good, wise, and happy - that the earlier my children begin to read it, the more steadily they pursue the practice of reading it throughout their lives, the more lively and confident will be my hopes that they will prove useful citizens of their country, respectable members of society.

ᕯ

JOHN QUINCY ADAMS, DEC. 24, 1814,
AFTER NEGOTIATING THE TREATY OF GHENT, LONDON:
You ask me what Bible I take as the standard of my faith-the

Hebrew, the Samaritan, the old English translation, or what? I answer, the Bible containing the Sermon on the Mount - any Bible...The New Testament I have repeatedly read in the original Greek, in the Latin, in the Geneva Protestant, in Sacy's Catholic French translations, in Luther's German translation, in the common English Protestant, and in the Douay Catholic translations. I take any one of them for my standard of faith...My hopes of a future life are all founded upon the Gospel of Christ.

❧

JOHN QUINCY ADAMS, DEC. 24, 1814, FROM LONDON AFTER NEGOTIATING THE TREATY OF GHENT:

The Sermon on the Mount commands me to lay up for myself treasures, not upon earth, but in Heaven. My hopes of a future life are all founded upon the Gospel of Christ.

❧

JOHN QUINCY ADAMS, MAR. 4, 1825, INAUGURAL:

I appear, my fellow-citizens, in your presence and in that of Heaven to bind myself by the solemnities of religious obligation to the faithful performance of the duties allotted to me...

Freedom of the press and of religious opinion should be inviolate; the policy of our country is peace and the ark of our salvation union are articles of faith upon which we are all now agreed...and knowing that "Except the Lord keep the city, the watchman waketh in vain," with fervent supplications for His favor, to His overruling providence I commit with humble but fearless confidence my own fate and the future destinies of my country.

❧

JOHN QUINCY ADAMS, DEC. 6, 1825, 1ST ANNUAL MESSAGE:

There has, indeed, rarely been a period in the history of civilized man in which the general condition of the Christian nations has been marked so extensively by peace and prosperity...Moral, political, intellectual improvement are duties assigned by the Author of Our Existence to social no less than to individual man...

The exercise of delegated powers is a duty as sacred and indispensable as the usurpation of powers not granted is criminal and odious...That the nation blessed with the largest portion of liberty must in proportion to its numbers be the most powerful nation upon the earth, and that the tenure of power by man is, in the moral purposes of his Creator, upon condition that it shall be exercised to ends of beneficence, to improve the condition of himself and fellow-men.

While foreign nations less blessed with that freedom which is power than ourselves are advancing with gigantic strides in the career of public improvement, were we to slumber in indolence or fold up our arms and proclaim to the world that we are palsied by the will of our constituents, would it not be to cast away the bounties of Providence and doom ourselves to perpetual inferiority?...May He who searches the hearts of the children of men prosper your exertions to secure the blessings peace and promote the highest welfare of our country.

∽

JOHN QUINCY ADAMS, DEC. 5, 1826, 2ND ANNUAL MESSAGE, UPON DEATHS OF THOMAS JEFFERSON & JOHN ADAMS:

Since your last meeting at this place, the fiftieth anniversary of the day when our independence was declared...two of the principal actors in that solemn scene - the hand that penned the ever-memorable Declaration and the voice that sustained it in debate - were by one summons, at the distance of 700 miles from each other, called before the Judge of All to account for their deeds done upon earth...

With but sense and sensibility left to breathe a last aspiration to Heaven of blessing upon their country, may we not humbly hope that to them too it was a pledge of transition from gloom to glory, and that while their mortal vestments were sinking into the clod of the valley their emancipated spirits were ascending to the bosom of their God!

∽

JOHN QUINCY ADAMS, DEC. 2, 1828,
4TH ANNUAL MESSAGE.

Savages, whom it was our policy and our duty to use our influence in converting to Christianity and in bringing within the pale of civilization...As brethren of the human race, rude and ignorant, we endeavored to bring them to the knowledge of religion and of letters.

The ultimate design was to incorporate in our own institutions that portion of them which could be converted to the state of civilization...We have had the rare good fortune of teaching them the arts of civilization and the doctrines of Christianity.

∽

JOHN QUINCY ADAMS, U.S. REPRESENTATIVE FROM MASSACHUSETTS (1830-48), BEING ONLY FORMER PRESIDENT TO SERVE AS CONGRESSMAN, LED FIGHT AGAINST SLAVERY FOR 14 YEARS:

Oh, if but one man could arise with a genius capable of supporting, and an utterance capable of communicating those eternal truths that belong to this question, to lay bare in all its nakedness that outrage upon the goodness of God - Human Slavery! Now is the time, and this is the occasion, upon which such a man would perform the duties of an angel upon earth!

∽

JOHN QUINCY ADAMS, JUL. 4, 1837, ON THE 61ST ANNIVERSARY OF THE DECLARATION OF INDEPENDENCE, NEWBURYPORT:

Why is it that, next to the birthday of the Savior of the World, your most joyous and most venerated festival returns on this day. Is it not that, in the chain of human events, the birthday of the nation is indissolubly linked with the birthday of the Savior? That it forms a leading event in the Progress of the Gospel dispensation? Is it not that the Declaration of Independence first organized the social compact on the foundation of the Redeemer's mission upon earth?

∽

JOHN QUINCY ADAMS, FEB. 27, 1844, AS U.S. CONGRESSMAN ADDRESSING THE AMERICAN BIBLE SOCIETY, OF WHICH HE WAS CHAIRMAN:

I deem myself fortunate in having the opportunity, at a stage of a long life drawing rapidly to its close, to bear at this place, the capital of our National Union, in the Hall of representatives of the North American people...to bear my solemn testimonial of reverence and gratitude to that book of books, the Holy Bible...The Bible carries with it the history of the creation, the fall and redemption of man, and discloses to him, in the infant born at Bethlehem, the Legislator and Saviour of the world.

ANDREW JACKSON

ANDREW JACKSON, JAN. 8, 1815, LETTER TO HIS FRIEND ROBERT HAYS REGARDING THE VICTORIOUS BATTLE OF NEW ORLEANS, DURING THE WAR OF 1812:

It appears that the unerring hand of Providence shielded my men from the shower of balls, bombs, and rockets, when every ball and bomb from our guns carried with them a mission of death.

ᔰ

ANDREW JACKSON, LETTER TO HIS WIFE, RACHEL, WRITTEN WHILE HE WAS AWAY IN WASHINGTON, DC:

I trust that the God of Isaac and of Jacob will protect you, and give you health in my absence. In Him alone we ought to trust; He alone can preserve and guide us through this troublesome world, and I am sure He will hear your Prayers.

We are told that the prayers of the righteous prevaileth much, and I add mine for your health and preservation until we meet again.

ᔰ

ANDREW JACKSON, MAR. 4, 1829, 1ST INAUGURAL, LESS THAN 3 MONTHS AFTER HIS WIFE DIED:

As long as our Government is administered for the good of the people, and is regulated by their will; as long as it secures to us the rights of person and of property, liberty of conscience and of the press, it will be worth defending...

And a firm reliance on the goodness of that Power whose providence mercifully protected our national infancy, and has since upheld our liberties in various vicissitudes, encourages me to offer up my ardent supplications that He will continue to make our beloved country the object of His divine care and gracious benediction.

∾

ANDREW JACKSON, DEC. 8, 1829, 1ST ANNUAL MESSAGE:

Upon this country more than any other has, in the providence of God, been cast the special guardianship of the great principle of adherence to written constitutions. If it fail here, all hope in regard to it will be extinguished.

That this was intended to be a government of limited and specific, and not general powers must be admitted by all, and it is our duty to preserve for it the character intended by its framers.

∾

ANDREW JACKSON, JAN. 20, 1830, TO CONGRESS:

Gentlemen: I respectfully submit to your consideration the accompanying communication from the Secretary of the Treasury, showing that according to the terms of an agreement between the United States and the United Society of Christian Indians the latter have a claim to an annuity of $400, commencing from the 1st of October, 1826, for which an appropriation by law for this amount, as long as they are entitled to receive it, will be proper.

∾

ANDREW JACKSON, JAN. 16, 1833, TO CONGRESS:

I fervently pray that the Great Ruler of Nations may so guide your deliberations and our joint measures as that they may prove salutary examples not only to the present but to future times.

∾

ANDREW JACKSON, MAR. 4, 1833, 2ND INAUGURAL:

Finally, it is my fervent prayer to that Almighty Being before whom I now stand, and who has kept us in His hands from the infancy of our Republic to the present day...that He will so overrule all my intentions and actions and inspire the hearts of my fellow-citizens that we may be preserved from dangers of all kinds and continue forever a united happy people.

✧

ANDREW JACKSON, APR. 15, 1834, PROTEST MESSAGE:

The Bank of the United States, a great moneyed monopoly, had attempted...controlling the elections...to control public opinion and...to concentrate in the hands of a body not directly amenable to the people a degree of influence and power dangerous to their liberties...The only ambition I can feel is to acquit myself to Him to whom I must soon render an account of my stewardship...If the Almighty Being who has hitherto sustained and protected me will but vouchsafe to make my feeble powers instrumental to such a result, I shall anticipate with pleasure the place to be assigned me in the history of my country.

✧

ANDREW JACKSON, SEP. 11, 1834, TO SON, ANDREW, JR:

I nightly offer up my prayers to the Throne of Grace for the health and safety of you all, and that we ought all to rely with confidence on the promises of our dear Redeemer, and give Him our hearts. This is all He requires and all that we can do, and if we sincerely do this, we are sure of salvation through his atonement.

✧

ANDREW JACKSON, 1834, TO ANDREW AND MARY HUTCHINGS ON THE DEATH OF THEIR FIRSTBORN:

My dear Hutchings...I am truly happy to find that you both have met this severe bereavement with that Christian meekness and submission as was your duty. This charming babe was only given you from your Creator and benefactor...He has a right to take away, and we ought humbly to submit to His will and be always ready to say, blessed be His name. We have one consolation under this severe bereavement, that this babe is now in the bosom of its Saviour.

❧

ANDREW JACKSON, JAN. 1835, TO KING OF ENGLAND, WHO EXPRESSED CONCERN OVER AN ASSASSINATION PLOT ON JACKSON; (A MAN, AT POINT BLANK RANGE, ATTEMPTED TO FIRE TWO PISTOLS, BUT GUNS MISFIRED):

A kind of Providence had been pleased to shield me against the recent attempt upon my life, and irresistibly carried many minds to the belief in a superintending Providence.

❧

ANDREW JACKSON, MAR. 25, 1835, LETTER:

Judge the tree by its fruit. All who profess Christianity believe in a Saviour, and that by and through Him we must be saved. We ought, therefore, to consider all good Christians whose walks correspond with their professions, be they Presbyterian, Episcopalian, Baptist, Methodist or Roman Catholic.

❧

ANDREW JACKSON, DEC. 30, 1836, TO MR. ANDREW DONELSON AFTER HEARING HIS WIFE, EMILY, HAD DIED:

My dear Andrew, we cannot recall her, we are commanded by our dear Saviour, not to mourn for the dead, but for the living. I am sure from my dream that she is happy, she has changed a world of woe, for a world of eternal happiness, and we ought to prepare, as we too, must follow...It becomes our duty to submit to this heavy bereavement with due submission, and control our passions, submit to the will of God who holds our lives in his hand and say with humble and contrite hearts, "The Lord's will be done on earth as it is in heaven."

❧

ANDREW JACKSON, MAR. 4, 1837, FAREWELL ADDRESS:

Providence has showered on this favored land blessings without number, and has chosen you as the guardians of freedom, to preserve it for the benefit of the human race. May He who holds in His hands the destinies of nations, make you worthy of the favors He has bestowed, and enable you, with pure hearts and hands and sleepless vigilance, to guard and defend to the end of time, the great charge He has committed to your keeping. My own race is nearly run; advanced age and failing health warns me that before long I must pass beyond the reach of human events...I thank God that my life has been spent in a land of liberty and that He has given me a heart to love my country with the affection of a son. And filled with gratitude for your constant and unwavering kindness, I bid you a last and affectionate farewell.

✦

ANDREW JACKSON, SEP. 20, 1838, ON RECEIVING NEWS THAT HIS OLD FRIEND, RALPH EARL, HAD DIED:

I must soon follow him, and hope to meet him and those friends who have gone before me in the realms of bliss through the mediation of a dear Redeemer, Jesus Christ.

✦

ANDREW JACKSON, TO FAMILY OF GENERAL COFFEE:

Rely on our dear Saviour. He will be father to the fatherless and husband to the widow. Trust in the mercy and goodness of Christ, and always be ready to say with heartfelt resignation, "may the Lord's will be done."

✦

ANDREW JACKSON, MAY 29, 1845, IN HIS WILL, WRITTEN JUST A FEW WEEKS BEFORE HIS DEATH:

Sir, I am in the hands of a merciful God. I have full confidence in his goodness and mercy...The Bible is true. I have tried to conform to its spirit as near as possible. Upon that Sacred Volume I rest my hope for eternal salvation, through the merits and blood of our blessed Lord and Saviour, Jesus Christ... First, I bequeath my body to the dust whence it comes, and my soul to God who gave it, hoping for a happy immortality through the atoning merits of our Lord Jesus Christ, the Saviour of the world.

✦

ANDREW JACKSON, JUN. 1, 1845, IN REPLY TO THOSE VISITING HIM IN HIS LAST ILLNESS:

When I have suffered sufficiently, the Lord will then take me to Himself - but what are all my sufferings compared to those of the Blessed Saviour, who died upon that cursed tree for me? Mine are nothing.

✦

ANDREW JACKSON, JUN. 8, 1845,
REFERRING TO THE BIBLE:

That book, Sir, is the Rock upon which our republic rests.

ᖇ

ANDREW JACKSON, JUN. 8, 1845, TO HIS FAMILY AND
SERVANTS JUST MOMENTS BEFORE HIS DEATH:

My dear children, do not grieve for me; it is true, I am going to leave you; I am well aware of my situation. I have suffered much bodily pain, but my sufferings are but as nothing compared with that which our blessed Redeemer endured upon the accursed Cross, that all might be saved who put their trust in Him...God will take care of you for me.

I am my God's. I belong to Him. I go but a short time before you, and...I hope and trust to meet you all in Heaven, both white and black.

ᖇ

ANDREW JACKSON, JUN. 8, 1845, HIS LAST WORDS:

Oh, do not cry. Be good children, and we will all meet in Heaven.

ᖇ

MARTIN VAN BUREN

MARTIN VAN BUREN, MAR. 4, 1837, INAUGURAL:

So sensibly, fellow-citizens, do these circumstances press themselves upon me that I should not dare to enter upon my path of duty did I not look for the generous aid of those who will be associated with me in the various and coordinate branches of the Government; did I not repose with unwavering reliance on the patriotism, the intelligence, and the kindness of a people who never yet deserted a public servant honestly laboring in their cause; and above all, did I not permit myself humbly to hope for the sustaining of an ever-watchful and beneficent Providence.

❧

MARTIN VAN BUREN, MAR. 4, 1837, INAUGURAL:

I only look to the gracious protection of that Divine Being whose strengthening support I humbly solicit, and whom I fervently pray to look down upon us all. May it be among the dispensations of His Providence to bless our beloved country with honors and length of days; may her ways be pleasantness, and all her paths peace!

∾

MARTIN VAN BUREN, SEP. 4, 1837,
TO SPECIAL SESSION OF CONGRESS:

In the event of my election I would not be able to cooperate in the reestablishment of a national bank...The reestablishment of such a bank...would impair the rightful supremacy of the popular will, injure the character and diminish the influence of our political system, and bring once more into existence a concentrated moneyed power, hostile to the spirit and threatening the permanency of our republican institutions...

The great agricultural interest has in many parts of the country suffered comparatively little, and, as if Providence intended to display the munificence of its goodness at the moment of our greatest need, and in direct contrast to the evils occasioned by the waywardness of man, we have been blessed throughout our extended territory....

We can only feel more deeply the responsibility of the respective trusts that have been confided to us, and under the pressure of difficulties unite in invoking the guidance and aid of the Supreme Ruler of Nations.

∾

MARTIN VAN BUREN, DEC. 5, 1837, 1ST ANNUAL MESSAGE:

We have reason to renew the expression of our devout gratitude to the Giver of All Good for His benign protection. Our country presents on every side the evidences of that continued favor under whose auspices it has gradually risen from a few feeble and dependent colonies to a prosperous and powerful confederacy.

∾

MARTIN VAN BUREN, DEC. 3, 1838, 2ND ANNUAL MESSAGE:

These blessings, which evince the care and beneficence of Providence, call for our devout and fervent gratitude. We have not less reason to be grateful for other bounties bestowed by the same Munificent Hand, and more exclusively our own.

∾

MARTIN VAN BUREN, DEC. 2, 1839, 3RD ANNUAL MESSAGE:

Prosperity which has been heretofore so bountifully bestowed upon us by the Author of All Good still continues...

Abuses as we are now encountering...seek to perpetuate their power...to gain for the few an ascendancy over the many by securing to them a monopoly of the currency...to nourish, in preference to the manly virtues that give dignity to human nature, a craving desire for luxurious enjoyment and sudden wealth, which renders those who seek them dependent on those who supply them; to substitute for republican simplicity and economical habits a sickly appetite for effeminate indulgence and an imitation of that reckless extravagance.

∽

MARTIN VAN BUREN, DEC. 2, 1839, 3RD ANNUAL MESSAGE:

By ceasing to run in debt and applying the surplus of our crops and incomes to the discharge of existing obligations...we shall see our country soon recover from a temporary depression...

Fortunately for us at this moment, when the balance of trade is greatly against us and the difficulty of meeting it enhanced by the disturbed state of our money affairs, the bounties of Providence have come to relieve us from the consequences of past errors...

Our surplus profits, the energy and industry of our population, and the wonderful advantages which Providence has bestowed upon our country...will in due time afford abundant means.

∽

MARTIN VAN BUREN, DEC. 5, 1840, 4TH ANNUAL MESSAGE:

Our devout gratitude is due to the Supreme Being for having graciously continued to our beloved country through the vicissitudes of another year the invaluable blessings of health, plenty, and peace.

∽

MARTIN VAN BUREN, WHO JOINED THE DUTCH REFORMED CHURCH, 1860, IN HIS LAST ILLNESS:

The atonement of Jesus Christ is the only remedy and rest for my soul.

∽

Martin Van Buren - 8th President

WILLIAM HENRY HARRISON

WILLIAM HENRY HARRISON, 1840, TO METHODIST CHURCH PASTOR IN CINCINNATI PRIOR TO HIS ELECTION:

I know there are some of my political opponents who will be ready to impugn my motives in attending this revival-meeting at this peculiar time; but I care not for the smiles or frowns of my fellow-countrymen. God knows my heart and understands my motives. A deep and an abiding sense of my inward spiritual necessities brings me to this hallowed place night after night.

∞

WILLIAM HENRY HARRISON, MAR. 4, 1841, INAUGURAL, DELIVERED ONLY 30 DAYS BEFORE HIS DEATH:

I too well understand the dangerous temptations to which I shall be exposed from the magnitude of the power which it has been the pleasure of the people to commit to my hands not to place my chief confidence upon the aid of that Almighty Power which has hitherto protected me and enabled me...We admit of no government by divine right, believing that so far as power is concerned the Beneficent Creator has made no distinction amongst men; that all are upon an equality, and that the only legitimate right to govern is an express grant of power from the governed.

∽

WILLIAM HENRY HARRISON, MAR. 4, 1841, INAUGURAL:

The maxim which our ancestors derived from the mother country that "freedom of the press is the great bulwark of civil and religious liberty" is one of the most precious legacies which they have left us.

∽

WILLIAM HENRY HARRISON, MAR. 4, 1841, INAUGURAL:

Limited as are the powers which have been granted, still enough have been granted to constitute a despotism if concentrated in one of the departments...more particularly...the Executive branch...

The tendency of power to increase itself, particularly when exercised by a single individual...would terminate in virtual monarchy...As long as the love of power is a dominant passion of the human bosom, and as long as the understanding of men can be warped and their affections changed by operations upon their passions and prejudices, so long will the liberties of a people depend on their constant attention to its preservation.

∽

WILLIAM HENRY HARRISON, MAR. 4, 1841, INAUGURAL:

The tendencies of all such governments in their decline is to monarchy, and the antagonist principle to liberty there is the spirit of faction - a spirit which assumes the character and in times of great excitement imposes itself upon the people as the genuine spirit of freedom, and, like the false christs whose coming was foretold by the Savior, seeks to, and were it possible would, impose upon the true and most faithful disciples of liberty. It is in periods like this that it behooves the people to be most watchful of those to whom they have intrusted power.

∽

WILLIAM HENRY HARRISON, MAR. 4, 1841, INAUGURAL:

I deem the present occasion sufficiently important and solemn to justify me in expressing to my fellow citizens a profound reverence for the Christian religion, and a thorough conviction that sound morals, religious liberty, and a just sense of religious responsibility are essentially connected with all true and lasting happiness;

And to that good Being who has blessed us by the gifts of civil and religious freedom, who watched over and prospered the labors of our fathers and has hitherto preserved to us institutions far exceeding in excellence those of any other people, let us unite in fervently commending every interest of our beloved country in all future time.

∽

WILLIAM HENRY HARRISON, 1841, LETTER TO WIFE, ANNA:

I retired into the presence of my Maker, and implored his gracious guidance in the faithful discharge of the duties of my high station.

∽

WILLIAM HENRY HARRISON, TO WHITE HOUSE VISITORS:

We shall be happy to see you at any time except on the Sabbath.

∽

WILLIAM HENRY HARRISON,
TO PRESBYTERIAN PASTOR NEAR HIS INDIANA HOME:

I think I enjoy religion and delight in the duties of a child of God, and have concluded to unite with the Church of God as soon as my health will permit me to go out.

∽

William Henry Harrison - 9th President

JOHN
TYLER

JOHN TYLER, APR. 9, 1841, UPON ASSUMING
PRESIDENCY AFTER DEATH OF PRESIDENT HARRISON:

For the first time in our history the person elected to the Vice-Presidency...has had devolved upon him the Presidential office...My earnest prayer shall be constantly addressed to the all-wise and all-powerful Being who made me, and by whose dispensation I am called to the high office of President...Confiding in the protecting care of an everwatchful and overruling Providence, it shall be my first and highest duty to preserve unimpaired the free institutions under which we live and transmit them to those who shall succeed me in their full force and vigor.

❧

JOHN TYLER, APR. 13, 1841, NATIONAL DAY OF FASTING
UPON THE DEATH OF PRESIDENT HARRISON:

When a Christian people feel themselves to be overtaken by a great public calamity, it becomes them to humble themselves under the dispensation of Divine Providence, to recognize His righteous government over the children of men, to acknowledge His goodness in time past, as well as their own unworthiness, and to supplicate His merciful protection for the future...to impress all minds with a sense of the uncertainty of human things and of the dependence of nations, as well as individuals, upon our Heavenly Parent...

We may all with one accord join in humble and reverential approach to Him in whose hands we are, invoking Him to inspire us with a proper spirit and temper of heart and mind under these frowns of His providence and still to bestow His gracious benedictions upon our Government and our country.

∽

JOHN TYLER, JUN. 13, 1841, TO MRS. ANNA SYMMES HARRISON, WIDOW OF LATE-PRESIDENT:

In conveying to you, my dear madam...sincere condolences on the late afflicting dispensations of Providence, permit me to mingle my feelings with theirs and tender you my fervent wishes for your health, happiness, and long life.

∽

JOHN TYLER, AUG. 16, 1841, VETO MESSAGE:

The bill entitled "An act to incorporate the subscribers to the Fiscal Bank of the United States"...has been considered...I can not conscientiously give it my approval...Under an impressive dispensation of Providence I succeeded to the Presidential office. Before entering upon the duties of that office I took an oath...

I could not give my sanction to a measure of the character described without surrendering all claim to the respect of honorable men, all confidence on the part of the people, all self-respect, all regard for moral and religious obligations, without an observance of which no government can be prosperous and no people can be happy.

∽

JOHN TYLER, DEC. 7, 1841, 1ST ANNUAL MESSAGE:

We are in the enjoyment of all the blessings of civil and religious liberty...We are all called upon by the highest obligations of duty to renew our thanks and our devotion to our Heavenly Parent, who has continued to vouchsafe to us the eminent blessings which surround us and who has so signally crowned the year with His goodness. If we find ourselves increasingly beyond example in numbers, in strength, in wealth, in knowledge, in everything which promotes human and social happiness, let us ever remember our dependence for all these on the protection and merciful dispensations of Divine Providence.

∽

JOHN TYLER, AUG. 30, 1842, PROTEST MESSAGE:

It is true that the succession of the Vice-President to the Chief Magistracy has never occurred before...But I found myself placed in this most responsible station by no usurpation or contrivance of my own. I was called to it, under Providence, by the supreme law of the land and the deliberately declared will of the people.

∽

JOHN TYLER, DEC. 6, 1842, 2ND ANNUAL MESSAGE:

We have continued reason to express our profound gratitude to the Great Creator of All Things for the numberless benefits conferred upon us as a people. Blessed with genial seasons, the husbandman has his garners filled with abundance, and the necessaries of life, not to speak of its luxuries, abound in every direction...

Such are the circumstances under which you now assemble in your respective chambers and which should lead us to unite in praise and thanksgiving to that Great Being who made us and who preserves us as a nation...The schoolmaster and the missionary are found side by side, and the remnants of what were once numerous and powerful nations may yet be preserved as the builders up of a new name for themselves and their posterity.

∽

JOHN TYLER, DEC. 1843, 3RD ANNUAL MESSAGE:

If any people ever had cause to render up thanks to the Supreme Being for parental care and protection extended to them in all the trials and difficulties to which they have been from time to time exposed, we certainly are that people.

From the first settlement of our forefathers on the continent, through the dangers attendant upon the occupation of a savage wilderness, through a long period of colonial dependence, through the War of the Revolution, in the wisdom which led to the adoption of the existing forms of republican government...the superintendence of an overruling Providence has been plainly visible. As preparatory, therefore, to entering once more upon the high duties of legislation, it becomes us humbly to acknowledge our dependence upon Him as our guide and protector and to implore a continuance of His parental watchfulness over our beloved country.

❧

JOHN TYLER, DEC. 3, 1844, 4TH ANNUAL MESSAGE:

We have continued cause for expressing our gratitude to the Supreme Ruler of the Universe for the benefits and blessings which our country, under His kind providence, has enjoyed...The guaranty of religious freedom, of the freedom of the press, of the liberty of speech, of the trial by jury, of the habeas corpus;...

In the progress of time the inestimable principles of civil liberty will be enjoyed by millions yet unborn...Our prayers should evermore be offered up to the Father of the Universe for His wisdom to direct us in the path of our duty so as to enable us to consummate these high purposes.

❧

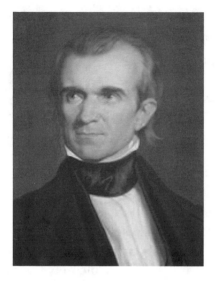

JAMES K.
POLK

JAMES K. POLK, MAR. 4, 1845, INAUGURAL:

I fervently invoke the aid of that Almighty Ruler of the Universe in whose hands are the destinies of nations and of men to guard this Heaven-favored land...The Republic of Texas has made known her desire to come into our Union, to form a part of our Confederacy and enjoy with us the blessings of liberty secured and guaranteed by our Constitution...I enter upon the discharge of the high duties which have been assigned to me by the people, again humbly supplicating that Divine Being, who has watched over and protected our beloved country from its infancy to the present hour.

∽

JAMES K. POLK, JUN. 16, 1845, UPON DEATH OF ANDREW JACKSON, ORDER NO. 27 TO ACTING SECRETARY OF WAR AND SECRETARY OF THE NAVY, GEORGE BANCROFT:

The President of the United States with heartfelt sorrow announces to the Army, the Navy, and the Marine Corps the death of

Andrew Jackson. On the evening of Sunday, the 8th day of June, about 6 o'clock, he resigned his spirit to his Heavenly Father...Heaven gave him length of days and he filled them with deeds of greatness...Thrice happy in death, for while he believed the liberties of his country imperishable and was cheered by visions of its constant advancement, he departed from this life in a full hope of a blessed immortality through the merits and atonement of the Redeemer.

∽

JAMES K. POLK, DEC. 2, 1845, 1ST ANNUAL MESSAGE:

Under the blessings of Divine Providence and the benign influence of our free institutions, it stands before the world a spectacle of national happiness...It becomes us in humility to make our devout acknowledgments to the Supreme Ruler of the Universe for the inestimable civil and religious blessings with which we are favored....Our experience has shown that when banking corporations have been the keepers of the public money, and been thereby made in effect the Treasury, the Government can have no guaranty that it can command the use of its own money for public purposes.

The late Bank of the United States proved to be faithless...Public money should not be mingled with the private funds of banks or individuals or to be used for private purposes. When it is placed in banks for safe-keeping, it is in effect loaned to them without interest, and is loaned by them upon interest to borrowers from them. The public money is converted into banking capital, and is used and loaned out for the private profit of bank stockholders. ...The framers of the Constitution could never have intended that the money paid into the Treasury should be thus converted to private use.

∽

JAMES K. POLK, MAY 13, 1846,
PROCLAMATION OF WAR WITH REPUBLIC OF MEXICO:

I do, moreover, exhort all the good people of the United States, as they love their country, as they feel the wrongs which have forced on them the last resort of injured nations, and they consult the best means, under the blessing of Divine Providence, of abridging its calamities.

∽

JAMES K. POLK, DEC. 8, 1846, 2ND ANNUAL MESSAGE:

Our devout and sincere acknowledgments are due to the gracious Giver of All Good for the numberless blessings which our beloved country enjoys.

∞

JAMES K. POLK, DEC. 7, 1847, 3RD ANNUAL MESSAGE:

The success of our admirable system is a conclusive refutation of the theories of those in other countries who maintain that a "favored few" are born to rule and that the mass of mankind must be governed by force. Subject to no arbitrary or hereditary authority, the people are the only sovereigns recognized by our Constitution...No country has been so much favored, or should acknowledge with deeper reverence the manifestations of Divine protection.

An all-wise Creator directed and guarded us in our infant struggle for freedom and has constantly watched over our surprising progress until we have become one of the great nations of the earth...In the enjoyment of the bounties of Providence at home such as have rarely fallen to the lot of any people, it is the cause of congratulation... Invoking the blessing of the Almighty Ruler of the Universe upon your deliberations, it will be my highest duty, no less than my sincere pleasure, to cooperate with you in all measures which may tend to promote the honor and enduring welfare of our common country..

∞

JAMES K. POLK, FEB. 24, 1848, EXECUTIVE ORDER:

It has pleased Divine Providence to call hence a great and patriotic citizen. John Quincy Adams is no more. At the advanced age of more than fourscore years, he was suddenly stricken from his seat in the House of Representatives...He had for more than a half a century filled the most important public stations.

∞

JAMES K. POLK, DEC. 5, 1848, 4TH ANNUAL MESSAGE:

Under the benignant providence of Almighty God the representatives of the States and of the people are again brought together to deliberate for the public good. The gratitude of the nation to the Sovereign Arbiter of All Human Events should be commensurate with the boundless blessings which we enjoy.

Peace, plenty, and contentment reign throughout our borders, and our beloved country presents a sublime moral spectacle to the world...Invoking the blessing of the Almighty upon your deliberations at your present important session, my ardent hope is that in a spirit of harmony and concord you may be guided to wise results, and such as my redound to the happiness, the honor, and the glory of our beloved country.

≼

JAMES K. POLK, JUN. 8, 1849, COMMENT A WEEK BEFORE HIS DEATH TO REV. EDGAR, NASHVILLE, TN, RESULTING IN HIS BAPTISM INTO THE METHODIST EPISCOPAL CHURCH, SOUTH, & RECEIVING THE LORD'S SUPPER:

Sir, if I had supposed, twenty years ago, that I should come to my death bed unprepared, it would have made me an unhappy man; and yet I am about to die, and have not made preparation. I have not been baptized. Tell me, sir, can there be any ground for a man thus situated to hope?

≼

ZACHARY TAYLOR

ZACHARY TAYLOR, FEB. 21, 1849,
ACKNOWLEDGEMENT OF BIBLE PRESENTED BY A
DELEGATION OF LADIES FROM FRANKFURT, KY,
PRINTED IN FRANKFORT COMMONWEALTH:

I accept with gratitude and pleasure your gift of this inestimable Volume. It was for the love of the truths of this great Book that our fathers abandoned their native shores for the wilderness. Animated by its lofty principles they toiled and suffered till the desert blossomed as a rose. The same truths sustained them in their resolutions to become a free nation; and guided by the wisdom of this Book they founded a government.

∽

ZACHARY TAYLOR, FEB. 21, 1849, ACKNOWLEDGEMENT OF BIBLE PRESENTED BY A DELEGATION OF LADIES FROM FRANKFURT, KY, FRANKFORT COMMONWEALTH:

If there were in that Book nothing but its great precept, "All things whatsoever ye would that men should do unto you, do ye even so to them," and if that precept were obeyed, our government might extend over the whole Continent.

&

ZACHARY TAYLOR, MAR. 5, 1849, INAUGURAL, DELIVERED A DAY LATER THAN USUAL AS HE REFUSED TO BE SWORN IN ON SUNDAY IN HONOR OF THE SABBATH:

Our geographical position, the genius of our institutions and our people, the advancing spirit of civilization, and, above all, the dictates of religion direct us to the cultivation of peaceful and friendly relations with all other powers...

In conclusion I congratulate you, my fellow-citizens, upon the high state of prosperity to which the goodness of Divine Providence has conducted our common country. Let us invoke a continuance of the same protecting care which has led us from small beginnings to the eminence we this day occupy.

&

ZACHARY TAYLOR, JUL. 3, 1849, NATIONAL DAY OF PRAYER PROCLAMATION DURING A CHOLERA EPIDEMIC:

At a season when the providence of God has manifested itself in the visitation of a fearful pestilence which is spreading itself throughout the land, it is fitting that a people whose reliance has ever been in His protection should humble themselves before His throne, and, while acknowledging past transgressions, ask a continuance of the Divine mercy. It is therefore earnestly recommended that the first Friday in August be observed throughout the United States as a day of fasting, humiliation, and prayer.

All business will be sustained in the various branches of the public service on that day; and it is recommended to persons of all religious denominations to abstain as far as practical from secular occupations and to assemble in their respective places of public worship, to acknowledge the Infinite Goodness which has watched over our existence as a nation, and so long crowned us with manifold blessings, and to implore the Almighty in His own good time to stay the destroying hand which is now lifted up against us.

❦

ZACHARY TAYLOR, JUL. 4, 1849, ADDRESS AT SABBATH-SCHOOL CELEBRATION IN THE CITY OF WASHINGTON:

The only ground of hope for the continuance of our free institutions is in the proper moral and religious training of the children, that they may be prepared to discharge aright the duties of men and citizens.

❦

ZACHARY TAYLOR, DEC. 4, 1849, 1ST ANNUAL MESSAGE:

During the past year we have been blessed by a kind Providence with an abundance of the fruits of the earth, and although the destroying angel for a time visited extensive portions of our territory with the ravages of a dreadful pestilence, yet the Almighty has at length deigned to stay His hand and to restore the inestimable blessing of general health to a people who acknowledged His power, deprecated His wrath, and implored His merciful protection...It is a proper theme of thanksgiving to Him who rules the destinies of nations.

❦

ZACHARY TAYLOR, DEC. 4, 1849, 1ST ANNUAL MESSAGE:

With a sedulous inculcation of that respect and love for the Union of the States which our fathers cherished and enjoined upon their children, and with the aid of that overruling Providence which has so long and so kindly guarded our liberties and institutions, we may reasonably expect to transmit them, with their innumerable blessings, to the remotest posterity.

❦

ZACHARY TAYLOR, DEC. 4, 1849, 1ST ANNUAL MESSAGE:

We have not been insensible to the distractions and wars which have prevailed in other quarters of the world. It is a proper theme of thanksgiving to Him who rules the destinies of nations that we have been able to maintain amidst all these contests an independent and neutral position toward all belligerent powers.

❦

Zachary Taylor - 12th President

MILLARD FILLMORE

MILLARD FILLMORE, JUL. 10, 1850, UPON ASSUMING THE PRESIDENCY AFTER THE DEATH OF PRESIDENT TAYLOR:

A great man has fallen among us, and a whole country is called to an occasion of unexpected, deep, and general mourning...

I appeal to you to aid me, under the trying circumstances which surround me, in the discharge of the duties from which, however much I may be oppressed by them, I dare not shrink; and I rely upon Him who holds in His hands the destinies of nations to endow me with the requisite strength for the task and to avert from our country the evils apprehended from the heavy calamity which has befallen us.

∽

MILLARD FILLMORE, AUG. 6, 1850, ADDRESS TO CONGRESS:

It is plain, therefore, on the face of these treaty stipulations that all Mexicans established in territories north or east of the line of demarcation already mentioned come within the protection of the ninth article, and that the treaty, being a part of the supreme law of the land, does extend over all such Mexicans, and assures to them perfect security in the free enjoyment of their liberty and property, as well as in the free exercise of their religion.

∽

MILLARD FILLMORE, DEC. 2, 1850, 1ST ANNUAL MESSAGE:

Being suddenly called in the midst of the last session of Congress by a painful dispensation of Divine Providence to the responsible station which I now hold, I contented myself with such communications...

Nations, like individuals in a state of nature, are equal and independent, possessing certain rights and owing certain duties to each other, arising from their necessary and unavoidable relations...

There are rights and duties, binding in morals, in conscience, and in honor...The great law of morality ought to have a national as well as a personal and individual application. We should act toward other nations as we wish them to act toward us.

∽

MILLARD FILLMORE, DEC. 2, 1850, 1ST ANNUAL MESSAGE:

I can not bring this communication to a close without invoking you to join me in humble and devout thanks to the Great Ruler of Nations for the multiplied blessings which He has graciously bestowed upon us. His hand, so often visible in our preservation, has stayed the pestilence...

Our liberties, religious and civil, have been maintained, the fountains of knowledge have all been kept open, and means of happiness widely spread and generally enjoyed greater than have fallen to the lot of any other nation.

And while deeply penetrated with gratitude for the past let us hope that His all-wise providence will so guide our counsels as that they shall result in giving satisfaction to our constituents, securing the peace of the country, and adding new strength to the united Government under which we live.

∽

MILLARD FILLMORE, DEC. 2, 1851, 2ND ANNUAL MESSAGE:

None can look back to the dangers which are passed or forward to the bright prospect before us without feeling a thrill of gratification, at the same time that he must be impressed with a grateful sense of our profound obligations to a beneficent Providence, whose paternal care is so manifest in the happiness of this highly favored land.

∽

MILLARD FILLMORE, DEC. 6, 1852,
3RD ANNUAL MESSAGE:

Our grateful thanks are due to an all-merciful Providence, not only for staying the pestilence which in different forms has desolated some of our cities, but for crowning the labors of the husbandman with an abundant harvest and the nation generally with the blessings of peace and prosperity...

We owe these blessings, under Heaven, to the happy Constitution and Government which were bequeathed to us by our fathers, and which it is our sacred duty to transmit in all their integrity to our children.

∽

MILLARD FILLMORE, DEC. 6, 1852,
3RD ANNUAL MESSAGE:

Our grateful thanks are due to an all-merciful Providence, not only for staying the pestilence which in different forms has desolated some of our cities, but for crowning the labors of the husbandman with an abundant harvest and the nation generally with the blessings of peace and prosperity...

Our own free institutions were not the offspring of our Revolution. They existed before. They were planted in the free charters of self-government under which the English colonies grew up, and our Revolution only freed us from the dominion of a foreign power whose government was at variance with those institutions.

But European nations have had no such training for self-government, and every effort to establish it by bloody revolutions has been, and must without that preparation continue to be, a failure.

Liberty unregulated by law degenerates into anarchy, which soon becomes the most horrid of all despotisms. We owe these blessings, under Heaven, to the happy Constitution and

Government which were bequeathed to us by our fathers, and which it is our sacred duty to transmit in all their integrity to our children.

❧

MILLARD FILLMORE, STATEMENT AFTER BEING INAUGURATED PRESIDENT, MEMBER OF THE EPISCOPAL CHURCH:

The Sabbath day I always kept as a day of rest. Besides being a religious duty, it was essential to health. On commencing my Presidential career, I found that the Sabbath had frequently been employed by visitors for private interviews with the President. I determined to put an end to this custom, and ordered my doorkeeper to meet all Sunday visitors with an indiscriminate refusal.

❧

FRANKLIN
PIERCE

FRANKLIN PIERCE, 1839, WHILE SERVING IN
THE U.S. SENATE, TO HIS LAW PARTNER:

I have dwelt somewhat more this winter upon the truths of divine revelation than usual and perhaps have struggled somewhat harder to think and act in conformity with the precepts and commands of the New Testament than ever before.

᎒

FRANKLIN PIERCE, MAR. 4, 1853, INAUGURAL, ONLY 2 MONTHS AFTER HIS 11-YEAR-ONLY SON, BENNIE, WAS KILLED AS THEIR CAMPAIGN TRAIN ROLLED OFF TRACKS:

Our fathers decided for themselves, both upon the hour to declare and the hour to strike. They were their own judges of the circumstances under which it became them to pledge to each other "their lives, their fortunes, and their sacred honor" for the acquisition of the priceless inheritance transmitted to us.

The energy with which that great conflict was opened was under the guidance of a manifest and beneficent Providence.

❧

FRANKLIN PIERCE, MAR. 4, 1853, INAUGURAL:

The dangers of a concentration of all power in the General government of a confederacy so vast as ours are too obvious to be disregarded. You have a right...to expect your agents in every department to regard strictly the limits imposed upon them by the Constitution...Liberty rests upon a proper distribution of power between the State and Federal authorities...With the Union my best and dearest earthly hopes are entwined. Without it what are we individually or collectively? What becomes of the noblest field ever opened for the advancement of our race in religion, in government, in the arts, and in all that dignifies and adorns mankind.

❧

FRANKLIN PIERCE, MAR. 4, 1853, INAUGURAL:

It is with me an earnest and vital belief that as the Union has been the source, under Providence, of our prosperity to this time, so it is the surest pledge of a continuance of the blessings we have enjoyed, and which we are sacredly bound to transmit undiminished to our children...But let not the foundation of our hope rest upon man's wisdom...It must be felt that there is no national security but in the nation's humble, acknowledged dependence upon God and His overruling providence...With all the cherished memories of the past gathering around me like so many eloquent voices of exhortation from Heaven, I can express no better hope for my country than that the kind Providence which smiled upon our fathers may enable their children to preserve the blessings they have inherited.

❧

FRANKLIN PIERCE, DEC. 5, 1853, 1ST ANNUAL MESSAGE:

Although disease, assuming at one time the characteristics of a widespread and devastating pestilence, has left its sad traces upon some portions of our country, we have still the most abundant cause for reverent thankfulness to God for an accumulation of signal mercies showered upon us as a nation. It is well that a consciousness of rapid advancement and increasing strength be habitually associated with an abiding sense of dependence upon Him who holds in His hands the destiny of men and of nations.

≪

FRANKLIN PIERCE, DEC. 5, 1853, 1ST ANNUAL MESSAGE:

Recognizing the wisdom of the broad principles of absolute religious toleration proclaimed in our fundamental law, and rejoicing in the benign influence which it has exerted upon our social and political condition, I should shrink from a clear duty if I failed to express my deepest conviction that we can place no secure reliance upon any apparent progress if it be not sustained by national integrity, resting upon the great truths affirmed and illustrated by Divine Revelation.

≪

FRANKLIN PIERCE, DEC. 5, 1853, 1ST ANNUAL MESSAGE:

The Federal Government has...limited powers conferred on it by the Constitution, chiefly as to those things in which the States have a common interest in their relations to one another and to foreign governments, while the great mass of interests which belong to cultivated men - the ordinary business of life...- rest securely upon the general reserved powers of the people of the several States...Happily, I have no occasion to suggest any radical changes in the financial policy of the Government. Ours is almost, if not absolutely, the solitary power of Christendom having a surplus revenue drawn immediately from imposts on commerce.

≪

FRANKLIN PIERCE, DEC. 4, 1854, 2ND ANNUAL MESSAGE:

In the present, therefore, as in the past, we find ample grounds for reverent thankfulness to the God of grace and providence for His protecting care and merciful dealings with us as a people...As individuals we can not repress sympathy with human suffering nor regret for the causes which produce it; as a nation we are reminded that whatever interrupts the peace or checks the prosperity of any part of Christendom tends more or less to involve our own...

We have to maintain inviolate the great doctrine of the inherent right of popular self-government...to harmonize a sincere and ardent devotion to the institutions of religious faith with the most universal religious toleration...whilst exalting the condition of the Republic, to assure to it the legitimate influence and the benign authority of a great example amongst all the powers of Christendom. Under the solemnity of these convictions the blessings of Almighty God is earnestly invoked to attend upon your deliberations and upon all the counsels and acts of Government, to the end that, with common zeal and common efforts, we may, in humble submission to the divine will, cooperate for the promotion of the supreme good of these United States.

∽

FRANKLIN PIERCE, DEC. 31, 1855, 3RD ANNUAL MESSAGE:

I rely confidently on the patriotism of the people, on the dignity and self-respect of the States, on the wisdom of Congress, and, above all, on the continued gracious favor of Almighty God to maintain against all enemies, whether at home or abroad, the sanctity of the Constitution and the integrity of the Union.

∽

FRANKLIN PIERCE, JAN. 16, 1857, TO THE SENATE:

I communicate to the Senate herewith, for its constitutional action, a treaty made and concluded at Fort Leavenworth, Kansas Territory, on the 16th day of December, 1856, between Indian Agent Benjamin F. Robinson, commissioner on the part of the United States, the principal men of the Christian Indians, and Gottleib F. Oehler, on behalf of the board of elders of the northern diocese of the Church of the United Brethren in the United States of America.

∽

JAMES BUCHANAN

JAMES BUCHANAN, WHILE U.S. MINISTER IN RUSSIA, 1832-1833, TO HIS BROTHER, A PRESBYTERIAN MINISTER:

I can sincerely say for myself that I desire to be a Christian, and I think I could withdraw from the vanities and follies of the world without suffering many pangs.

I have thought much upon the subject since my arrival in this strange land and sometimes almost persuade myself that I am a Christian: but I am often haunted by the spirit of skepticism. My true feeling upon many occasions is: "Lord, I would believe; help thou my unbelief." Yet I am far from being an unbeliever.

∽

JAMES BUCHANAN, FEB. 29, 1844,
TO HIS BROTHER FROM WASHINGTON, DC:

I am a believer; but not with that degree of firmness of faith calculated to exercise a controlling influence on my conduct. I ought constantly to pray, "Help Thou my unbelief."

I trust that the Almighty Father, through the merits and atonement of His Son, will yet vouchsafe to me a clearer and stronger faith than I possess.

❧

JAMES BUCHANAN, MAR. 4, 1857, INAUGURAL:

In entering upon this great office I must humbly invoke the God of our fathers for wisdom and firmness to execute its high and responsible duties...We should never forget...those exiles from foreign shores who may seek in this country to improve their condition and to enjoy the blessings of civil and religious liberty...

We ought to cultivate peace, commerce, and friendship with all nations, and this not merely as the best means of promoting our own material interests, but in a spirit of Christian benevolence toward our fellow-men, wherever their lot may be cast...In all our acquisitions the people, under the protection of the American flag, have enjoyed civil and religious liberty...

I shall now proceed to take the oath prescribed by the Constitution, whilst humbly invoking the blessing of Divine Providence on this great people.

❧

JAMES BUCHANAN, DEC. 8, 1857, 1ST ANNUAL MESSAGE:

First and above all, our thanks are due to Almighty God for the numerous benefits which He has bestowed upon this people, and our united prayers ought to ascend to Him that He would continue to bless our great Republic in time to come as He has blessed it in time past.

❧

JAMES BUCHANAN, JAN. 7, 1858,
MESSAGE TO THE SENATE:

The crime well deserves the punishment inflicted upon it by our laws. It violates the principles of Christianity, morality, and humanity, held sacred by all civilized nations and by none more than by the people of the United States...The avowed principle which lies at the foundation of the law of nations is contained in the Divine command that "all things whatsoever ye would that men should do to you do ye even so to them."

Tried by this unerring rule, we should be severely condemned if we shall not use our best exertions to arrest such expeditions against our feeble sister republic of Nicaragua.

᪣

JAMES BUCHANAN, FEB. 2, 1858, ADDRESS TO CONGRESS:
I have thus performed my duty on this important question, under a deep sense of responsibility to God and my country. My public life will terminate within a brief period, and I have no other object of earthly ambition than to leave my country in a peaceful and prosperous condition.

᪣

JAMES BUCHANAN, DEC. 6, 1858, 2ND ANNUAL MESSAGE:
We have much reason for gratitude to that Almighty Providence which has never failed to interpose for our relief at the most critical periods of our history...Immediately upon the formation of a new Territory people from different States and from foreign countries rush into it for the laudable purpose of improving their condition. Their first duty to themselves is to open and cultivate farms, to construct roads, to establish schools, to erect places of religious worship.

᪣

JAMES BUCHANAN, DEC. 20, 1858, TO THE SENATE:
Under the act of JAN. 17, 1858, the courts of inquiry were directed to investigate "the physical, mental, professional, and moral fitness" of each officer who applied to them for relief...In performance of my duty I found the greatest difficulty in deciding what should be considered as "moral fitness" for the Navy...There has been but one perfect standard of morality on earth, and how far a departure from His precepts and example must proceed in order to disqualify an officer for the naval service is a question on which a great difference of honest opinion must always exist.

᪣

JAMES BUCHANAN, DEC. 19, 1859, 3RD ANNUAL MESSAGE:
We are obliged as a Christian and moral nation to consider what would be the effect upon unhappy Africa itself if we should reopen the slave trade. This would give the trade an impulse and extension which it has never had, even in its palmiest days.

The numerous victims required to supply it would convert the whole slave coast into a perfect pandemonium, for which this country would be held responsible in the eyes both of God and man...

When a market for African slaves shall no longer be furnished in Cuba, and thus all the world be closed against this trade, we may then indulge a reasonable hope for the gradual improvement of Africa...In this manner Christianity and civilization may gradually penetrate the existing gloom.

⍥

JAMES BUCHANAN, DEC. 3, 1860, 4TH ANNUAL MESSAGE:

Self-preservation is the first law of nature, and has been implanted in the heart of man by his Creator for the wisest purpose; and no political union, however fraught with blessings and benefits in all other respects, can long continue if the necessary consequence be to render the homes and the firesides of nearly half the parties to it habitually and hopelessly insecure.

Sooner or later the bonds of such a union must be severed. It is my conviction that this fatal period has not yet arrived, and my prayer to God is that He would preserve the Constitution and the Union throughout all generations...

As sovereign States, they, and they alone, are responsible before God...What, in the meantime, is the responsibility and true position of the Executive?

He is bound by solemn oath, before God and the country, "to take care that the laws be faithfully executed," and from this obligation he can not be absolved by any human power...

When we take a retrospect of what was then our condition and contrast this with its material prosperity at the time of the late Presidential elections, we have abundant reason to return our grateful thanks to that merciful Providence which has never forsaken us as a nation in all our past trials...

My prayer to God is that He would preserve the Constitution and the Union throughout all generations...It is with great satisfaction I communicate the fact that since the date of my last annual message not a single slave has been imported into the United States in violation of the laws prohibiting the African Slave trade...

It surely ought to be the prayer of every Christian and patriot that such expeditions may never again receive countenance in our country or depart from our shores.

∽

JAMES BUCHANAN, DEC. 14, 1860, NATIONAL DAY OF HUMILIATION, FASTING & PRAYER PROCLAMATION:

The Union of the States is at the present moment threatened with alarming and immediate danger...In this the hour of our calamity and peril to whom shall we resort for relief but to the God of our fathers? His omnipotent arm only can save us from the awful effects of our own crimes and follies - our own ingratitude and guilt toward our Heavenly Father.

Let us, then, with deep contrition and penitent sorrow unite in humbling ourselves before the Most High, in confessing our individual and national sins, and in acknowledging the justice of our punishment. Let us implore Him to remove from our hearts that false pride of opinion which would impel us to persevere in wrong.

∽

JAMES BUCHANAN, DEC. 14, 1860, NATIONAL DAY OF HUMILIATION, FASTING & PRAYER PROCLAMATION:

Let us with deep reverence beseech Him to restore the friendship and good will which prevailed in former days among the people of the several States, and, above all, to save us from the horrors of civil war and "blood guiltiness."

Let our fervent prayers ascend to His throne that He would not desert us in this hour of extreme peril, but remember us as He did our fathers in the darkest days of the Revolution...

An omnipotent Providence may overrule existing evils for permanent good. He can make the wrath of man to praise Him, and the remainder of wrath He can restrain.

Let me invoke every individual, in whatever sphere of life he may be placed, to feel a personal responsibility to God and his country for keeping this day holy and for contributing all in his power to remove our actual and impending calamities.

∽

JAMES BUCHANAN, NEARING THE END OF HIS LIFE, IN A LETTER TO A FRIEND:

We are both at a period of life when it is our duty to relax our grasp on the world fast receding, and fix our thoughts, desires, and affections on One who knows no change. I trust in God that, through the merits and atonement of His Son, we may both be prepared for the inevitable change.

∽

ABRAHAM LINCOLN

ABRAHAM LINCOLN, AUG. 15, 1846, ILLINOIS GAZETTE:

I have never denied the truth of the Scriptures; and I have never spoken with intentional disrespect of religion in general, or of any denomination of Christians in particular...I do not think I could, myself, be brought to support a man for office whom I knew to be an open enemy of, and scoffer at religion.

༄

ABRAHAM LINCOLN, SEP. 11, 1858, AT EDWARDSVILLE, IL:

Our reliance is in the love of liberty which God has planted in us. Our defense is in the spirit which prized liberty as the heritage of all men, in all lands everywhere. Destroy this spirit and you have planted the seeds of despotism at your own doors. Familiarize yourselves with the chains of bondage and you prepare your own limbs to wear them. Accustomed to trample on the rights of others, you have lost the genius of your own independence and become the fit subjects of the first cunning tyrant who rises among you.

༄

ABRAHAM LINCOLN, APR 6, 1859, TO H.L. PIERCE

This is a world of compensation; and he who would be no slave must consent to have no slave. Those who deny freedom to others deserve it not for themselves, and under a just God, cannot long retain it.

∽

ABRAHAM LINCOLN, FEB. 23, 1861, WILLIAM DODGE:

With the support of the people and the assistance of the Almighty, I shall undertake to perform it....Freedom is the natural condition of the human race, in which the Almighty intended men to live. Those who fight the purpose of the Almighty will not succeed. They always have been, they always will be, beaten.

∽

ABRAHAM LINCOLN, MAR. 4, 1861, 1ST INAUGURAL:

The candid citizen must confess that if the policy of the Government upon vital questions affecting the whole people is to be irrevocably fixed by decisions of the Supreme Court, the instant they are made...the people will have ceased to be their own rulers, having to that extent practically resigned their Government into the hands of the eminent tribunal.

∽

ABRAHAM LINCOLN, MAR. 4, 1861, 1ST INAUGURAL:

Intelligence, patriotism, Christianity, and a firm reliance on Him who has never yet forsaken this favored land, are still competent to adjust in the best way all our present difficulty.

∽

ABRAHAM LINCOLN, AUG. 12, 1861, DAY OF HUMILIATION, PRAYER & FASTING AFTER UNION DEFEAT AT BULL RUN:

Whereas when our own beloved country, once, by the blessings of God, united, prosperous and happy, is now afflicted with faction and civil war, it is peculiarly fit for us to recognize the hand of God in this terrible visitation, and in sorrowful remembrance of our own faults and crimes as a nation and as individuals, to humble ourselves before Him and to pray for His mercy - to pray that we may be spared further punishment, though most justly deserved...that the inestimable boon of civil and religious liberty...may be restored.

ॐ
ABRAHAM LINCOLN, APR. 10, 1862, PROCLAMATION:

It has pleased Almighty God to vouchsafe signal victories to the land and naval forces...and at the same time to avert from our country the dangers of foreign intervention and invasion.

It is therefore recommended to the people of the United States that at their next weekly assemblages in their accustomed places of public worship...they especially acknowledge and render thanks to our Heavenly Father for these inestimable blessings, that they then and there implore spiritual consolation in behalf of all who have been brought into affliction by the casualties and calamities of sedition and civil war.

ॐ
ABRAHAM LINCOLN, SEP. 22, 1862, ADDRESSING CABINET AFTER CONFEDERATE DEFEAT AT ANTIETAM:

I made a solemn vow before God, that if General Lee were driven back from Pennsylvania, I would crown the result by the declaration of freedom to the slaves.

ॐ
ABRAHAM LINCOLN, NOV. 15, 1862, GENERAL ORDER:

The President, Commander in Chief of the Army and Navy, desires and enjoins the orderly observance of the Sabbath by the officers and men in the military and naval service. The importance for man and beast of the prescribed weekly rest, the sacred rights of Christian soldiers and sailors, a becoming deference to the best sentiment of a Christian people, and a due regard for the Divine Will demand that Sunday labor in the Army and Navy be reduced to the measure of strict necessity.

The discipline and character of the national forces should not suffer nor the cause they defend be imperiled by the profanation of the day or name of the Most High. "At this time of public distress," adopting the words of Washington in 1776, "men may find enough to do in the service of God and their country without abandoning themselves to vice and immorality."

The first general order issued by the Father of his Country after the Declaration of Independence indicates the spirit in which our institutions were founded and should ever be defended:

"The General hopes and trusts that every officer and man will endeavor to live and act as becomes a Christian soldier defending the dearest rights and liberties of his country."

∽

ABRAHAM LINCOLN, DEC. 1, 1862, 2ND ANNUAL MESSAGE:

In giving freedom to the slave, we assure freedom to the free - honorable alike in what we give and what we preserve. We shall nobly save - or meanly lose - the last, best hope of earth.

Other means may succeed; this could not fail. The way is plain, peaceful, generous, just - a way which if followed the world will forever applaud and God must forever bless.

∽

ABRAHAM LINCOLN, MAR. 30, 1863, NATIONAL DAY OF HUMILIATION, FASTING & PRAYER PROCLAMATION:

It is the duty of nations as well as of men to own their dependence upon the overruling power of God, to confess their sins and transgressions in humble sorrow yet with assured hope that genuine repentance will lead to mercy and pardon, and to recognize the sublime truth, announced in the Holy Scriptures and proven by all history: that those nations only are blessed whose God is the Lord.

∽

ABRAHAM LINCOLN, MAR. 30, 1863, NATIONAL DAY OF HUMILIATION, FASTING & PRAYER PROCLAMATION:

We have forgotten God. We have forgotten the gracious Hand which preserved us in peace, and multiplied and enriched and strengthened us; and we have vainly imagined, in the deceitfulness of our hearts, that all these blessings were produced by some superior wisdom and virtue of our own.

Intoxicated with unbroken success, we have become too self-sufficient to feel the necessity of redeeming and preserving grace, too proud to pray to the God that made us! It behooves us then to humble ourselves before the offended Power, to confess our national sins and to pray for clemency and forgiveness.

∽

ABRAHAM LINCOLN, JUL. 15, 1863, NATIONAL DAY OF THANKSGIVING, PRAISE & PRAYER PROCLAMATION:

It is meet and right to recognize and confess the presence of the Almighty Father and the power of His hand equally in these triumphs and in these sorrows...

I invite the people of the United States to assemble on that occasion in their customary places of worship and in the forms approved by their own consciences render the homage due to the Divine Majesty for the wonderful things He has done in the nation's behalf and invoke the influence of His Holy Spirit to subdue the anger which has produced and so long sustained a needless and cruel rebellion.

∽

ABRAHAM LINCOLN, NOV. 19, 1863, COMMEMORATING THE BATTLE OF GETTYSBURG, WHERE OVER 50,000 SOLDIERS WERE KILLED OR WOUNDED ON JUL. 1-3, 1863:

Fourscore and seven years ago our fathers brought forth upon this continent a new nation, conceived in liberty, and dedicated to the proposition that all men are created equal.

Now we are engaged in a great civil war, testing whether that nation, or any nation so conceived and so dedicated, can long endure. We are met on a great battlefield of that war. We have come to dedicate a portion of that field as a final resting place for those who here gave their lives that that nation might live. It is altogether fitting and proper that we should do this.

But in a larger sense we cannot dedicate, we cannot consecrate, we cannot hallow this ground. The brave men, living and dead, who struggled here, have consecrated it far above our poor power to add or detract. The world will little note, nor long remember, what we say here, but it can never forget what they did here. It is for us, the living, rather to be dedicated here to the unfinished work which they who fought here have thus far so nobly advanced.

It is rather for us to be here dedicated to the great task remaining before us - that from these honored dead we take increased devotion to that cause for which they gave the last full measure of devotion - that we here highly resolve that these dead shall not have died in vain - that this nation, under God, shall have a new birth of freedom - and that government of the people, by the people, for the people, shall not perish from the earth.

❦

ABRAHAM LINCOLN, JUL. 7, 1864, NATIONAL DAY OF HUMILIATION & PRAYER PROCLAMATION:

I do hereby further invite and request the heads of the Executive Departments of this Government, together with all legislators, all judges and magistrates, and all other persons exercising authority in the land, whether civil, military, or naval, and all soldiers, seamen, and marines in the national service, and all the other loyal and law-abiding people of the United States, to assemble in their preferred places of public worship on that day, and there and then to render to the Almighty and Merciful Ruler of the Universe such homages and such confessions and to offer to Him such supplications as the Congress of the United States have in their aforesaid resolution so solemnly, so earnestly, and so reverently recommended.

❦

ABRAHAM LINCOLN, MAR. 4, 1865, 2ND INAUGURAL, 45 DAYS BEFORE HIS ASSASSINATION:

Both read the same Bible and pray to the same God...The prayers of both could not be answered. That of neither has been answered fully. The Almighty has His own purposes. "Woe unto the world because of offenses"...

Yet, if God will that it continue until all the wealth piled by the bondsmen's two hundred and fifty years of unrequited toil shall be sunk, and until every drop of blood drawn with the lash shall be paid by another drawn with the sword, as was said three thousand years ago, so still it must be said "the Judgements of the Lord are true and righteous."

❦

ABRAHAM LINCOLN, SEP. 5, 1864, WASHINGTON CHRONICLE, TO A COMMITTEE OF COLORED PEOPLE FROM BALTIMORE, ACKNOWLEDGING A GIFT OF A BIBLE:

In regard to this Great Book, I have but to say, I believe the Bible is the best gift God has given to man. All the good Saviour gave to the world was communicated through this Book. But for this Book we could not know right from wrong. All things most desirable for man's welfare, here and hereafter, are to be found portrayed in it.

❦

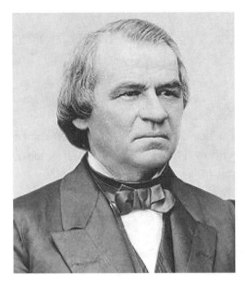

ANDREW JOHNSON

ANDREW JOHNSON, APR. 15, 1865, UPON ASSUMING THE
PRESIDENCY FOLLOWING LINCOLN'S ASSASSINATION:
Duties have been mine; consequences are God's.

ᐓ

ANDREW JOHNSON, APR. 25, 1865, NATIONAL DAY OF
HUMILIATION & MOURNING PROCLAMATION
ISSUED UPON DEATH OF PRESIDENT LINCOLN:

Whereas our country has become one great house of mourning, where the head of the family has been taken away, and believing that a special period should be assigned for again humbling ourselves before Almighty God,...

Now, therefore, in order to mitigate that grief on earth which can only be assuaged by communion with the Father in Heaven...I recommend my fellow-citizens then to assemble in their respective places of worship, there to unite in solemn service to Almighty God in memory of the good man who has been removed.

✍

ANDREW JOHNSON, APR. 29, 1865, RECOMMENDATIONS REGARDING NATIONAL DAY OF HUMILIATION & PRAYER PROCLAMATION:

My proclamation of the 25th instant Thursday, the 25th day of next month, was recommended as a day for special humiliation and prayer in consequence of the assassination of Abraham Lincoln...but whereas my attention has since been called to the fact that the day aforesaid is sacred to large numbers of Christians as one of rejoicing for the ascension of the Savior:

Now, therefore, be it known that I, Andrew Johnson, President of the United States, do hereby suggest that the religious services recommended as aforesaid should be postponed until Thursday, the 1st day of June next.

✍

ANDREW JOHNSON, OCT. 28, 1865, NATIONAL DAY OF THANKSGIVING PROCLAMATION:

Whereas it has pleased Almighty God during the year which is now coming to an end to relieve our beloved country from the fearful scourge of civil war and to permit us to secure the blessings of peace, unity, and harmony, with a great enlargement of civil liberty; and

Whereas our Heavenly Father has also during the year graciously averted from us the calamities of foreign war, pestilence, and famine, while our granaries are full of the fruits of an abundant season; and

Whereas righteousness exalteth a nation, while sin is a reproach to any people...

I...recommend to the people thereof that they do set apart and observe the first Thursday of December next as a day of national thanksgiving to the Creator of the Universe for these great deliverances and blessings.

✍

ANDREW JOHNSON, DEC. 4, 1865, 1ST ANNUAL MESSAGE:

The House of Representatives answered Washington by the voice of Madison: "We adore the Invisible Hand which has led the American people, through so many difficulties"...

Who of them will not acknowledge, in the words of Washington, that "every step by which the people of the United States have advanced to the character of an independent nation seems to have been distinguished by some token of providential agency"? Who will not join with me in the prayer that the Invisible Hand which has led us through the clouds that gloomed around our path will not so guide us onward to a perfect restoration?

∾

ANDREW JOHNSON, OCT. 8, 1866, NATIONAL DAY OF THANKSGIVING & PRAISE PROCLAMATION:

Almighty God, our Heavenly Father, has been pleased to vouchsafe to us as a people another year Almighty God, our Heavenly Father, has been pleased to vouchsafe to us as a people another year of that national life which is an indispensable condition of peace, security, and progress...

In offering these national thanksgivings, praises, and supplications we have the divine assurance that "the Lord remaineth a king forever; them that are meek shall He guide in judgement and such as are gentle shall He learn His way; the Lord shall give strength to His people, and the Lord shall give to His people the blessing of peace"...

I...recommend...a day of thanksgiving and praise to Almighty God, with due remembrance that "in His temple doth every man speak of His honor."

∾

ANDREW JOHNSON, SEP. 7, 1867, OATH PRESCRIBED IN PROCLAMATION OF AMNESTY & PARDON TO PARTICIPANTS OF THE CONFEDERATE INSURRECTION:

Nevertheless, that every person who shall seek to avail himself of this proclamation shall take and subscribe the following oath...

"I, _____ _____, do solemnly swear (or affirm), in presence of Almighty God, that I will henceforth faithfully support, protect, and defend the Constitution of the United States and the Union of the States thereunder, and that I will in like manner abide by and faithfully support all laws and proclamations which have been made during the late rebellion with reference to the emancipation of slaves.

So help me God."

⁕

ANDREW JOHNSON, DEC. 3, 1867, 3RD ANNUAL MESSAGE:

We must all acknowledge that the restoration of the States to their proper legal relations with the Federal Government and with one another, according to the terms of the original compact, would be the greatest temporal blessing which God, in His kindest Providence, could bestow upon this nation...

Christianity and civilization have made such progress that recourse to a punishment so cruel and unjust would meet with condemnation of all unprejudiced and right-minded men.

⁕

ANDREW JOHNSON, OCT. 12, 1868, NATIONAL DAY OF PUBLIC PRAISE, THANKSGIVING & PRAYER PROCLAMATION:

The annual period of rest, which we have reached in health and tranquility, and which is crowned with so many blessings, is by universal consent a convenient and suitable one for cultivating personal piety and practicing public devotion.

I therefore recommend...a day for public praise, thanksgiving, and prayer to the Almighty Creator and Divine Ruler of the Universe, by whose ever-watchful, merciful, and gracious Providence alone states and nations, no less than families and individual men, do live and move and have their being.

⁕

ANDREW JOHNSON, DEC. 9, 1868, 4TH ANNUAL MESSAGE:

Let us earnestly hope that before the expiration of our respective terms of service, now rapidly drawing to a close, an All-Wise Providence will so guide our counsels as to strengthen and preserve the Federal Union, inspire reverence for the Constitution, restore prosperity and happiness to our whole people, and promote "on earth peace, good will toward men."

⁕

ULYSSES S. GRANT

ULYSSES S. GRANT, MAR. 4, 1869, 1ST INAUGURAL:

In conclusion I ask patient forbearance one toward another throughout the land, and a determined effort on the part of every citizen to do his share toward cementing a happy union; and I ask the prayers of the nation to Almighty God in behalf of this consummation.

✌

ULYSSES S. GRANT, OCT. 5, 1869, NATIONAL DAY OF THANKSGIVING, PRAISE & PRAYER PROCLAMATION:

It becomes a people thus favored to make acknowledgment to the Supreme Author from whom such blessings flow of their gratitude and their dependence, to render praise and thanksgiving for the same, and devoutly to implore a continuance of God's mercies...

I, Ulysses S. Grant, President of the United States, do recommend that Thursday, the 18th day of November next, be observed as a day of thanksgiving and of praise and of prayer to Almighty God, the Creator and the Ruler of the Universe;

and I do further recommend to all the people of the United States to assemble on that day in their accustomed places of public worship and to unite in the homage and praise due to the bountiful Father of All Mercies and in fervent prayer for the continuance of the manifold blessings He has vouchsafed to us as a people.

∽

ULYSSES S. GRANT, DEC. 6, 1869, 1ST ANNUAL MESSAGE:

The Society of Friends is well known as having succeeded in living in peace with the Indians in the early settlement of Pennsylvania...They are known for their opposition to all strife, violence, and war, and are generally noted for their strict integrity and fair dealings. These considerations induced me to give the management of a few reservations of Indians to them and to throw the burden of the selection of agents upon the Society itself. The result has proven most satisfactory.

∽

ULYSSES S. GRANT, DEC. 5, 1870, 2ND ANNUAL MESSAGE:

Such religious denominations as had heretofore established missionaries among the Indians, and perhaps to some other denominations who would undertake the work on the same terms - i.e., as a missionary work.

The societies selected are allowed to name their own agents, subject to the approval of the Executive, and are expected to watch over them and aid them as missionaries, to Christianize and civilize the Indians, and to train him in the arts of peace.

∽

ULYSSES S. GRANT, JAN. 1, 1871, TO HOUSE & SENATE:

It would seem highly desirable that the civilized Indians of the country should be encouraged in establishing for themselves forms of Territorial government compatible with the Constitution of the United States...This is the first indication of the aborigines desiring to adopt our form of government, and it is highly desirable that they become self-sustaining, self-relying, Christianized, and civilized.

∽

ULYSSES S. GRANT, DEC. 4, 1871, 3RD ANNUAL MESSAGE:

Many tribes of Indians have been induced to settle upon reservations, to cultivate the soil, to perform productive labor of various kinds, and to partially accept civilization. They are being cared for in such a way, it is hoped, as to induce those still pursuing their old habits of life to embrace the only opportunity which is left them to avoid extermination. I recommend liberal appropriations to carry out the Indian peace policy, not only because it is humane, Christianlike, and economical, but because it is right.

◅

ULYSSES S. GRANT, DEC. 2, 1872, 4TH ANNUAL MESSAGE:

I can not doubt that the continued maintenance of slavery in Cuba is among the strongest inducements to the continuance of this strife. A terrible wrong is the natural cause of a terrible evil...It is greatly to be hoped that the present liberal Government of Spain will voluntarily adopt this view.

The law of emancipation...was the recognition of right, and was hailed as such, and exhibited Spain in harmony with sentiments of humanity and of justice and in sympathy with the other powers of the Christian and civilized world.

◅

ULYSSES S. GRANT, MAR. 4, 1873, 2ND INAUGURAL:

Under Providence, I have been called a second time to act as Executive over this great nation...I do believe that our Great Maker is preparing the world, in His own good time, to become one nation, speaking one language, and then armies and navies will no longer be required.

◅

ULYSSES S. GRANT, OCT. 27, 1875, NATIONAL DAY OF THANKSGIVING PROCLAMATION:

In accordance with a practice at once wise and beautiful, we have been accustomed, as the year is drawing to a close, to devote an occasion to the humble expression of our thanks to Almighty God for the ceaseless and distinguished benefits bestowed upon us as a nation and for His mercies and protection during the closing year.

Amid the rich and free enjoyment of all our advantages, we should not forget the source from whence they are derived and the extent of our obligation to the Father of All Mercies. We have full reason to renew our thanks to Almighty God...By His continuing mercy civil and religious liberty have been maintained.

INSPIRING FAITH FROM LEADERS OF THE PAST

ൟ

ULYSSES S. GRANT, JUN. 6, 1876, FROM WASHINGTON TO EDITOR OF THE SUNDAY SCHOOL TIMES, PHILADELPHIA:

My advice to Sunday schools, no matter what their denomination, is: Hold fast to the Bible as the sheet anchor of your liberties; write its precepts in your hearts, and practice them in your lives. To the influence of this Book are we indebted for all the progress made in true civilization, and to this must we look as our guide in the future. "Righteousness exalteth a nation; but sin is a reproach to any people."

ൟ

ULYSSES S. GRANT, OCT., 26, 1876,
NATIONAL THANKSGIVING DAY PROCLAMATION:

We have especial occasion to express our hearty thanks to Almighty God that by His providence and guidance our Government, established a century ago, has been enabled to fulfill the purpose of its founders in offering an asylum to the people of every race, securing civil and religious liberty to all within its borders, and meting out to every individual alike justice and equality before the law. It is, moreover, especially our duty to offer our humble prayers to the Father of All Mercies for a continuance of His divine favor to us as a nation and as individuals.

ൟ

ULYSSES S. GRANT, 1884, RESPONSE TO AFFECTION
DISPLAYED BY THE AMERICAN PUBLIC DURING HIS
FIGHT WITH THROAT CANCER, WHILE WRITING HIS
MEMOIRS, AT BEHEST OF MARK TWAIN,
WHO PUBLISHED THEM:

I did not go riding yesterday, although invited and permitted by my physicians, because it was the Lord's day, and because I felt that if a relapse should set in, the people who are praying for me would feel that I was not helping their faith by riding out on Sunday...

Yes, I know, and I feel very grateful to the Christian people of the land for their prayers in my behalf. There is no sect or religion, as shown in the Old or New Testament, to which this does not apply.

ൟ

RUTHERFORD B. HAYES

RUTHERFORD B. HAYES, MAR. 5, 1877, INAUGURAL,
WHICH HE DELIVERED A DAY LATER THAN USUAL,
REFUSING TO BE SWORN IN ON SUNDAY IN HONOR OF
THE SABBATH. HE REPEATED THE OATH, HIS PALM
PLACED ON PSALM 118:13, AND KISSED THE BIBLE:

Looking for the guidance of that Divine Hand by which the destinies of nations and individuals are shaped, I call upon you, Senators, Representatives, judges, fellow-citizens, here and everywhere, to unite with me in an earnest effort to secure to our country the blessings, not only of material property, but of justice, peace, and union.

⤎

RUTHERFORD B. HAYES, OCT. 29, 1877, NATIONAL DAY
OF THANKSGIVING & PRAYER PROCLAMATION:

The completed circle of summer and winter, seedtime and harvest, has brought us to the accustomed season at which a religious people celebrates with praise and thanksgiving the enduring mercy of Almighty God...

Let us with one spirit and with one voice lift up praise and thanksgiving to God for His manifold goodness to our land, His manifest care for our nation...

I earnestly recommend that, withdrawing themselves from secular cares and labors, the people of the United States do meet together on that day in their respective places of worship, there to give thanks and praise to Almighty God for His mercies and to devoutly beseech their continuance.

∽

RUTHERFORD B. HAYES, DEC. 3, 1877, 1ST ANNUAL MESSAGE:

The Government of the Samoan Islands has sent an envoy...to invite the Government of the United States to recognize and protect their independence, to establish commercial relations with their people, and to assist them in their steps toward regulated and responsible government. The inhabitants of these islands, having made considerable progress in Christian civilization and the development of trade, are doubtful of their ability to maintain peace and independence without the aid of some stronger power.

∽

RUTHERFORD B. HAYES, OCT. 30, 1878, NATIONAL DAY OF THANKSGIVING & PRAYER PROCLAMATION:

The general prevalence of the blessings of health through our wide land has made more conspicuous the sufferings and sorrows which the dark shadow of pestilence has cast upon a portion of our people. This heavy affliction even the Divine Ruler has tempered to the suffering communities in the universal sympathy and succor which have flowed to their relief, and the whole nation may rejoice in the unity of spirit in our people by which they cheerfully share one another's burdens.

Now, therefore, I, Rutherford B. Hayes, President of the United States, do appoint Thursday, the 28th day of November next, as a day of national thanksgiving and prayer; and I earnestly recommend that, withdrawing themselves from secular cares and labors, the people of the United States do meet together on that day in their respective places of worship, there to give thanks and praise to Almighty God for His mercies and to devoutly beseech their continuance.

❦

RUTHERFORD B. HAYES, DEC. 2, 1878,
2ND ANNUAL MESSAGE:

Our heartfelt gratitude is due to the Divine Being who holds in His hands the destinies of nations for the continued bestowal during the last year of countless blessings upon our country.

❦

RUTHERFORD B. HAYES, NOV. 3, 1879, NATIONAL DAY
OF THANKSGIVING & PRAYER PROCLAMATION:

At no recurrence of the season, which the devout habit of a religious people has made the occasion for giving thanks to Almighty God and humbly invoking His continued favor, has the material prosperity enjoyed by our whole country been more conspicuous, more manifold, or more universal...I earnestly recommend that, withdrawing themselves from secular cares and labors, the people of the United States do meet together on that day in their respective places of worship, there to give thanks and praise to Almighty God for His mercies and to devoutly beseech their continuance.

❦

RUTHERFORD B. HAYES, DEC. 1, 1879,
3RD ANNUAL MESSAGE:

The members of the Forty-sixth Congress have assembled in their first regular session under circumstances calling for mutual congratulations and grateful acknowledgment to the Giver of All Good for the large and unusual measure of national prosperity which we now enjoy.

❦

RUTHERFORD B. HAYES, NOV. 1, 1880,
NATIONAL DAY OF THANKSGIVING PROCLAMATION:

At no period in their history since the United States became a nation has this people had so abundant and universal reasons for joy and gratitude at the favor of Almighty God or been subject to so profound an obligation to give thanks for His loving kindness and humbly to implore His continued care and protection....

Let the thanks of a happy and united people, as with one voice, ascend in devout homage to the Giver of All Good.

I therefore recommend that on Thursday, the 25th day of November next, the people meet in their respective places of worship to make their acknowledgments to Almighty God for His bounties and His protection and to offer to Him prayers for their continuance.

∽

RUTHERFORD B. HAYES, MAR. 13, 1892,
LAST WILL & TESTAMENT:

I commit my soul to the mercy of God through our Lord and Saviour Jesus Christ, and I exhort my dear children humbly to try to guide themselves by the teachings of the New Testament in its broad spirit, and to put no faith in any man's narrow construction of its letter here or there.

∽

BENJAMIN HARRISON, JAN. 18, 1893, MESSAGE FROM HIS
EXECUTIVE MANSION IN WASHINGTON, DC,
UPON THE DEATH OF RUTHERFORD B. HAYES:

To the people of the United States: The death of Rutherford B. Hayes, who was President of the United States from March 4, 1877, to March 4, 1881, at his home in Fremont, Ohio, at 11 p.m. yesterday, is an event the announcement of which will be received with very general and very sincere sorrow. His public service extended over many years and over a wide range of official duty.

He was a patriotic citizen, a lover of the flag and of our free institutions, an industrious and conscientious civil officer, a soldier of dauntless courage, a loyal comrade and friend, a sympathetic and helpful neighbor, and the honored head of a happy Christian home.

∽

JAMES GARFIELD

JAMES GARFIELD, APR. 15, 1865, ADDRESS DELIVERED
IN NEW YORK WHILE A U.S. CONGRESSMAN,
AFTER RECEIVING NEWS OF
PRESIDENT LINCOLN'S ASSASSINATION:

Fellow citizens! Clouds and darkness are around Him. His pavilion is dark waters and thick clouds of the skies! Justice and judgment are the establishment of His throne! Mercy and truth shall go before His face. Fellow citizens! God reigns and the Government at Washington still lives!

⤝

JAMES GARFIELD, 1871, DESCRIBING OTTO EDUARD
LEOPOLD VON BISMARCK, CHANCELLOR OF
THE NEWLY UNITED GERMAN EMPIRE:

I am struck with the fact that Bismarck, the great statesman of Germany, probably the foremost man in Europe today, stated as an unquestioned principle, that the support, the defense, and propagation of the Christian Gospel is the central object of the German government.

❧

JAMES GARFIELD, JUL. 4, 1876, ADDRESS COMMEMORATING THE 100TH ANNIVERSARY OF THE DECLARATION OF INDEPENDENCE, DELIVERED WHILE SERVING AS THE U.S. CONGRESSMAN CHAIRING THE COMMITTEE ON APPROPRIATIONS:

Now more than ever before, the people are responsible for the character of their Congress. If that body be ignorant, reckless, and corrupt, it is because the people tolerate ignorance, recklessness, and corruption.

If it be intelligent, brave, and pure, it is because the people demand these high qualities to represent them in the national legislature...If the next centennial does not find us a great nation...it will be because those who represent the enterprise, the culture, and the morality of the nation do not aid in controlling the political forces.

❧

JAMES GARFIELD, 1876, ENDING A LETTER TO A FRIEND, ON DEATH OF HIS FRIEND'S YOUNG SON, EDWARD:

In the hope of the Gospel, which is so precious in this hour of affliction, I am affectionately your brother in Christ.

❧

JAMES GARFIELD, MAR. 4, 1881, INAUGURAL:

Let our people find a new meaning in the divine oracle which declares that "a little child shall lead them," for our own little children will soon control the destinies of the Republic. My countrymen, we do not now differ in our judgement concerning the controversies of past generations, and fifty years hence our children will not be divided in their opinions concerning our controversies.

They will surely bless their fathers and their fathers' God that the Union was preserved, that slavery was overthrown, and that both races were made equal before the law.

❧

JAMES GARFIELD, MAR. 4, 1881, INAUGURAL:

Before continuing the onward march let us pause on this height for a moment to strengthen our faith and renew our hope...The emancipated race has already made remarkable progress.

With unquestioning devotion to the Union, with a patience and gentleness not born of fear, they have "followed the light as God gave them to see the light."...Above all, upon our efforts to promote the welfare of this great people and their Government I reverently invoke the support and blessings of Almighty God.

∽

JAMES GARFIELD, STATEMENT:

The world's history is a Divine poem, of which the history of every nation is a canto, and every man a word. Its strains have been pealing along down the centuries, and though there have been mingled the discords of warring cannons and dying men, yet to the Christian philosopher and historian - the humble listener - there has been a Divine melody running through the song which speaks of hope and halcyon days to come.

∽

JAMES GARFIELD, JUL. 2, 1881, AFTER HAVING BEEN IN OFFICE 4 MONTHS, WAS SHOT IN THE BACK WHILE IN THE WASHINGTON, DC, RAILROAD STATION AND DIED SEP. 19, 1881. SECRETARY OF STATE JAMES G. BLAINE, WRITING FROM LONG BRANCH, N.J., SENT THIS ANNOUNCEMENT TO JAMES RUSSELL LOWELL, U.S. MINISTER IN LONDON:

James A. Garfield, President of the United States, died at Elberon, N.J., last night at ten minutes before 11 o'clock. For nearly eighty days he suffered great pain, and during the entire period exhibited extraordinary patience, fortitude, and Christian resignation. Fifty millions of people stand as mourners by his bier.

∽

JAMES GARFIELD, MAR. 4, 1850, ENTRY IN HIS JOURNAL RECOUNTING HIS CONVERSION AT AGE 18:

Today I was buried with Christ in baptism and arose to walk in newness of life.

∽

James Garfield - 20th President

CHESTER A. ARTHUR

CHESTER A. ARTHUR, SEP. 22, 1881, ADDRESS UPON
ASSUMING PRESIDENCY AFTER GARFIELD'S DEATH:
    For the fourth time in the history of the Republic its Chief
Magistrate has been removed by death. All hearts are filled with grief
and horror at the hideous crime which has darkened our land, and the
memory of the murdered President...Summoned to these high duties
and responsibilities and profoundly conscious of their magnitude and
gravity, I assume the trust imposed by the Constitution, relying for aid
on Divine Guidance and the virtue, patriotism, and intelligence of the
American people.

                                      ᕯ

CHESTER A. ARTHUR, SEP. 22, 1881, NATIONAL DAY OF
HUMILIATION & MOURNING PROCLAMATION
AFTER THE DEATH OF PRESIDENT GARFIELD:
    Whereas in His inscrutable wisdom it has pleased God to
remove from us the illustrious head of the nation, James A. Garfield,
late President of the United States; and

Whereas It is fitting that the deep grief which fills all hearts should manifest itself with one accord toward the Throne of Infinite Grace, and that we should bow before the Almighty and seek from Him that consolation in our affliction and that sanctification of our loss which He is able and willing to vouchsafe:

Now, therefore, in obedience to sacred duty and in accordance with the desire of the people, I, Chester A. Arthur, President of the United States of America, do hereby appoint Monday next, the 26th day of September - on which day the remains of our honored and beloved dead will be consigned to their last resting place on earth - to be observed throughout the United States as a day of humiliation and mourning;

And I earnestly recommend all the people to assemble on that day in their respective places of divine worship, there to render alike their tribute of sorrowful submission to the will of Almighty God and of reverence and love for the memory and character of our late Chief Magistrate.

∽

CHESTER A. ARTHUR, NOV. 4, 1881, NATIONAL DAY OF THANKSGIVING & PRAYER PROCLAMATION:

It has long been the pious custom of our people, with the closing of the year, to look back upon the blessings brought to them in the changing course of the seasons and to return solemn thanks to the All-Giving Source from whom they flow...

The countless benefits which have showered upon us during the past twelvemonth call for our fervent gratitude and make it fitting that we should rejoice with thankfulness that the Lord in His infinite mercy has most signally favored our country and our people.

∽

CHESTER A. ARTHUR, NOV. 4, 1881, NATIONAL DAY OF THANKSGIVING & PRAYER PROCLAMATION:

For all these things it is meet that the voice of the nation should go up to God in devout homage. Wherefore, I, Chester A. Arthur, President of the United States, do recommend that all the people observe Thursday, the 24th day of November instant, as a day of national thanksgiving and prayer, by ceasing, so far as may be, from their secular labors and meeting in their several places of worship, there to join in ascribing honor and praise to Almighty God, whose goodness has been so manifest in our history and in our lives, and offering earnest prayers that His bounties may continue to us and to our children.

∽

CHESTER A. ARTHUR, DEC. 6, 1881, 1ST ANNUAL MESSAGE:
For these manifestations of His favor we owe to Him who holds our destiny in His hands the tribute of our grateful devotion. To that mysterious exercise of His will which has taken from us the loved and illustrious citizen who was but lately the head of the nation we bow in sorrow and submission.

∽

CHESTER A. ARTHUR, DEC. 6, 1881, 1ST ANNUAL MESSAGE:
Russia should be...assuring to peaceable Americans who visit the Empire the consideration which is due to them as citizens of a friendly state. This is especially needful with respect to American Israelites, whose classification with the native Hebrew has evoked energetic remonstrances.

∽

CHESTER A. ARTHUR, DEC. 6, 1881, 1ST ANNUAL MESSAGE:
The insecurity of life and property in many parts of Turkey has given rise to correspondence with the Porte looking particularly to the better protection of American missionaries in the Empire. The condemned murderer of the eminent missionary Dr. Justin W. Parsons has not yet been executed, although this Government has repeatedly demanded that exemplary justice be done.

∽

CHESTER A. ARTHUR, DEC. 6, 1881, 1ST ANNUAL MESSAGE:
For many years the Executive...has urged the necessity of stringent legislation for the suppression of polygamy in the Territories, and especially in the Territory of Utah. The existing statute for the punishment of this odious crime, so revolting to the moral and religious sense of Christendom, has been persistently and contemptuously violated ever since its enactment.

∽

CHESTER A. ARTHUR, OCT. 25, 1882, NATIONAL DAY OF THANKSGIVING & PRAYER PROCLAMATION:

For wise and generous provision to effect the intellectual and moral education of our youth; for the influence upon the conscience of a restraining and transforming religion, and for the joys of home - for these and for many other blessings we should give thanks.

Wherefore I do recommend that the day above designated be observed throughout the country as a day of national thanksgiving and prayer, and that the people, ceasing from their daily labors and meeting in accordance with their several forms of worship draw near to the throne of Almighty God, offering to Him praise and gratitude for the manifold goodness which He has vouchsafed to us and praying that His blessings and His mercies may continue.

∽

CHESTER A. ARTHUR, DEC. 4, 1882, 2ND ANNUAL MESSAGE:

Our long-established friendliness with Russia has remained unshaken. It has prompted me to proffer the earnest counsels of this Government that measures by adopted for suppressing the proscription which the Hebrew race in that country has lately suffered. It has not transpired that any American citizen has been subjected to arrest or injury, but our courteous remonstrance has nevertheless been courteously received.

There is reason to believe that the time is not far distant when Russia will be able to secure toleration to all faiths within her borders...The closing year has been replete with blessings, for which we owe to the Giver of All Good our reverent acknowledgment.

∽

CHESTER A. ARTHUR, OCT. 26, 1883, NATIONAL DAY OF THANKSGIVING PROCLAMATION:

In furtherance of the custom of this people at the closing of each year to engage, upon a day set apart for that purpose, in a special festival of praise to the Giver of All Good, I, Chester A. Arthur, President of the United States, do hereby designate Thursday, the 29th day of November next, as a day of national thanksgiving. The year which is drawing to an end has been replete with evidences of Divine Goodness...

I do therefore recommend that on the day above appointed the people rest from their accustomed labors and, meeting in their several places of worship, express their devout gratitude to God that He hath dealt so bountifully with this nation and pray that His grace and favor abide with it forever.

ᕗ

CHESTER A. ARTHUR, FEB. 8, 1884,
FROM HIS EXECUTIVE MANSION IN WASHINGTON, D.C:

General William T. Sherman, General of the Army, having this day reached the age of 64 years, is, in accordance with law, placed upon the retired list of the Army without reduction in his current pay and allowances...

The President deems this a fitting occasion to give expression in this manner to the gratitude felt toward General Sherman by his fellow-citizens, and to the hope that Providence may grant him many years of health and happiness in the relief from the active duties of his profession.

ᕗ

CHESTER A. ARTHUR, NOV. 7, 1884,
NATIONAL DAY OF THANKSGIVING PROCLAMATION:

The season in nigh when it is the yearly wont of this people to observe a day appointed for that purpose by the President as an especial occasion for thanksgiving unto God. Now, therefore, in recognition of this hallowed custom, I, Chester A. Arthur, President of the United States, do hereby designate as such day of general thanksgiving Thursday, the 27th day of this present November.

And I do recommend that throughout the land the people, ceasing from their accustomed occupations, do then keep holiday at their several homes and their several places of worship, and with heart and voice pay reverent acknowledgment to the Giver of All Good for the countless blessings wherewith He hath visited this nation.

ᕗ

GROVER CLEVELAND

GROVER CLEVELAND, MAR. 4, 1885, 1ST INAUGURAL:

On this auspicious occasion we may well renew the pledge of our devotion to the Constitution, which, launched by the founders of the Republic and consecrated by their prayers and patriotic devotion, has for almost a century borne the hopes and the aspirations of a great people...

And let us not trust to human effort alone, but humbly acknowledge the power and goodness of Almighty God who presides over the destiny of nations, and who has at all times been revealed in our country's history, let us invoke His aid and His blessings upon our labors.

❦

GROVER CLEVELAND, JUL. 23, 1885,
PROCLAMATION AT DEATH OF ULYSSES S. GRANT:

The President of the United States has just received the sad tidings of the death of that illustrious citizen and ex-President of the United States, General Ulysses S. Grant...

The destined end has come at last, and his spirit has returned to the Creator who sent it forth.

֍

GROVER CLEVELAND, NOV. 2, 1885, NATIONAL DAY OF THANKSGIVING & PRAYER PROCLAMATION:

The American people have always abundant cause to be thankful to Almighty God, whose watchful care and guiding hand have been manifested in every stage of their national life, guarding and protecting them in time of peril and safely leading them in the hour of darkness and of danger.

It is fitting and proper that a nation thus favored should on one day in every year, for that purpose especially appointed, publicly acknowledge the goodness of God and return thanks to Him for all His gracious gifts.

֍

GROVER CLEVELAND, NOV. 2, 1885, NATIONAL DAY OF THANKSGIVING & PRAYER PROCLAMATION:

On that day let all secular business be suspended, and let the people assemble in their usual places of worship and with prayer and songs of praise devoutly testify their gratitude to the Giver of Every Good and Perfect Gift for all that He has done for us in the year that has passed; for our preservation as a united nation and for our deliverance from the shock and danger of political convulsion;

for the blessings of peace and for our safety and quiet while wars and rumors of wars have agitated and afflicted other nations of the earth; for our security against the scourge of pestilence, which in other lands has claimed its dead by thousands and filled the streets with mourners; for plenteous crops which reward the labor of the husbandman and increase our nation's wealth, and for the contentment throughout our borders which follows in the train of prosperity and abundance.

֍

GROVER CLEVELAND, NOV. 2, 1885, NATIONAL DAY OF THANKSGIVING & PRAYER PROCLAMATION:

And let us by no means forget while we give thanks and enjoy the comforts which have crowned our lives that truly grateful hearts are inclined to deeds of charity, and that a kind and thoughtful remembrance of the poor will double the pleasures of our condition and render our praise and thanksgiving more acceptable in the sight of the Lord.

ॐ

GROVER CLEVELAND, DEC. 8, 1885, 1ST ANNUAL MESSAGE:

The strength, the perpetuity, and the destiny of the nation rest upon our homes, established by the law of God, guarded by parental care, regulated by parental authority, and sanctified by parental love...

The mothers of our land, who rule the nation as they mold the characters and guide the actions of their sons, live according to God's Holy Ordinances, and each, secure and happy in the exclusive love of the father of her children, sheds the warm light of true womanhood, unperverted and unpolluted, upon all within her pure and wholesome family circle...

The fathers of our families are the best citizens of the Republic. Wife and children are the sources of patriotism, and conjugal and parental affection beget devotion to the country. The man who is surrounded in his single home with his wife and children has a stake in the country which inspires him with respect for its laws and courage for its defense.

ॐ

GROVER CLEVELAND, NOV. 1, 1886, NATIONAL DAY OF THANKSGIVING & PRAYER PROCLAMATION:

It has long been the custom of the people of the United States, on a day in each year especially set apart for that purpose by their Chief Executive, to acknowledge the goodness and mercy of God and to invoke His continued care and protection.

In observance of such custom, I, Grover Cleveland, President of the United States, do hereby designate and set apart Thursday, the 25th day of November instant, to be observed and kept as a day of thanksgiving and prayer.

On that day let all our people forego their accustomed employments and assemble in their usual places of worship to give thanks to the Ruler of the Universe for our continued enjoyment of the blessings of a free government, for a renewal of business prosperity throughout our land, for the return which has rewarded the labor of those who till the soil, and for our progress as a people in all that makes a nation great.

And while we contemplate the infinite power of God in earthquake, flood, and storm let the grateful hearts of those who have been shielded from harm through His mercy be turned in sympathy and kindness toward those who have suffered through His visitations.

Let us also in the midst of our thanksgiving remember the poor and needy with cheerful gifts and alms so that our service may by deeds of charity be made acceptable in the sight of the Lord.

∽

GROVER CLEVELAND, JUL. 13, 1887, CENTENNIAL CELEBRATION, CLINTON, NEW YORK:

That the office of Presidency of the United States does represent the sovereignty of sixty millions of free people, is, to my mind, a statement full of solemnity; for this sovereignty I conceive to be the working out or enforcement of the divine right of man to govern himself and a manifestation of God's plan concerning the human race.

∽

GROVER CLEVELAND, OCT. 25, 1887, NATIONAL DAY OF THANKSGIVING & PRAYER PROCLAMATION:

The goodness and the mercy of God, which have followed the American people during all the days of the past year, claim their grateful recognition and humble acknowledgment.

By His omnipotent power He has protected us from war and pestilence and from every national calamity; by His gracious favor the earth has yielded a generous return to the labor of the husbandman, and every path of honest toil has led to comfort and contentment; by His loving kindness the hearts of our people have been replenished with fraternal sentiment and patriotic endeavor, and by His unerring guidance we have been directed in the way of national prosperity.

∽

GROVER CLEVELAND, OCT. 25, 1887, NATIONAL DAY OF THANKSGIVING & PRAYER PROCLAMATION:

A day of thanksgiving and prayer, to be observed by all the people of the land.

On that day let all secular work and employment be suspended, and let our people assemble in their accustomed places of worship and with prayer and songs of praise give thanks to our Heavenly Father for all that He has done for us, while we humbly implore the forgiveness of our sins and a continuance of His mercy.

Let families and kindred be reunited on that day, and let their hearts, filled with kindly cheer and affectionate reminiscence, be turned in thankfulness to the Source of all their pleasures and the Giver of all that makes the day glad and joyous.

∽

GROVER CLEVELAND, NOV. 1, 1888, NATIONAL DAY OF THANKSGIVING & PRAYER PROCLAMATION:

On that day let all our people suspend their ordinary work and occupations, and in their accustomed places of worship, with prayer and songs of praise, render thanks to God for all His mercies, for the abundant harvests which have rewarded the toil of the husbandman during the year that has passed, and for the rich rewards that have followed the labors of our people in their shops and their marts of trade and traffic. Let us give thanks for peace and for social order and contentment within our borders, and for our advancement in all that adds to national greatness.

And mindful of the afflictive dispensations with which a portion of our land has been visited, let us, while we humble ourselves before the power of God, acknowledge His mercy in setting bounds to the deadly march of pestilence, and let our hearts be chastened by sympathy with our fellow-countrymen who have suffered and who mourn.

And as we return thanks for all the blessings which we have received from the hand of our Heavenly Father, let us not forget that He has enjoined upon us charity; and on this day of thanksgiving let us generously remember the poor and needy, so that our tribute of praise and gratitude may be acceptable in the sight of the Lord.

⋲

GROVER CLEVELAND, MEMORIZED THE WESTMINSTER CONFESSION & PILGRIM'S PROGRESS, BEING THE SON OF PRESBYTERIAN MINISTER RICHARD FALLEY CLEVELAND-PASTOR OF CHURCHES IN NEW JERSEY, NEW YORK & DISTRICT SECRETARY OF THE AMERICAN HOME MISSION SOCIETY:

I have always felt that my training as a minister's son has been more valuable to me as a strengthening influence than any other incident in life.

⋲

BENJAMIN HARRISON

BENJAMIN HARRISON, MAR. 4, 1889, INAUGURAL:

Entering thus solemnly into covenant with each other, we may reverently invoke and confidently extend the favor and help of Almighty God - that He will give to me wisdom, strength, and fidelity, and to our people a spirit of fraternity and a love of righteousness and peace...

God has placed upon our head a diadem and has laid at our feet power and wealth beyond definition or calculation. But we must not forget that we take these gifts upon the condition that justice and mercy shall hold the reins of power and the upward avenues of hope shall be free to all people.

∽

BENJAMIN HARRISON, APR. 4, 1889, NATIONAL DAY OF PRAYER & THANKSGIVING PROCLAMATION ON THE CENTENNIAL OF WASHINGTON'S INAUGURATION:

George Washington took the oath of office as Chief Magistrate of the new-born Republic. This impressive act was preceded at 9 o'clock in the morning in all the churches of the city by prayer for God's blessing on the Government and its first President...

In order that the joy of the occasion may be associated with a deep thankfulness in the minds of the people for all our blessings in the past and a devout supplication to God for their gracious continuance in the future, the representatives of the religious creeds, both Christian and Hebrew, have memorialized the Government to designate an hour for prayer and thanksgiving on that day.

৵

BENJAMIN HARRISON, JUN. 7, 1889, GENERAL ORDER ISSUED FROM THE EXECUTIVE MANSION:

In November, 1862, President Lincoln quoted the words of Washington to sustain his own views, and announced in a general order that - "The President, Commander in Chief of the Army and Navy, desires and enjoins the orderly observance of the Sabbath by the officers and men in the military and naval service.

The importance for man and beast of the prescribed weekly rest, the sacred rights of Christian soldiers and sailors, a becoming deference to the best sentiment of a Christian people, and a due regard for the divine will demand that Sunday labor in the Army and Navy be reduced to the measure of strict necessity." The truth so concisely stated can not be too faithfully regarded, and the pressure to ignore it is far less now than in the midst of war.

To recall the kindly and considerate spirit of the orders issued by these great men in the most trying times of our history, and to promote contentment and efficiency, the President directs that Sunday-morning inspection will be merely of the dress and general appearance, without arms; and the more complete inspection under arms, with all men present, as required in paragraph 950, Army Regulations, 1889, will take place on Saturday.

৵

BENJAMIN HARRISON, NOV. 1, 1889, NATIONAL DAY OF THANKSGIVING & PRAYER PROCLAMATION:

A highly favored people, mindful of their dependence on the bounty of Divine Providence, should seek fitting occasion to testify gratitude and ascribe praise to Him who is the author of their many blessings. It behooves us, then, to look back with thankful hearts over the past year and bless God for His infinite mercy in vouchsafing to our land enduring peace, to our people freedom from pestilence and famine, to our husbandmen abundant harvests, and to them that labor a recompense of their toil.

❧

BENJAMIN HARRISON, NOV. 1, 1889, NATIONAL DAY OF THANKSGIVING & PRAYER PROCLAMATION:

Now, therefore, I, Benjamin Harrison, President of the United States of America, do earnestly recommend that Thursday, the 28th day of this present month of November, be set apart as a day of national thanksgiving and prayer, and that the people of our country, ceasing from the cares and labors of their working day, shall assemble in their respective places of worship and give thanks to God, who has prospered us on our way and made our paths the paths of peace, beseeching Him to bless the day to our present and future good, making it truly one of thanksgiving for each reunited home circle as for the nation at large.

❧

BENJAMIN HARRISON, DEC. 3, 1889, FROM HIS EXECUTIVE MANSION IN WASHINGTON, 1ST ANNUAL MESSAGE:

The recommendations of this international conference of enlightened statesmen will doubtless have the considerate attention of Congress...But while the commercial results which it is hoped will follow this conference are worthy of pursuit and of the great interests they have excited, it is believed that the crowning benefit will be found in the better securities which may be devised for the maintenance of peace among all American nations and the settlement of all contentions by methods that a Christian civilization can approve.

❧

BENJAMIN HARRISON, FEB. 10, 1890, PROCLAMATION REGARDING THE SIOUX NATION OF INDIANS IN DAKOTA:

It is therein provided that if any land in said Great Sioux Reservation is occupied and used by any religious society at the date of said act for the purpose of missionary or educational work among the Indians, whether situated outside of or within the limits of any of the separate reservations, the same, not exceeding 160 acres in any one tract, shall be granted to said society for the purposes and upon the terms and conditions therein named.

∞

BENJAMIN HARRISON, NOV. 8, 1890, NATIONAL DAY OF PRAYER & THANKSGIVING PROCLAMATION:

By the grace and favor of Almighty God the people of this nation have been led to the closing days of the passing year, which has been full of the blessings of peace and the comforts of plenty. Bountiful compensation has come to us for the work of our minds and of our hands in every department of human industry.

Now, therefore, I, Benjamin Harrison, President of the United States of America, do hereby appoint Thursday, the 27th day of the present month of November, to be observed as a day of prayer and thanksgiving; and I do invite the people upon that day to cease from their labors, to meet in their accustomed houses of worship, and to join in rendering gratitude and praise to our beneficent Creator for the rich blessings He has granted to us as a nation and in invoking the continuance of His protection and grace for the future.

∞

BENJAMIN HARRISON, NOV. 13, 1891, NATIONAL DAY OF JOYFUL THANKSGIVING PROCLAMATION:

It is a very glad incident of the marvelous prosperity which has crowned the year now drawing to a close that its helpful and reassuring touch has been felt by all our people. It has been as wide as our country, and so special that every home has felt its comforting influence.

It is too great to be the work of man's power and too particular to be the device of his mind. To God, the beneficent and all-wise, who makes the labors of men to be fruitful, redeem their losses by His grace, and the measure of whose giving is as much beyond the thoughts of man as it is beyond his deserts, the praise and gratitude of the people of this favored nation are justly due.

Now, therefore, I, Benjamin Harrison, President of the United States of America, do hereby appoint Thursday, the 26th day of November present, to be a day of joyful thanksgiving to God for the bounties of His providence, for the peace in which we are permitted to enjoy them, and for the preservation of those institutions of civil and religious liberty which He gave our fathers the wisdom to devise and establish and us the courage to preserve. Among the appropriate observances of the day are rest from toil, worship in the public congregations, the renewal of family ties about our American firesides, and thoughtful helpfulness toward those who suffer lack of the body or of the spirit.

∽

BENJAMIN HARRISON, DEC. 9, 1891, 3RD ANNUAL MESSAGE:

This Government has found occasion to express in a friendly spirit, but with much earnestness, to the Government of the Czar its serious concern because of the harsh measures now being enforced against the Hebrews in Russia.

By the revival of anti-Semitic laws, long in abeyance, great numbers of those unfortunate people have been constrained to abandon their homes and leave the Empire by reason of the impossibility of finding subsistence within the pale to which it is sought to confine them.

The immigration of these people to the United States - many others countries being closed to them - is largely increasing and is likely to assume proportions which may make it difficult to find home and employment for them here and to seriously affect the labor market. It is estimated that over 1,000,000 will be forced from Russia within a few years.

The Hebrew is never a beggar; he has always kept the law - life by toil - often under severe and oppressive civil restrictions. It is also true that no race, sect, or class has more fully cared for its own than the Hebrew race...This consideration, as well as the suggestion of humanity, furnishes ample ground for the remonstrances which we have presented to Russia.

∽

BENJAMIN HARRISON, JAN. 5, 1892,
MESSAGE TO SENATE & HOUSE OF REPRESENTATIVES:

The famine prevailing in some of the Provinces of Russia is so severe and widespread as to have attracted the sympathetic interest of a large number of our liberal and favored people. In some of the great grain-producing States of the West movements have already been organized to collect flour and meal for the relief of these perishing Russian families, and the response has been such as to justify the belief that a ship's cargo can very soon be delivered at the seaboard through the generous cooperation of the transportation lines.

It is most appropriate that a people whose storehouses have been so lavishly filled with all the fruits of the earth by the gracious favor of God should manifest their gratitude by large gifts to His suffering children in other lands.

∽

BENJAMIN HARRISON, AS COLONEL OF THE 70TH INDIANA INFANTRY REGIMENT DURING THE CIVIL WAR, LETTER TO HIS WIFE, CARRIE:

I hope you all remember us at home and that many prayers go up to God daily for my Regiment and for me. Ask Him for me in prayer, my dear wife, first that He will enable me to bear myself as a good soldier of Jesus Christ; second that He will give me valor and skill to conduct myself so as to honor my country and my friends, and lastly, if consistent with His holy will, I may be brought "home again" to the dear loved ones.

∽

GROVER CLEVELAND

GROVER CLEVELAND, MAR. 4, 1893, 2ND INAUGURAL:

My Fellow-Citizens: In obedience to the mandate of my countrymen I am about to dedicate myself to their service under the sanction of a solemn oath.

Deeply moved by the expression of confidence and personal attachment which has called me to this service, I am sure my gratitude can make no better return than the pledge I now give before God and these witnesses of unreserved and complete devotion to the interests and welfare of those who have honored me...

It can not be doubted that our stupendous achievements as a people and our country's robust strength have given rise to heedlessness of those laws governing our national health which we can no more evade than human life can escape the laws of God and nature...

Above all, I know there is a Supreme Being who rules the affairs of men and whose goodness and mercy have always followed the American people, and I know He will not turn from us now if we humbly and reverently seek His powerful aid.

∽

GROVER CLEVELAND, NOV. 3, 1893, NATIONAL DAY OF THANKSGIVING & PRAISE PROCLAMATION:

While the American people should every day remember with praise and thanksgiving the divine goodness and mercy which have followed them since their beginning as a nation, it is fitting that one day in each year should be especially devoted to the contemplation of the blessings we have received from the hand of God and to the grateful acknowledgment of His loving kindness...

On that day let us forego our ordinary work and employments and assemble in our usual places of worship, where we may recall all that God has done for us and where from grateful hearts our united tribute of praise and song may reach the Throne of Grace.

Let the reunion of kindred and the social meeting of friends lend cheer and enjoyment to the day, and let generous gifts of charity for the relief of the poor and needy prove the sincerity of our thanksgiving.

∽

GROVER CLEVELAND, NOV. 1, 1894, NATIONAL DAY OF THANKSGIVING & PRAYER PROCLAMATION:

The American people should gratefully render thanksgiving and praise to the Supreme Ruler of the Universe, who has watched over them with kindness and fostering care during the year that has passed; they should also with humility and faith supplicate the Father of All Mercies for continued blessings according to their needs, and they should by deeds of charity seek the favor of the Giver of Every Good and Perfect Gift.

Let us pray that these blessings may be multiplied unto us, that our national conscience may be quickened to a better recognition of the power and goodness of God, and that in our national life we may clearer see and closer follow the path of righteousness.

∽

GROVER CLEVELAND, NOV. 1, 1894, NATIONAL DAY OF THANKSGIVING & PRAYER PROCLAMATION:

On that day let our ordinary work and business be suspended and let us meet in our accustomed places of worship and give thanks to Almighty God for our preservation as a nation, for our immunity from disease and pestilence, for the harvests that have rewarded our husbandry, for a renewal of national prosperity, and for every advance in virtue and intelligence that has marked our growth as a people.

And with our thanksgiving let us pray that these blessings may be multiplied unto us, that our national conscience may be quickened to a better recognition of the power and goodness of God, and that in our national life we may clearer see and closer follow the path of righteousness.

And in our places of worship and praise, as well as in the happy reunions of kindred and friends on that day, let us invoke divine approval by generously remembering the poor and needy. Surely He who has given us comfort and plenty will look upon our relief of the destitute and our ministrations of charity as the work of hearts truly grateful and as proofs of the sincerity of our thanksgiving.

∽

GROVER CLEVELAND, DEC. 11, 1894, MESSAGE FROM HIS EXECUTIVE MANSION TO THE SENATE:

I have received a copy of the following resolution of the Senate, passed the 3d instant: Resolved, That the President be requested, if in his judgement it be not incompatible with the public interest, to communicate to the Senate any information he may have received in regard to alleged cruelties committed upon Armenians in Turkey, and especially whether any such cruelties have been committed upon citizens who have declared their intention to become naturalized in this country or upon persons because of their being Christians.

And further, to inform the Senate whether any expostulations have been addressed by this Government to the Government of Turkey in regard to such matters or any proposals made by or to this Government to act in concert with other Christian powers regarding the same.

∽

GROVER CLEVELAND, NOV. 4, 1895, NATIONAL DAY OF THANKSGIVING & PRAYER PROCLAMATION:

The constant goodness and forbearance of Almighty God which have been vouchsafed to the American people during the year which is just past call for their sincere acknowledgment and devout gratitude. To the end, therefore, that we may with thankful hearts unite in extolling the loving care of our Heavenly Father, I, Grover Cleveland, President of the United States, do hereby appoint and set apart Thursday, the 28th day of the present month of November, as a day of thanksgiving and prayer...

On that day let us forego our usual occupations and in our accustomed places of worship join in rendering thanks to the Giver of Every Good and Perfect Gift for the bounteous returns that have rewarded our labors...and for the other blessings that have been showered upon us from an open hand. And with our thanksgiving let us humbly beseech the Lord to so incline the hearts of our people unto Him that He will not leave us nor forsake us as a nation, but will continue to us His mercy and protecting care.

∽

GROVER CLEVELAND, DEC. 2, 1895,
3RD ANNUAL MESSAGE:

Reported massacres of Christians in Armenia and the development there and in other districts of a spirit of fanatic hostility to Christian influences naturally excited apprehension for the safety of the devoted men and women who, as dependents of the foreign missionary societies in the United States, reside in Turkey, under the guaranty of law and usage and in the legitimate performance of their educational and religious mission.

No efforts have been spared in their behalf, and their protection in person and property has been earnestly and vigorously enforced by every means within our power...

Orders have been carried out, and our latest intelligence gives assurance of the present personal safety of our citizens and missionaries. Though thus far no lives of American citizens have been sacrificed, there can be no doubt that serious loss and destruction of mission property have resulted from riotous conflicts and outrageous attacks.

By treaty several of the most powerful European powers have secured a right and have assumed a duty not only in behalf of their own citizens and in furtherance of their own interests, but as agents of the Christian world.

Their right to enforce such conduct of Turkish government as will refrain fanatical brutality, and if this fails their duty is to so interfere as to insure against such dreadful occurrences in Turkey as have lately shocked civilization.

❧

GROVER CLEVELAND, NOV. 4, 1896, NATIONAL DAY OF THANKSGIVING & PRAYER PROCLAMATION:

The United States should never be unmindful of the gratitude they owe the God of Nations for His watchful care, which has shielded them from dire disaster and pointed out to them the way of peace and happiness.

Nor should they ever refuse to acknowledge with contrite hearts their proneness to turn away from God's teaching and to follow with sinful pride after their own devices. To the end that these thoughts may be quickened it is fitting that on a day especially appointed we should join together in approaching the Throne of Grace with praise and supplication.

❧

GROVER CLEVELAND, DEC. 7, 1896, 8TH ANNUAL MESSAGE:

It would afford me satisfaction if I could assure the Congress that the disturbed condition in Asiatic Turkey had during the past year assumed a less hideous and bloody aspect...

Instead...we have been afflicted by continued and not infrequent reports of the wanton destruction of homes and the bloody butchery of men, women, and children, made martyrs to their profession of Christian faith. While none of our citizens in Turkey have thus far been killed or wounded, though often in the midst of dreadful scenes of danger, their safety in the future is by no means assured...

The outbreaks of blind fury which lead to murder and pillage in Turkey occur suddenly and without notice...We have made claims against the Turkish Government for the pillage and destruction of missionary property at Harpoot and Marash during the uprisings at those places...

A number of Armenian refugees having arrived at our ports...it is hoped that hereafter no obstacle will be interposed to prevent the escape of all those who seek to avoid the perils which threaten them in Turkish dominions... I do not believe that the present somber prospect in Turkey will be long permitted to offend the sight of Christendom.

It so mars the humane and enlightened civilization that belongs to the close of the nineteenth century that it seems hardly possible that the earnest demand of good people throughout the Christian world for its corrective treatment will remain unanswered.

❧

GROVER CLEVELAND,
THE WRITINGS AND SPEECHES
OF GROVER CLEVELAND:

The citizen is a better business man if he is a Christian gentleman, and, surely, business is not the less prosperous and successful if conducted on Christian principles...All must admit that the reception of the teachings of Christ results in the purest patriotism, in the most scrupulous fidelity to public trust, and in the best type of citizenship.

Those who manage the affairs of government are by this means reminded that the law of God demands that they should be courageously true to the interests of the people, and that the Ruler of the Universe will require of them a strict account of their stewardship.

❧

WILLIAM MCKINLEY

WILLIAM MCKINLEY, MAR. 4, 1897, 1ST INAUGURAL:

I assume the arduous and responsible duties of President of the United States, relying upon the support of my countrymen and invoking the guidance of Almighty God. Our faith teaches that there is no safer reliance than upon the God of our fathers, who has so singularly favored the American people in every national trial, and who will not forsake us so long as we obey His commandments and walk humbly in His footsteps...

It is consoling and encouraging to realize that free speech, a free press, free thought, free schools, the free and unmolested right of religious liberty and worship, and free and fair elections are dearer and more universally enjoyed to-day than ever before...

Illiteracy must be banished from the land if we shall attain that high destiny as the foremost of the enlightened nations of the world which, under Providence, we ought to achieve...

I would have all my countrymen observe: "I will faithfully execute the office of the President of the United States, and will, to the best of my ability, preserve, protect, and defend the Constitution of the United States." This is the obligation I have reverently taken before the Lord Most High. To keep it will be my single purpose, my constant prayer.

✑

WILLIAM MCKINLEY, OCT. 29, 1897, NATIONAL DAY OF THANKSGIVING & PRAYER PROCLAMATION:

In remembrance of God's goodness to us during the past year, which has been so abundant, "let us offer unto Him our thanksgiving and pay our vows unto the Most High." Under His watchful providence industry has prospered, the conditions of labor have been improved...

For these great benefits it is our duty to praise the Lord in a spirit of humility and gratitude and to offer up to Him our most earnest supplications. That we may acknowledge our obligation as a people to Him who has so graciously granted us the blessings of free government and material prosperity.

✑

WILLIAM MCKINLEY, APR. 11, 1898, MESSAGE TO CONGRESS:

Official information was received by me that the latest decree of the Queen Regent of Spain directs General Blanco, in order to prepare and facilitate peace, to proclaim a suspension of hostilities...

If this measure attains a successful result, then our aspirations as a Christian, peace-loving people will be realized. If it fails, it will be only another justification for our contemplated action.

✑

WILLIAM MCKINLEY, APR. 20, 1898, APPROVING A JOINT RESOLUTION OF CONGRESS:

The abhorrent conditions which have existed for more than three years in the island of Cuba, so near our own borders, have shocked the moral sense of the people of the United States, have been a disgrace to Christian civilization, culminating, as they have, in the destruction of a United States battle ship [U.S.S. Maine], with 266 of its officers and crew, while on a friendly visit in the harbor of Havana, and can not longer be endured, as has been set forth by the President of the United States in his message to Congress of April 11, 1898, upon which the action of Congress was invited: Therefore, Resolved by the Senate and House of Representatives of the United States of America in Congress assembled, First. That the people of the island of Cuba are and of a right ought to be free.

∽

WILLIAM MCKINLEY, MAY 9, 1898, MESSAGE TO CONGRESS:

The 4th of May Commodore Dewey had taken possession of the naval station at Cavite [Manila, Philippine Islands], destroying the fortifications there, and at the entrance of the bay and paroling their garrisons.

The waters of the bay are under his complete control. He has established hospitals within the American lines, where 250 of the Spanish sick and wounded are assisted and protected.

The magnitude of this victory can hardly be measured by the ordinary standard of naval warfare. Outweighing any material advantage is the moral effect of this initial success.

At this unsurpassed achievement the great heart of our nation throbs, not with boasting or with greed of conquest, but with deep gratitude that this triumph has come in a just cause and that by the grace of God an effective step has thus been taken toward the attainment of the wished-for peace.

∽

WILLIAM MCKINLEY, 1898, STATEMENT OF HIS DECISION TO ANNEX THE PHILIPPINE ISLANDS:

I walked the floor of the White House night after night until midnight, and I am not ashamed to tell you...that I went down no my knees and prayed Almighty God for light and guidance more than one night. And one night late it came to me...that there was nothing left for us to do but to take them all, and to educate the Filipinos, and uplift them and civilize and Christianize them.

∽

WILLIAM MCKINLEY, JUL. 6, 1898, NATIONAL DAY OF THANKSGIVING PROCLAMATION:

The unprecedented success which attended the operations of the United States fleet in the bay of Manila...are added the tidings of the no less glorious achievements of the naval and military arms of our beloved country at Santiago de Cuba, it is fitting that we should...reverently bow before the throne of divine grace and give devout praise to God, who holdeth the nations in the hollow of His hands and worketh upon them the marvels of His high will, and who has thus far vouchsafed to us the light of His face and led our brave soldiers and seamen to victory.

∽

WILLIAM MCKINLEY, JUL. 6, 1898, NATIONAL DAY OF THANKSGIVING PROCLAMATION:

I therefore ask the people of the United States, upon next assembling for divine worship in their respective places of meeting, to offer thanksgiving to Almighty God, who in His inscrutable ways, now leading our hosts upon the waters to unscathed triumph...With the nation's thanks let there be mingled the nation's prayers that our gallant sons may be shielded from harm...Let us pray with earnest fervor that He, the Dispenser of All Good, may speedily remove from us the untold afflictions of war and bring to our dear land the blessings of restored peace.

∽

WILLIAM MCKINLEY, OCT. 28, 1898, NATIONAL DAY OF THANKSGIVING PROCLAMATION:

The approaching November brings to mind the custom of our ancestors, hallowed by time and rooted in our most sacred traditions, of giving thanks to Almighty God for all the blessings He has vouchsafed to us during the year...The skies have been for a time darkened by the cloud of war, but as we were compelled to take up the sword in the cause of humanity we are permitted to rejoice that the conflict has been of brief duration and the losses we have had to mourn, though grievous and important, have been so few, considering the great results accomplished, as to inspire us with gratitude and praise to the Lord of Hosts. We may laud and magnify His Holy Name.

∽

WILLIAM MCKINLEY, OCT. 28, 1898, NATIONAL DAY OF THANKSGIVING PROCLAMATION:

I do therefore invite all my fellow-citizens, as well those who may be at sea or sojourning in foreign lands as those at home, to set apart and observe Thursday, the 24th day of November, as a day of national thanksgiving, to come together in their several places of worship for a service of praise and thanks to Almighty God for all the blessings of the year...and to pray that the divine guidance which has brought us heretofore to safety and honor may be graciously continued in the years to come.

WILLIAM MCKINLEY, DEC. 5, 1898, 2ND ANNUAL MESSAGE:

It is a pleasure for me to mention...the American National Red Cross, both in relief measures preparatory to the campaigns, in sanitary assistance at several of the camps of assemblage, and later, under the able and experienced leadership of the president of the society, Miss Clara Barton, on the fields of battle and in the hospitals at the front in Cuba.

Working in conjunction with the governmental authorities...the enthusiastic cooperation of many patriotic women and societies in the various States, the Red Cross has fully maintained its already high reputation...

To the members and officers of this society and all who aided them in their philanthropic work the sincere and lasting gratitude of the soldiers and the public is due and is freely accorded. In tracing these events we are constantly reminded of our obligations to the Divine Master for His watchful care over us and His safe guidance, for which the nation makes reverent acknowledgment and offers humble prayer for the continuance of His favor.

WILLIAM MCKINLEY, OCT. 29, 1900, NATIONAL DAY OF THANKSGIVING & PRAISE PROCLAMATION:

It has pleased the Almighty God to bring our nation in safety and honor through another year. The works of religion and charity have everywhere been manifest....

We have been generally exempt from pestilence and other great calamities; and even the tragic visitation which overwhelmed the city of Galveston made evident the sentiments of sympathy and Christian charity by virtue of which we are one united people.

Now, therefore, I, William McKinley, President of the United States, do hereby appoint and set apart Thursday, the 29th of November next, to be observed by all the people of the United States, at home or abroad, as a day of thanksgiving and praise to Him who holds the nations in the hollow of His hand.

I recommend that they gather in their several places of worship and devoutly give Him thanks for the prosperity wherewith He has endowed us, for seed-time and harvest, for the valor, devotion and humanity of our armies and navies, and for all His benefits to us as individuals and as a nation; and that they humbly pray for the continuance of His Divine favor, for concord and amity with other nations, and for righteousness and peace in all our ways.

✥

WILLIAM MCKINLEY, MAR. 4, 1901, 2ND INAUGURAL:

I enter upon its administration appreciating the great responsibilities which attach to this renewed honor and commission, promising unreserved devotion on my part to their faithful discharge and reverently invoking for my guidance the direction and favor of Almighty God. "Hope maketh not ashamed." The prophets of evil were not the builders of the Republic, nor in its crises since have they saved or served it.

The faith of the fathers was a mighty force in its creation, and the faith of their descendants has wrought its progress and furnished its defenders...As hereunto, so hereafter will the nation demonstrate its fitness to administer any new estate which events devolve upon it, and in the fear of God will "take occasion by the hand and make the bounds of freedom wider yet."

✥

THEODORE ROOSEVELT

THEODORE ROOSEVELT, SEP. 14, 1901, NATIONAL DAY OF MOURNING & PRAYER ISSUED UPON ASSUMING THE PRESIDENCY AFTER DEATH OF PRESIDENT MCKINLEY:

The President of the United States has been struck down; a crime not only against the Chief Magistrate, but against every law-abiding and liberty-loving citizen.

President McKinley crowned a life of largest love for his fellow men, of earnest endeavor for their welfare, by a death of Christian fortitude; and both the way in which he lived his life and the way in which, in the supreme hour of trial, he met death will remain forever a precious heritage of our people...

Now, therefore, I, Theodore Roosevelt, President of the United States of America, do appoint Thursday next, September 19, the day in which the body of the dead President will be laid in its last earthly resting place, as a day of mourning and prayer throughout the United States.

I earnestly recommend all the people to assemble on that day in their respective places of divine worship, there to bow down in submission to the will of Almighty God, and to pay out of full hearts the homage of love and reverence to the memory of the great and good President, whose death has so sorely smitten the nation.

∽

THEODORE ROOSEVELT, DEC. 3, 1901, 1ST ANNUAL MESSAGE:

We need every honest and efficient immigrant fitted to become an American citizen, every immigrant who comes here to stay, who brings here a strong body, a stout heart, a good head, and a resolute purpose, to do his duty well in every way and to bring up his children as law-abiding and God-fearing members of the community. In the midst of our affliction we reverently thank the Almighty that we are at peace with the nations of mankind; and we firmly intend that our policy shall be such as to continue unbroken these international relations of mutual respect and good will.

∽

THEODORE ROOSEVELT, OCT. 29, 1902, NATIONAL DAY OF THANKSGIVING PROCLAMATION:

We now abundantly enjoy material well-being, and under the favor of the Most High we are striving earnestly to achieve moral and spiritual uplifting. The year that has just closed has been one of peace and of overflowing plenty.

Rarely has any people enjoyed greater prosperity than we are now enjoying. For this we render heartfelt and solemn thanks to the Giver of Good; and we seek to praise Him not by words only but by deeds, by the way in which we do our duty to ourselves and to our fellow men.

∽

THEODORE ROOSEVELT, OCT. 24, 1903, NATIONAL DAY OF PRAISE & THANKSGIVING PROCLAMATION:

During the last year the Lord has dealt bountifully with us, giving us peace at home and abroad and the chance for our citizens to work for their welfare unhindered by war, famine or plague. It behooves us not only to rejoice greatly because of what has been given us, but to accept it with a solemn sense of responsibility, realizing that under Heaven it rests with us ourselves to show that we are worthy to use aright what has thus been entrusted to our care.

In no other place and at no other time has the experiment of government of the people, by the people, for the people, been tried on so vast a scale as here in our own country in the opening years of the 20th Century. Failure would not only be a dreadful thing for us, but a dreadful thing for all mankind, because it would mean loss of hope for all who believe in the power and the righteousness of liberty.

Therefore, in thanking God for the mercies extended to us in the past, we beseech Him that He may not withhold them in the future.

∽

THEODORE ROOSEVELT, NOV. 1, 1904, NATIONAL DAY OF THANKSGIVING PROCLAMATION:

I...do recommend that on that day they cease from their ordinary occupations and gather in their several places of worship or in their homes, devoutly to give thanks unto Almighty God for the benefits he has conferred upon us as individuals and as a nation, and to beseech Him that in the future His Divine favor may be continued to us.

∽

THEODORE ROOSEVELT, DEC. 6, 1904, 4TH ANNUAL MESSAGE:

No Christian and civilized community can afford to show a happy-go-lucky lack of concern for the youth of to-day; for, if so, the community will have to pay a terrible penalty of financial burden and social degradation in the to-morrow.

∽

THEODORE ROOSEVELT, DEC. 6, 1904, 4TH ANNUAL MESSAGE:

There should be severe child-labor and factory-inspection laws. It is very desirable that married women should not work in factories. The prime duty of the man is to work, to be the breadwinner; the prime duty of the woman is to be the mother, the housewife.

All questions of tariff and finance sink into utter insignificance when compared with the tremendous, the vital importance of trying to shape conditions so that these two duties of the man and of the woman can be fulfilled under reasonably favorable circumstances. It is equally true that among the men of whom we are most proud as Americans no distinction whatever can be drawn between those who themselves or whose parents came over in sailing ships or steamer from across the water and those whose ancestors' stepped ashore into the wooded wilderness at Plymouth or at the mouth of the Hudson, the Delaware, or the James nearly three centuries ago.

No fellow-citizen of ours is entitled to any peculiar regard because of the way in which he worships his Maker.

<&

THEODORE ROOSEVELT, DEC. 6, 1904, 4TH ANNUAL MESSAGE:

There is no enemy of free government more dangerous and none so insidious as the corruption of the electorate. No one defends or excuses corruption, and it would seem to follow that none would oppose vigorous measures to eradicate it.

I recommend the enactment of a law directed against bribery and corruption in Federal elections...and provisions for the publication not only of the expenditures for nomination and elections of all candidates but also of all contributions received and expenditures made by political committees.

<&

THEODORE ROOSEVELT, DEC. 6, 1904, 4TH ANNUAL MESSAGE:

There are kinds of peace which are highly undesirable, which are in the long run as destructive as any war. Tyrants and oppressors have many times made a wilderness and called it peace.

Many times peoples who were slothful or timid or shortsighted, who had been enervated by ease or by luxury, or misled by false teachings, have shrunk in unmanly fashion from doing duty that was stern and that needed self-sacrifice, and have sought to hide from their own minds their shortcomings, their ignoble motives, by calling them love of peace. The peace of tyrannous terror, the peace of craven weakness, the peace of injustice, all these should be shunned as we shun unrighteous war...

One of our great poets has well and finely said that freedom is not a gift that tarries long in the hands of cowards. Neither does it tarry long in the hands of those too slothful, too dishonest, or too unintelligent to exercise it. The eternal vigilance which is the price of liberty must be exercised, sometimes to guard against outside foes; although of course far more often to guard against our own selfish or thoughtless shortcomings.

❧

THEODORE ROOSEVELT, DEC. 6, 1904, 4TH ANNUAL MESSAGE:

A people like ours...shows by its consistent practice its belief in the principles of civil and religious liberty...It is inevitable that such a nation should desire eagerly to give expression to its horror on an occasion like that of the massacre of the Jews in Kishenef, or when it witnesses such systematic and long-extended cruelty and oppression as the cruelty and oppression of which the Armenians have been the victims, and which have won for them the indignant pity of the civilized world...

It has proved very difficult to secure from Russia the right for our Jewish fellow-citizens to receive passports and travel through Russian territory. Such conduct is not only unjust and irritating toward us, but it is difficult to see its wisdom from Russia's standpoint...If an American Jew or an American Christian misbehaves himself in Russia he can at once be driven out; but the ordinary American Jew, like the ordinary American Christian, would behave just about as he behaves here.

❧

THEODORE ROOSEVELT, JAN. 30, 1905, MESSAGE TO CONGRESS:

The institution of marriage is, of course, at the very foundation of our social organization, and all influences that affect that institution are of vital concern to the people of the whole country.

There is a widespread conviction that the divorce laws are dangerously lax and indifferently administered in some of the States, resulting in the diminishing regard for the sanctity of the marriage relation.

The hope is entertained that co-operation amongst the several States can be secured to the end that there may be enacted upon the subject of marriage and divorce uniform laws, containing all possible safeguards for the security of the family.

❧

THEODORE ROOSEVELT, MAR. 4, 1905, INAUGURAL:

No people on earth have more cause to be thankful than ours, and this is said reverently, in no spirit of boastfulness in our own strength, but with gratitude to the Giver of Good who has blessed us...We wish peace, but we wish the peace of justice, the peace of righteousness...If we fail, the cause of free self-government throughout the world will rock to its foundations, and therefore our responsibility is heavy, to ourselves, to the world as it is today, and to the generations yet unborn.

❧

THEODORE ROOSEVELT, 1917, INSCRIPTION ON THE COVER OF NEW TESTAMENTS GIVEN TO SOLDIERS PREPARING THE SET SAIL DURING WORLD WAR I:

Remember: the most perfect machinery of government will not keep us as a nation from destruction if there is not within us a soul. No abounding material prosperity shall avail us if our spiritual senses atrophy...

Do Justice and fight valiantly against those that stand for the reign of Molech and Beelzebub on this earth. Love mercy; treat your enemies well; succor the afflicted; treat every woman as if she were your own sister; care for the little children; and be tender to the old and helpless. Walk humbly; you will do so if you study the life and teachings of the Savior, walking in His steps.

❧

WILLIAM HOWARD TAFT

WILLIAM HOWARD TAFT, MAR. 4, 1909, INAUGURAL:

I invoke the considerate sympathy and support of my fellow-citizens and the aid of the Almighty God in the discharge of my responsible duties.

✦

WILLIAM HOWARD TAFT, NOV. 15, 1909,
NATIONAL DAY OF THANKSGIVING PROCLAMATION:

The people of the United States are wont to meet in their usual places of worship on a day of thanksgiving appointed by the Civil Magistrate to return thanks to God for the great mercies and benefits which they have enjoyed. During the past year we have been highly blessed....It is altogether fitting that we should humbly and gratefully acknowledge the Divine Source of these blessings.

Therefore, I hereby appoint...a day of general thanksgiving, and I call upon the people on that day, laying aside their usual vocations, to repair to their churches and unite in appropriate services of praise and thanks to Almighty God.

❧

WILLIAM HOWARD TAFT, NOV. 5, 1910, NATIONAL DAY OF THANKSGIVING & PRAYER PROCLAMATION:

These blessings have not descended upon us in restricted measure, but overflow and abound. They are the blessings and bounty of God...

I...in accordance with the wise custom of the civil magistrate since the first settlements in this land and with the rule established from the foundation of this Government...do appoint Thursday, November 24, 1910, as a day of National Thanksgiving and Prayer, enjoining the people upon that day to meet in their churches for the praise of Almighty God and to return heartfelt thanks to Him for all His goodness and loving-kindness.

❧

WILLIAM HOWARD TAFT, NOV. 7, 1912, NATIONAL DAY OF THANKSGIVING PROCLAMATION:

A God-fearing nation, like ours, owes it to its inborn and sincere sense of moral duty to testify its devout gratitude to the All-Giver for the countless benefits its has enjoyed. For many years it has been customary at the close of the year for the national Executive to call upon his fellow countrymen to offer praise and thanks to God for the manifold blessings vouchsafed to them....

Wherefore I, William Howard Taft, President of the United States of America, in pursuance of long-established usage and in response to the wish of the American people, invite my countrymen, wheresoever they may sojourn, to join on Thursday, the 28th day of this month of November, in appropriate ascription of praise and thanks to God for the good gifts that have been our portion, and in humble prayer that His great mercies toward us may endure.

❧

WILLIAM HOWARD TAFT, DEC. 6, 1912, ANNUAL MESSAGE:

We have no desire for war. We would go as far as any nation in the world to avoid war, but we are a world power, our responsibilities in the Pacific and the Atlantic, our defense of the Panama Canal, together with our enormous world trade and our missionary outposts on the frontiers of civilization, require us to recognize our position as one of the foremost in the family of nations, and to clothe ourselves with sufficient naval power to give force to our reasonable demands, and to give weight to our influence in those directions of progress that a powerful Christian nation should advocate.

∽

WILLIAM HOWARD TAFT, 1908,
AT A MISSIONARY CONFERENCE:

No man can study the movement of modern civilization from an impartial standpoint, and not realize that Christianity and the spread of Christianity are the basis of hope of modern civilization in the growth of popular self government.

The spirit of Christianity is pure democracy. It is equality of man before God - the equality of man before the law, which is, as I understand it, the most God-like manifestation that man has been able to make.

∽

William Howard Taft - 27th President

WOODROW WILSON

WOODROW WILSON, 1911, GOVERNOR OF NEW JERSEY, ADDRESS AT A DENVER RALLY:

A nation which does not remember what it was yesterday, does not know what it is today, nor what it is trying to do. We are trying to do a futile thing if we do not know where we came from or what we have been about....The Bible...is the one supreme source of revelation of the meaning of life, the nature of God and spiritual nature and needs of men. It is the only guide of life which really leads the spirit in the way of peace and salvation. America was born a Christian nation. America was born to exemplify that devotion to the elements of righteousness which are derived from the revelations of Holy Scripture.

⤝

WOODROW WILSON, MAR. 4, 1913, 1ST INAUGURAL:

The feelings with which we face this new age of right and opportunity sweep across our heartstrings like some air out of God's own presence, where justice and mercy are reconciled and the judge and the brother are one...

This is not a day of triumph; it is a day of dedication...Men's hearts wait upon us; men's lives hang in the balance; men's hopes call upon us to day what we will do. Who shall live up to the great trust? Who dare fail to try? I summon all honest men, all patriotic, all forward-looking men to my side. God helping me, I will not fail them.

∾

WOODROW WILSON, JUL. 4, 1913, AT GETTYSBURG, PA:

Here is the nation God has builded by our hands. What shall we do with it? Who stands ready to act again and always in the spirit of this day of reunion and hope and patriotic fervor? The day of our country's life has but broadened into morning. Do not put uniforms by. Put the harness of the present on.

Lift your eyes to the great tracts of life yet to be conquered in the interest of righteous peace, of that prosperity which lies in a people's heart and outlasts all wars and errors of men. Come, let us be comrades and soldiers yet, to serve our fellow men in quiet counsel, where the blare of trumpets is neither heard nor heeded and where the things are done which make blessed the nations of the world in peace and righteousness and love.

∾

WOODROW WILSON, OCT. 23, 1913, NATIONAL DAY OF THANKSGIVING & PRAYER PROCLAMATION:

The season is at hand in which it has been our long respected custom as a people to turn in praise and thanksgiving to Almighty God for His manifold mercies and blessings to us as a nation. The year that has just passed has been marked in a peculiar degree by manifestations of His gracious and beneficent providence...

We have seen the practical completion of a great work at the Isthmus of Panama which not only exemplifies the nation's abundant capacity of its public servants but also promises the beginning of a new age, of new contacts, new neighborhoods, new sympathies, new bonds, and new achievements of co-operation and peace.

"Righteousness exalteth a nation" and "peace on earth, good will towards men" furnish the only foundation upon which can be built the lasting achievements of the human spirit...Now, Therefore, I, Woodrow Wilson, President of the United States of America, do hereby designate Thursday the twenty-seventh of November next as a day of thanksgiving and prayer, and invite the people throughout the land to cease from their wonted occupations and in their several homes and places of worship render thanks to Almighty God.

❧

WOODROW WILSON, JUL. 4, 1914,
ADDRESS AT INDEPENDENCE HALL, PHILADELPHIA:

The way to success in this great country, with its fair Judgements, is to show that you are not afraid of anybody except God and His final verdict. If I did not believe that, I would not believe in democracy. If I did not believe that, I would not believe that people can govern themselves. If I did not believe that the moral judgement would be the last judgment, the final judgment, in the minds of men as well as the tribunal of God, I could not believe in popular government.

❧

WOODROW WILSON, SEP. 8, 1914, NATIONAL DAY OF
PRAYER & SUPPLICATION AT ONSET OF WORLD WAR I:

Whereas great nations of the world have taken up arms against one another and war now draws millions of men into battle...And Whereas in this as in all things it is our privilege and duty to seek counsel and succor of Almighty God, humbling ourselves before Him, confessing our weakness and our lack of any wisdom. equal to these things...

Therefore, I, Woodrow Wilson, President of the United States of America, do designate...a day of prayer and supplication and do request all God-fearing persons to repair on that day to their places of worship there to unite their petitions to Almighty God that, overruling the counsel of men, setting straight the things they can not govern or alter, taking pity on the nations now in the throes of conflict, in His mercy and goodness showing a way where men can see none....Praying also to this end that He forgive us our sins, our ignorance of His holy will, our wilfulness and many errors, and lead us in the paths of obedience.

❧

WOODROW WILSON, OCT. 24, 1914, THE POWER OF
CHRISTIAN YOUNG MEN, AT 70TH ANNIVERSARY OF
YOUNG MEN'S CHRISTIAN ASSOCIATION, PITTSBURGH, PA:

I wonder if we attach sufficient importance to Christianity...If you will think about what you ought to do for other people, your character will take care of itself...And that is the reason of Christianity. Christ came into the world to save others, not to save himself; and no man is a true Christian who does not think constantly of how he can lift his brother.

∽

WOODROW WILSON, OCT. 24, 1914, AT 70TH ANNIVERSARY OF YOUNG MEN'S CHRISTIAN ASSOCIATION:

An association of Christian young men is an association meant to put its shoulders under the world and lift it...who regard themselves as their brother's keeper....Christian young men are the strongest kind of young men, and when they associate themselves together they have the incomparable strength of organization...a common instrument for sending the light of Christianity out into the world...Drawing young men who were strangers into places where they could have companionship...that kept them straight...by surrounding themselves with an atmosphere of purity...something of a glimpse of the great ideal which Christ lifted when He was elevated upon the cross.

∽

WOODROW WILSON, OCT. 24, 1914, AT 70TH ANNIVERSARY OF YOUNG MEN'S CHRISTIAN ASSOCIATION:

I do believe, that at 70 the YMCA is just reaching its majority, and that from this time on a dream greater even than George Williams ever dreamed will be realized in the great accumulating momentum of Christian men throughout the world...Is it not very important...to work...upon Christian forbearance and Christian principles, upon the idea that it is impossible by sophistication to establish that a thing that is wrong is right? And yet, while we are going to judge with the absolute standard of righteousness, we are going to judge with Christian feeling, being men of a like sort ourselves, suffering the same passions; and while we do not condemn we are going to seek to say and to live the truth. What I am hoping for is...a great rush of Christian principle upon the strongholds of evil and of wrong in the world.

∽

WOODROW WILSON, OCT. 24, 1914, AT 70TH ANNIVERSARY OF YOUNG MEN'S CHRISTIAN ASSOCIATION:

The Young Men's Christian Association...can point out to its members the things that are wrong. It can guide the feet of those who are going astray; and when its members have realized the power of the Christian principle, then they will not be men if they do not unite to see that the rest of the world experiences the same emancipation...Eternal vigilance is the price, not only of liberty, but of a great many other things....It is the price of one's own soul...

What shall a man give in exchange for his own soul?...There is a text in Scripture...It says godliness is profitable in this life as well as in the life that is to come; and if you do not start it in this life, it will not reach the life that is to come...This world is intended as the place in which we shall show that we know how to grow in the stature of manliness and of righteousness. I have come here to bid Godspeed to the great work of the Young Men's Christian Association.

⚓

WOODROW WILSON, NOV. 5, 1915, ON 50TH ANNIVERSARY OF MANHATTAN CLUB, NY:

The mission of America in the world is essentially a mission of peace on earth and good will among men (Luke 2:14)...We are a God-fearing people. We agree to differ about methods of worship, but we are united in believing in Divine Providence and in worshipping the God of Nations. We are the champions of religious right here and everywhere that it may be our privilege to give in our countenance and support...Here is the nation God has builded by our hands. What shall we do with it? Who is there who does not stand ready at all times to act in her behalf in a spirit of devoted and disinterested patriotism?

⚓

WOODROW WILSON, JAN. 11, 1916, PROCLAMATION OF A CONTRIBUTION DAY FOR THE STRICKEN JEWISH PEOPLE:

In the various countries now engaged in war there are nine millions of Jews, the great majority of whom are destitute of food, shelter, and clothing...Millions of them have been driven from their homes without warning, deprived of an opportunity to make provision for their most elementary wants, causing starvation, disease and untold suffering...I, Woodrow Wilson, President of the United States...appoint...a day upon which the people of the United States may make such contributions as they feel disposed for the aid of the stricken Jewish people. Contributions may be addressed to the American Red Cross, Washington, DC, which will care for their proper distribution...Done at the City of Washington this eleventh day of January, in the year of Our Lord one thousand nine hundred and sixteen.

❧

WOODROW WILSON, MAR. 5, 1917, 2ND INAUGURAL:

We are being forged into a new unity amidst the fires that now blaze throughout the world. In their ardent heat we shall, in God's Providence, let us hope, be purged of faction and division, purified of the errant humors of party and of private interest, and shall stand forth in the days to come with a new dignity of national pride and spirit...I know now what the task means. I realize to the full the responsibility which it involves. I pray God I may be given the wisdom and the prudence to do my duty in the true spirit of this great people.

❧

WOODROW WILSON, JAN. 20, 1918, EXECUTIVE ORDER TO THE ARMY & NAVY ENJOINING SABBATH OBSERVANCE:

The President, commander in chief of the Army and Navy, following the reverent example of his predecessors, desires and enjoins the orderly observance of the Sabbath by the officers and men in the military and naval service of the United States. The importance for man and beast of the prescribed weekly rest, the sacred rights of Christian soldiers and sailors, a becoming deference to the best sentiment of a Christian people, and a due regard for the Divine Will demand that Sunday labor in the Army and Navy be reduced to the measure of strict necessity. Such an observance of Sunday is dictated by the best traditions of our people and by the convictions of all who look to Divine Providence for guidance and protection, and, in repeating in this order the language of President Lincoln, the President in confident that he is speaking alike to the hearts and to the consciences of those under his authority.

❧

WOODROW WILSON, MAY 18, 1918, AT OPENING OF 2ND RED CROSS DRIVE, NEW YORK CITY:

We are members...of the American Red Cross, of a great

fraternity and fellowship which extends all over the world, and this cross which these ladies bore here today is an emblem of Christianity itself...When you think of this, you realize how the people of the United States are being drawn together into a great intimate family whose heart is being used for the service of the soldiers not only, but for the long night of suffering and terror, in order that they and men everywhere may see the dawn of a day of righteousness and justice and peace.

᰷

WOODROW WILSON, MAY 11, 1918, NATIONAL DAY OF HUMILIATION, PRAYER & FASTING DURING WORLD WAR I:

Whereas the Congress of the United States..."Resolved by the Senate (the House of Representatives concurring), That, it being the duty peculiarly incumbent in a time of war humbly and devoutly to acknowledge our dependence on Almighty God and to implore His aid and protection, the President of the United States be, and he is hereby, respectfully requested to recommend a day of public humiliation, prayer and fasting, to be observed by the people of the United States with religious solemnity and the offering of fervent supplications to Almighty God for the safety and welfare of our cause, His blessings on our arms, and a speedy restoration of an honorable and lasting peace to the nations of the earth;"

And Whereas it has always been the reverent habit of the people of the United States to turn in humble appeal to Almighty God for His guidance in the affairs of their common life; Now, Therefore, I, Woodrow Wilson, President of the United States of America, do hereby proclaim...a day of public humiliation, prayer and fasting, and do exhort my fellow-citizens of all faiths and creeds to assemble on that day in their several places of worship and there, as well as in their homes, to pray Almighty God that He may forgive our sins and shortcomings as a people and purify our hearts to see and love the truth, to accept and defend all things that are just and right, and to purpose only those righteous acts and judgements which are in conformity with His will; beseeching Him that He will give victory to our armies as they fight for freedom.

᰷

WOODROW WILSON, SEP. 1, 1918, TO RABBI STEPHEN WISE:

I have watched with deep and sincere interest the reconstructive work which the Weizmann commission has done in Palestine...and I welcome an opportunity to express the satisfaction I have felt in the progress of the Zionist movement in the United States and in the allied countries since the declaration of Mr. Balfour, on behalf of the British Government, of Great Britain's approval of the establishment in Palestine of a national home for the Jewish people...Americans will be deeply moved by the report that even in this time of stress the Weizmann commission has been able to lay the foundation of the Hebrew University at Jerusalem, with the promise that that bears of spiritual rebirth.

✑

WOODROW WILSON, MAY 24, 1920, ASKING CONGRESS FOR MANDATE FOR ARMENIA UNDER LEAGUE OF NATIONS:

The Senate Committee on Foreign Relations has clearly established the truth of the reported massacres and other atrocities from which the Armenian people have suffered...The people of the United States are deeply impressed by the deplorable conditions of insecurity, starvation and misery now prevalent in Armenia...The voice of the American people expressing their genuine convictions and deep Christian sympathies...I urgently advise and request that the Congress grant the Executive power to accept for the United States a mandate over Armenia....

The sympathy with Armenia has proceeded from no single portion of our people, but has come with extraordinary spontaneity and sincerity from the whole of the great body of Christian men and women in this country...At their hearts this great and generous people have made the cause of Armenia their own...I am conscious that I am urging upon Congress a very critical choice, but I make the suggestion in the confidence that I am speaking in the spirit and in accordance with the wishes of the greatest of the Christian peoples. The sympathy for Armenia among our people has sprung from untainted consciences, pure Christian faith and an earnest desire to see Christian people everywhere succored in their time of suffering.

✑

WOODROW WILSON, STATEMENT:

When you have read the Bible, you will know that it is the Word of God, because you will have found it the key to your own heart, your own happiness, and your own duty.

WARREN G. HARDING

WARREN G. HARDING, MAR. 4, 1921, INAUGURAL:

I must utter my belief in the Divine Inspiration of the founding fathers. Surely there must have been God's intent in the making of this newworld Republic...Let us express renewed and strengthened devotion, in grateful reverence for the immortal beginning, and utter our confidence in the supreme fulfillment...America is ready...to participate in any seemly program likely to lessen the probability of war, and promote that brotherhood of mankind which must be God's highest conception of human relationship...

My most reverent prayer for America is for industrial peace...We want an America of homes...where mothers, freed from the necessity for long hours of toil beyond their own doors, may preside as befits the hearthstone of American citizenship. We want the cradle of American childhood rocked under conditions so wholesome and so hopeful that no blight may touch it...I would rejoice to acclaim the era of the Golden Rule.

❧

WARREN G. HARDING, MAR. 4, 1921, INAUGURAL:

The world upheaval has added heavily to our tasks. But with the realization comes the surge of high resolve, and there is reassurance in belief in the God-given destiny of our Republic. If I felt that there is to be sole responsibility in the Executive for the America of tomorrow I should shrink from the burden. But here are a hundred millions, with common concern and shared responsibility, answerable to God and country...

I accept my part with single-mindedness of purpose and humility of spirit, and implore the favor and guidance of God in His Heaven...I have taken the solemn oath of office on that passage of Holy Writ wherein it is asked: "What doth the Lord require of thee but to do justly, and to love mercy, and to walk humbly with thy God." This I plight to God and country.

᭡

WARREN G. HARDING, MAY 3, 1921,
NATIONAL MEMORIAL DAY PROCLAMATION:

Whereas this nation has been conceived in prayer and devotion by men and women who were moved under God to found a nation where principles of right should form the lasting cornerstone; and Whereas there principles purchased at the price of great sacrifice have been fostered by a worthy posterity...I...invite my fellow citizens to pay homage on this day to a noble dead who sleep in homeland, beneath the sea or on foreign field that we who survive might enjoy the blessings of peace and happiness.

᭡

WARREN G. HARDING, SEP. 30, 1921,
NATIONAL ARMISTICE DAY PROCLAMATION:

The remains of this unknown American...will be buried in the said Memorial Amphitheatre at Arlington on the eleventh day of November...I...call upon all devout and patriotic citizens of the United States to pause from their accustomed occupations and labors on Friday the eleventh day of November next from twelve o'clock noon to two minutes past the hour for a period of silent prayer of thanks to the Giver of All Good for these valuable and valorous lives and of supplication for His Divine mercy and for His blessings upon our beloved country.

᭡

WARREN G. HARDING, NOV. 11, 1921, BURYING AN UNKNOWN SOLDIER IN ARLINGTON CEMETERY:

In the death gloom of gas, the bursting of shells and rain of bullets, men face more intimately the great God over all...I can sense the prayers of our people, of all peoples, that this Armistice Day shall mark the beginning of a new and lasting era of peace on earth, good will among men. Let me join in that prayer.

Our Father who art in heaven, hallowed be Thy name. Thy kingdom come, Thy will be done on earth, as it is in heaven. Give us this day our daily bread and forgive us our trespasses as we forgive those who trespass against us. And lead us not into temptation, but deliver us from evil, for Thine is the kingdom, and the power, and the glory, forever Amen.

∼

WARREN G. HARDING, NOV. 12, 1921, TO CONFERENCE AT CONTINENTAL MEMORIAL HALL, WASHINGTON:

Inherent rights are of God, and the tragedies of the world originate in their attempted denial.

∼

WARREN G. HARDING, DEC. 23, 1921, OF THE AMERICAN DELEGATION DRAWING UP THE FOUR-POWER TREATY:

They are working out the greatest contribution to peace and good-will which has ever marked the Christmas time in all the Christian era.

∼

WARREN G. HARDING, MAY 30, 1922, AT DEDICATION OF LINCOLN MEMORIAL, WASHINGTON, D.C:

In every moment of peril, in every hour of discouragement, whenever the clouds gather, there is the image of Lincoln to rivet our hopes and to renew our faith...Here was the great purpose, here the towering hope, here the supreme faith. He treasured the inheritance handed down by the founding fathers, the ark of the covenant wrought through their heroic sacrifices, and builded in their inspired genius...
His faith was inspiring, his resolution commanding, his sympathy reassuring, his simplicity enlisting, his patience unfailing. He was Faith, Patience and Courage, with his head above the clouds, unmoved by

the storms which raged about his feet...He knew he had freed a race of bondmen and had given to the world the costly proof of the perpetuity of the American union...

Lincoln came almost as humbly as The Child of Bethlehem. His parents were unlettered, his home was devoid of every element of culture and refinement. He was no infant prodigy, no luxury facilitated or privilege hastened his development, but he had a God-given intellect, a love for work, a willingness to labor and a purpose to succeed...His work was so colossal, in the face of such discouragement, that none will dispute that he was incomparably the greatest of our presidents...Amid it all there was a gentleness, a kindness, a sympathetic sorrow, which suggest a divine intent to blend mercy with power in supreme attainment.

✎

WARREN G. HARDING, NOV. 20, 1922,
AMERICAN EDUCATION WEEK PROCLAMATION:

"Without a vision the people perish" (Pr. 29:18). Without education, there can be little vision. Of education it may be said that "It is twice blest; it blesseth him that gives and him that takes." It will be greatly worth the effort if, as an incident to the observance of Education Week, we can impress this thought upon the young manhood and womanhood of the nation and redirect their interest and patriotic zeal to the idea of making a proper contribution to educational work...The strength and security of the nation will always rest in the intelligent body of its people...Civic organizations and religious bodies may render special service by their cooperation; and particularly it is recommended that parents enlist themselves in behalf of closer understanding between school and home...

In Consideration and Witness Whereof, I have hereunto set my hand and caused the seal of the United States to be affixed. Done at the City of Washington this twentieth day of November, in the year of Our Lord one thousand nine hundred and twenty-two, and of the Independence of the United States the one hundred and forty-seventh.

✎

WARREN G. HARDING, JUN. 21, 1923, ON INTERNATIONAL
COURT OF JUSTICE, DELIVERED IN ST. LOUIS, MO:

In his never-to-be-forgotten Farewell Address, in which the first president compressed the gospel of our mutual interest at home and our proper relations abroad, he said: "Observe good faith and justice toward all nations. Cultivate peace and harmony with all. Religion and morality enjoin this conduct. And can it be that good policy does not equally enjoin it?"...

This solemn admonition was addressed by George Washington to his fellow-countrymen one hundred and twenty-seven years ago. That it has been heeded scrupulously we are proud to assume the world believes. That we have, indeed, observed good faith and have exalted justice above all other agencies of civilization, barring only Christianity, surely none can deny with truth...

Very recently a striking message was flashed through the air from Rome to Washington. "Tell America," said the vigorous Prime Minister, "that I like her, like her because she is strong, simple, and direct. I wish Italy to be the same and shall try to make her so." God speed him! And God grant that America shall never forfeit the high honor borne by that sentiment tribute...I shall call upon your patriotism. I shall beseech your humanity. I shall invoke your Christianity. I shall reach to the very depths of your love for your fellow man of whatever race or creed throughout the world.

I shall speak, as I speak now, with all the earnestness and power of the sincerity that is in me and in perfect faith that God will keep clear and receptive your understanding. I could not do otherwise. My soul yearns for peace. My heart is anguished by the sufferings of war. My spirit is eager to serve...If, in our search for everlasting peace, we but let lead, and follow humbly but dauntlessly, the "Kindly Light" of divine inspiration to all human brotherhood, gleaming like a star in the heavens, from the most beautiful hymn ever written, God will not let us fail.

∽

WARREN G. HARDING, JUN. 25, 1923, IN DENVER, CO:

There is another phase of law-observance to which reference is impelling. I am thinking of the law of the Golden Rule, a statute from the Man of Nazareth, who brought new peace and new hope to mankind, and proclaimed service to men the highest tribute to God.

Service is both the inspiration and the accomplishment of quite everything worth while which impels us onward and upward. With service which the Nazarene would approve are associated all our ideals and our finer aspirations...

We may rejoice in the flood tides of material good fortune, we may becomingly boast the measureless resources of the republic through God's bounty in creation and man's genius in development, but we aren't living the becoming life unless we are seeking to advance humankind as we achieve for ourselves. I would like the ages of envy and hate, and conquest and pillage, and armed greed and mad ambitions to be followed by understanding and peace, by the rule of law where force had reigned...the observance of the Golden Rule as the law of human righteousness.

∽

WARREN G. HARDING, JUN. 29, 1923,
ADDRESS DELIVERED IN HELENA, MONTANA:

We must recognize that the tendency is to take the modern mother more and more away from the control, the training, the intellectual guidance and spiritual direction of her children...Frankly, I am one of those old-fashioned people who would be glad if the way could be found to maintain the traditional relations of father, mother, children, and home...The mother who tirelessly seeks rightly to train her own children, to instill into them that indefinable essence which we know as good breeding, will be performing this service not alone for her own children, but in only less measure for the children who come from homes less blessed with the finer things of life...

The teacher, and the authorities back of her, must be equally ready to cooperate with the home and the mother. In the home must still be performed the duty of instilling into the child those fundamental concepts of religion and of faith which are essential to rightly shaping the character of citizens, and therefore of the nation.

It would be an irreparable mistake if in surrendering to society a larger responsibility for the child's intellectual and physical well being, we should forget the necessity for proper religious training. That duty must be performed in the home; it will always be peculiarly the duty of the mother....

Mankind never has stood more in need than it does now of the consolations and reassurances which derive from a firm religious faith.

We are living in a time of many uncertainties, of weakened faith in the efficiency of institutions, of industrial systems, of economic hypotheses, of dictum and dogma in whatever sphere. Yet we all know that there are certain fundamental truths of life and duty and destiny which will stand eternal...There must be no mistake whereby we shall confuse the things which are of eternity with those which are of time. We must not let our engrossment with the things of matter and of mind distract us from a proper concern for those which are of the spirit and the soul...

Twenty centuries of the Christian era and its great story of human progress, and the countless centuries before the light of Christianity flamed...is the best the world has revealed, and I preach the gospel of holding fast to that which has proven good, ever trying in good conscience to make it better, and consider and treat as an enemy every man who chooses our land as a haven in which to assail the very institutions which shelter him...In the recognized test which our civilization is now undergoing America's supreme task is one of preservation. I call upon America to protect and preserve.

∽

WARREN G. HARDING, JUL. 3, 1923, ADDRESS AT THE OREGON TRAIL MONUMENT, MEACHAM, OREGON, ONE MONTH PRIOR TO HIS DEATH, HONORING MEDICAL MISSIONARY DR. MARCUS WHITMAN, WHOSE STATUE STANDS IN THE U.S. CAPITOL STATUARY HALL:

Of the many rooms in the White Houses...the one most fascinating to me is...the President's Study...Before my mind's eye as I stood in that heroic chamber a few days ago appeared the vivid picture.

I beheld seated at his desk, immaculately attired, the embodiment of dignity and courtliness, John Tyler, 10th President of the United States.

Facing him, from a chair constructed for a massive frame, his powerful spirit gleaming through his cavernous eyes, was the lion-visaged Daniel Webster, Secretary of State.

The door opened and there appeared before the amazed statesmen a strange and astonishing figure. It was that of a man of medium height and sturdy build, deep chested, broad shouldered, yet lithe in movement and soft in step. He was clad in a coarse fur coat, buckskin breeches, fur leggings, and boot moccasins, looking much worse for the wear.

But it was the countenance of the visitor, as he stood for an instant in the doorway, that riveted the perception of the two Chiefs of State. It was that of a religious enthusiast, tenaciously earnest yet revealing no suggestion of fanaticism, bronzed from exposure to pitiless elements and seamed with deep lines of physical suffering, a rare combination of determination and gentleness - obviously a man of God, but no less a man among men.

Such was Marcus Whitman, the missionary hero of the vast, unsettled, unexplored Oregon country, who had come out of the West to plead that the State should acquire for civilization the Empire that the churches were gaining for Christianity...Then turning to President [Tyler], he added quietly but beseechingly: "All I ask is that you will not barter away Oregon or allow English interference until I can lead a bank of stalwart American settlers across the plains. For this I shall try to do!" "Dr. Whitman," he rejoined sympathetically, "your long ride and frozen limbs testify to your courage and your patriotism. Your credentials establish your character. Your request is granted!"

∽

WARREN G. HARDING, JUL. 3, 1923, ADDRESS AT THE OREGON TRAIL MONUMENT, MEACHAM, OREGON:

Never in the history of the world has there been a finer example of civilization following Christianity. The missionaries led under the banner of the cross, and the settlers moved close behind under the star-spangled symbol of the nation. Among all the records of the evangelizing efforts as the forerunner of human advancement, there is none so impressive as this of the early Oregon mission and its marvelous consequences.

To the men and women of that early day whose first thought was to carry the gospel to the Indians - to the Lees, the Spauldings, the Grays, the Walkers, the Leslies, to Fathers DeSmet & Blanchet &

DeMars & to all the others of that glorious company who found that in serving God they were also serving their country & their fellowmen - to them we pay today our tribute. To them we owe a debt of gratitude, which we can never pay, save partially through recognition such as you and I have accorded today.

 క

WARREN G. HARDING, JUL. 3, 1923, ADDRESS AT THE OREGON TRAIL MONUMENT, MEACHAM, OREGON:

I thank you from my heart for permitting me to participate in doing homage to those brave souls. I rejoice particularly in the opportunity afforded me of voicing my appreciation both as President of the United States and as one who honestly tries to be a Christian soldier, of the signal service of the martyred Whitman.

క

WARREN G. HARDING, STATEMENT :

Service is both the inspiration and the accomplishment of quite everything worthwhile which impels us onward and upward. With service which the Nazarene would approve are associated all our ideals and our finer aspirations.

క

WARREN G. HARDING, STATEMENT:

I have always believed in the inspiration of the Holy Scriptures, whereby they have become the expression to man of the Word and Will of God.

క

CALVIN COOLIDGE

CALVIN COOLIDGE, MAY 31, 1923, MEMORIAL DAY
ADDRESS ENTITLED THE DESTINY OF AMERICA:

Settlers came here from mixed motives, some for pillage and
adventure, some for trade and refuge, but those who have set their
imperishable mark upon our institutions came from far higher motives.
Generally defined, they were seeking a broader freedom. They were
intent upon establishing a Christian commonwealth in accordance to
the principle of self-government.

They were an inspired body of men. It has been said that God
sifted the nations that He might send choice grain into the wilderness.
They had a genius for organized society on the foundations of piety,
righteousness, liberty, and obedience of the law.

They brought with them the accumulated wisdom and
experience of the ages...Who can fail to see in it the hand of destiny?
Who can doubt that it has been guided by a Divine Providence?

❧

CALVIN COOLIDGE, AUG. 4, 1923, NATIONAL DAY OF MOURNING & PRAYER PROCLAMATION:

In the inscrutable wisdom of Divine Providence, Warren Gamaliel Harding, twenty-ninth President of the United States, has been taken from us...Now, therefore, I, Calvin Coolidge, President of the United States, do appoint...a day of mourning and prayer throughout the United States. I earnestly recommend the people to assemble on that day in their respective places of divine worship, there to bow down in submission to the will of Almighty God, and to pay out of full hearts the homage of love and reverence to the memory of the great and good President whose death has so sorely smitten the nation.

❧

CALVIN COOLIDGE, SEP. 1923, TO RIGHT REVEREND JAMES E. FREEMAN, BISHOP OF WASHINGTON:

The foundation of all progress, all government and all civilization...is religion. Our country is not lacking in material resources...It cannot be said to be lacking in intelligence. But certainly it has need of a greater practical application of the truths of religion. It is only in that direction that there is hope of the solution of our economic and social problems. Whatever inspires and strengthens the religious belief and religious activity of the people, whatever ministers to their spiritual life is of supreme importance. Without it all other efforts will fail. With it, there lies the only hope of success. The strength of our country is the strength of its religious convictions.

❧

CALVIN COOLIDGE, STATEMENT:

The foundations of our society and our government rest so much on the teachings of the Bible that it would be difficult to support them if faith in these teachings would cease to be practically universal in our country.

❧

CALVIN COOLIDGE, JUN. 6, 1924, HOWARD UNIVERSITY:

It has come to be a legend...that Howard University was the outgrowth of the inspiration of a prayer meeting...The accomplishments of the colored people in the United States...can not but make us realize that there is something essential in our civilization which gives it a special power. I think we shall be able to agree that this particular element is the Christian religion, whose influence always and everywhere has been a force for the illumination and advancement of the peoples who have come under its sway.

&

CALVIN COOLIDGE, JUL. 4, 1924, CONVENTION OF NATIONAL EDUCATION ASSOCIATION, WASHINGTON, D.C:

America is turning from the things that are seen to the things that are unseen...which we must recognize as the guiding hand of Providence...Unless our material resources are supported by moral and spiritual resources, there is not foundation for progress. A trained intelligence can do much, but there is no substitute for morality, character, and religious convictions. Unless these abide, American citizenship will be found unequal to its task.

&

CALVIN COOLIDGE, JUL. 25, 1924, TO BOY SCOUTS BOUND FOR AN INTERNATIONAL GATHERING IN COPENHAGEN:

The three fundamentals of scouthood: The first is a reverence for nature...Second is a reverence for law...Third is a reverence for God. It is hard to see how a great man can be an atheist. Without the sustaining influence of faith in a divine power we could have little faith in ourselves...Doubters do not achieve; skeptics do not contribute; cynics to not create. Faith is the great motive power, and no man realizes his full possibilities unless he has the deep conviction that life is eternally important, and that his work, well done, is part of an unending plan.

&

CALVIN COOLIDGE, SEP. 21, 1924, TO THE HOLY NAME SOCIETY IN WASHINGTON, D.C:

More than six centuries ago, when...there was much ignorance, much wickedness and much warfare...when the condition of the common people appeared to be sunk in hopelessness...when the speech of men was too often profane and vulgar, until the earth rang with the tumult of those who took the name of the Lord in vain, the foundation of this day was laid in the formation of the Holy Name Society...It sought to rededicate the minds of the people to a true conception of the sacredness of the name of the Supreme Being. It was an effort to save all reference to the Deity from curses and blasphemy, and to restore the lips of men to reverence and praise...This is the beginning of a proper conception of ourselves, of our relationship to each other, and our relationship to our Creator....

The mind does not unfold, the creative faculty does not mature, the spirit does not expand, save under the influence of reverence...It is along the path of reverence and obedience that the race has reached the goal of freedom, of self-government, of a higher morality, and a more abundant spiritual life...He who gives license to his tongue only discloses the contents of his own mind. By the excess of his words he proclaims his lack of discipline...

The worst evil that could be inflicted upon the youth of the land would be to leave them without restraint and completely at the mercy of their own uncontrolled inclinations. Under such conditions education would be impossible, and all orderly development intellectually or morally would be hopeless. I do not need to picture the result. We know too well what weakness and depravity follow when the ordinary processes of discipline are neglected...

The very first paragraph of the Declaration of Independence asserted that they proposed "to assume, among the powers of the earth, the separate and equal station to which the laws of nature and of nature's God entitle them." And as they closed that noble document...they again revealed what they believed to be the ultimate source of authority by stating that they were also "appealing to the Supreme Judge of the World for the rectitude of"...their "intentions."

When finally our Constitution was adopted, it contained specific provision that the President and members of the Congress and of state legislatures, and all executive and judicial officials, should be qualified for the discharge of their office by oath or affirmation. By the statute law of the United States, and I doubt not by all States, such oaths are administered by a solemn appeal to God for help in the keeping of their covenants.

I scarcely need to refer to the fact that the Houses of Congress...open their daily sessions with prayer. The foundations of our independence and our Government rests upon basic religious convictions. Back of the authority of our laws is the authority of the Supreme Judge of the

World, to whom we still appeal for their final justification...

The principle of equality...follows inevitably from belief in the brotherhood of man through the fatherhood of God. When once the right of the individual to liberty and equality is admitted, there is no escape from the conclusion that he alone is entitled to the rewards of his own industry...

It seems to me perfectly plain that the authority of law, the right to equality, liberty and property, under American institutions, have for their foundation reverence for God. If we could imagine that to be swept away, these institutions of our American government could not long survive...But I know they will continue to stand. We may perish, but they will endure. They are founded on the Rock of Ages.

∽

CALVIN COOLIDGE, OCT. 15, 1924, UNVEILING EQUESTRIAN STATUE OF BISHOP FRANCIS ASBURY:

"All things work together for good to them that love God"...In the direction of the affairs of our country there has been an influence...which we can only ascribe to a Divine Providence...

Our government rests upon religion. It is from that source that we derive our reverence for truth and justice, for equality and liberty, and for the rights of mankind. Unless the people believe in these principles they cannot believe in our government. There are only two main theories of government in the world. One rests on righteousness, the other rests on force. One appeals to reason, the other appeals to the sword. One is exemplified in a republic, the other is represented by a despotism.

The history of government on this earth has been almost entirely a history of the rule of force held in the hands of a few. Under our Constitution America committed itself to the practical application of the rule of reason, with the power in the hands of the people...

The generation which fought the American Revolution had seen a very extensive religious revival. They had heard the preaching of Jonathan Edwards...of George Whitefield. The religious experiences of those days made a profound impression upon the great body of the people...By calling the people to righteousness they were a direct preparation for self-government.

It was for a continuation of this work that Francis Asbury was raised up...

Just as our Declaration of Independence asserts that all men are created free, so it seems to me the founders of this movement were inspired by the thought that all men were worthy to hear the Word, worthy to be sought out and brought to salvation. It was this motive that took their preachers among the poor and neglected, even to criminals in the jails. As our ideal has been to bring all men to freedom, so their ideal was to bring all men to salvation...

Just as the time was approaching when our country was about to begin the work of establishing a government which was to represent the rule of the people, where not a few but the many were to control public affairs, where the vote of the humblest was to count for as much as the most exalted, Francis Asbury came to America to preach religion...

At the age of 17, he began his preaching. In 1771, when he was 26 years old, responding to a call for volunteers, he was sent by John Wesley to America. Landing in Philadelphia, he began that ministry which in the next 45 years was to take him virtually all through the colonies and their western confines and into Canada, from Maine on the north, almost to the Gulf of Mexico on the south.

He came to America five years after the formation of the first Methodist Society in the city of New York...At that time it is reported that there were 316 members of his denomination in this country...He traveled some 6,000 miles each year, or in all about 270,000 miles, preaching about 15,500 sermons and ordaining more than 4,000 clergymen, besides presiding at no less than 224 Annual Conferences. The highest salary that he received was $80 each year for this kind of service, which meant exposure to summer heat and winter cold, traveling alone through the frontier forests, sharing the rough fare of the pioneer's cabin, until his worn-out frame was laid at last to rest...He left behind him as one evidence of his labors 695 preachers and 214,235 members of his denomination...The 316 with which he began has now grown to more than 800,000.

His problem during the Revolutionary War was that of continuing to perform his duties without undertaking to interfere in civil or military affairs.

He had taken for the text of his first sermon in America these very significant words: "For I determined not to know anything among you save Jesus Christ and Him crucified."

When several of his associates left for England in 1775, he decided to stay. "I can by no means agree to leave such a field for gathering souls to Christ as we have in America," he writes, "therefore I am determined by the grace of God not to leave them, let the consequence by what it may."..He had no lack of loyalty to the early form of American government. When the inauguration of Washington took place April 30, 1789, ...a congratulatory address to the new President...was adopted, and the Bishop...in person, read it to Washington...

With the pioneers, his missionaries visited the hovels of the poor so that all men might be brought to a knowledge of the truth...It was because of what Bishop Asbury and his associates preached...that our country has developed so much freedom and contributed so much to the civilization of the world...The government of a country never gets ahead of the religion of a country. There is no way by which we can substitute the authority of law for the virtue of man...

Real reforms which society in these days is seeking will come as a result of our religious convictions, or they will not come at all. Peace, justice, humanity, charity - these cannot be legislated into being. They are the result of a Divine Grace...It is more than probable that Nancy Hanks, the mother of Lincoln, had heard him in her youth. Adams and Jefferson must have known him, and Jackson must have seen in him a flaming spirit as unconquerable as his own.

How many temples of worship dot our landscape; how many institutions of learning...all trace the inspiration of their existence to the sacrifice and service of this lone circuit rider. He is entitled to rank as one of the builders of our nation. On the foundation of a religious civilization which he sought to build, our country has enjoyed greater blessing of liberty and prosperity than was ever before the lot of man.

These cannot continue if we neglect the work which he did. We cannot depend on the government to do the work of religion. I do not see how anyone could recount the story of this early Bishop without feeling a renewed faith in our own country.

❧

CALVIN COOLIDGE, OCT. 26, 1924, TO FEDERATION OF JEWISH PHILANTHROPIC SOCIETIES OF NEW YORK CITY:

Your Federation for the Support of Jewish Philanthropic Societies in New York is the central financial agency...for no less than 91 various philanthropies...among them are hospitals, orphanages, a great relief society, a loaning organization, a home for Aged and Infirm. The Young Men's Hebrew Association and the Young Women's Hebrew Association do social and educational work of the greatest value...

Jewish people have always...been particularly devoted to the ideal of taking care of their own. This Federation is one of the monuments to their independence and self-reliance. They have sought to protect and preserve that wonderful inheritance of tradition, culture, literature and religion, which has placed the world under so many obligations to them...You are making good citizens...You are strengthening the Government...You are demonstrating the supremacy of the spiritual life and helping establish the Kingdom of God on earth.

❧

CALVIN COOLIDGE, NOV. 3, 1924, RADIO ADDRESS FROM THE WHITE HOUSE TO THE NATION:

I therefore urge upon all the voters of our country, without reference to party, that they assemble tomorrow at their respective voting places in the exercise of the high office of American citizenship, that they approach the ballot box in the spirit that they would approach a sacrament, and there, disregarding all appeals to passion and prejudice, dedicating themselves truly and wholly to the welfare of their country, they make their choice of public officers solely in the light of their own conscience. When an election is so held, when a choice is so made, it results in the real rule of the people, it warrants and sustains the belief that the voice of the people is the voice of God.

❧

CALVIN COOLIDGE, MAR. 4, 1925, INAUGURAL:

If we wish to continue to be distinctly American, we must continue...to pursue a conscientious and religious life...Peace will come when there is realization that only under a reign of law, based on righteousness and supported by the religious conviction of the brotherhood of man, can there be any hope of a complete and satisfying life. Parchment will fail, the sword will fail, it is only the spiritual nature of man that can be triumphant...

America seeks no earthly empires built on blood and force. No ambition, no temptation, lures her to thought of foreign dominions. The legions which she sends forth are armed, not with the sword, but with the Cross. The higher state to which she seeks the allegiance of all mankind is not of human, but Divine origin. She cherishes no purpose save to merit the favor of Almighty God.

∽

CALVIN COOLIDGE, MAY 3, 1925, LAYING CORNERSTONE OF THE JEWISH COMMUNITY CENTER, WASHINGTON, DC:

A century and a half ago marked the beginning of the American Revolution...There were well-nigh as many divergencies of religious faith as there were of origin, politics and geography...From its beginning, the new continent had seemed destined to be the home of religious tolerance. Those who claimed the right of individual choice for themselves finally had to grant it to others...

One of the factors which I think weighed heaviest on the side of unity - the Bible was the one work of literature that was common to all of them. The Scriptures were read and studied everywhere. There are many testimonies that their teachings became the most important intellectual and spiritual force for unification. I remember...of the historian W.E.H. Lecky, the observation the "Hebraic mortar cemented the foundations of American democracy." Lecky had in mind this very influence of the Bible in drawing together the feelings and sympathies of the widely scattered communities...

From New Hampshire to Georgia, they found a common ground of faith and reliance in the Scriptural writings. In those days books were few, and even those of a secular character were largely the product of a scholarship which used the Scriptures...The young American nation owed to the sacred writing that the Hebrew people gave to the world.

This biblical influence was strikingly impressive in all the New England colonies...In the Connecticut Code of 1650, the Mosaic model is adopted.

The magistrates were authorized to administer justice "according to the laws here established, and, for want of them, according to the word of God." In the New Haven Code of 1655, there were 79 topical statutes for the Government, half of which contained references to the Old Testament.

The founders of the New Haven, John Davenport and Theophilus Eaton, were expert Hebrew scholars. The extent to which they leaned upon the moral and administrative system, laid down by the Hebrew lawgivers, was responsible for their conviction that the Hebrew language and literature ought to be made as familiar as possible to all the people. So it was that John Davenport arranged that in the first public school in New Haven the Hebrew language should be taught.

The preachers of those days, saturated in the religion and literature of the Hebrew prophets, were leaders, teachers, moral mentors and even political philosophers for their flocks. A people raised under such leadership, given to much study and contemplation of the Scriptures, inevitably became more familiar with the great figures of Hebrew history, with Joshua, Samuel, Moses, Joseph, David, Solomon, Gideon, Elisha - than they were with the stories of their own ancestors as recorded in the pages of profane history.

The sturdy old divines of those days found the Bible a chief source of illumination for their arguments in support of the patriot cause. They knew the Book...and were eminently capable in the exposition of all its justifications for rebellion. To them...Exodus from Egypt was indeed an inspired precedent...It required no great stretch of logical processes to demonstrate that the children of Israel, making bricks without straw in Egypt, had their modern counterpart in the people of the colonies, enduring the imposition of taxation without representation!

And the Jews themselves...scattered throughout the colonies, were true to the teachings of their own prophets. The Jewish faith is predominantly the faith of liberty. From the beginning to the conflict between the colonies and the mother country, they were overwhelmingly on the side of the rising revolution...

Among the merchants who unhesitatingly signed the non-importation resolution of 1765: Isaac Moses, Benjamin Levy, Samson Levy, David Franks, Joseph Jacobs, Hayman Levy, Jr., Mathias Bush, Michael

Gratz, Bernard Gratz, Isaac Franks, Moses Mordecai, Benjamin Jacobs, Samuel Lyon and Manuel Mordecai Noah.

When the time came for raising and sustaining an army, they were ready to serve...There is a romance in the story of Haym Solomon, Polish Jew financier of the Revolution. Born in Poland, he was made prisoner by the British forces in New York, and when he escaped set up in business in Philadelphia. He negotiated for Robert Morris all the loans raised in France and Holland, pledged his personal faith and fortune for enormous amounts, and personally advanced large sums to such men as James Madison, Thomas Jefferson, Baron Steuben, General St. Clair, and many other patriot leaders who testified that without his aid they could not have carried on in the cause.

A considerable number of Jews became officers in the continental forces. The records show at least four Jews who served as Lieutenant Colonels, three and Majors and certainly six, probably more, as Captains. Major Benjamin Nones has been referred to as the Jewish Lafayette. He came from France in 1777, enlisted in the continentals as a volunteer private, served on the staffs of both Washington and Lafayette, and later was attached to the command of Baron De Kalb, in which were a number of Jews. When De Kalb was fatally wounded in the thickest of the fighting at the Battle of Camden, the three officers who were at hand to bear him from the field were Major Nones, Captain De La Motta, and Captain Jacob De Leon, all of the Jews...

Jews of the Carolinas and Georgia were ardent supporters of the Revolution. One corps of infantry raised in Charleston, South Carolina, was composed preponderantly of Jews, and they gave a splendid account of themselves in the fighting in that section. It is easy to understand why a people with the historic background of the Jew should thus overwhelmingly and unhesitatingly have allied themselves with the cause of freedom. From earliest colonial times, America has been a new land of promise to this long- persecuted race.

The Jewish community of the United States is...the second most numerous in the world...The 14,000 Jews who live in this Capital City...are planting here a home for community service...Here will be the seat of organized influence for the preservation and dissemination of all...the culture and philosophy of this "peculiar people" who have so greatly given to the advancement of humanity...

Every inheritance of the Jewish people, every teaching of their secular history and religious experience, draws them powerfully to the side of charity, liberty and progress...This capacity for adaptation in detail, without sacrifice of essentials, has been one of the special lessons which the marvelous history of the Jewish people has taught...

The patriots who laid the foundation of this Republic drew their faith from the Bible. May they give due credit to the people among whom the Holy Scriptures came into being. And as they ponder the assertion that "Hebraic mortar cemented the foundations of American democracy," they cannot escape the conclusion that if American democracy is to remain the greatest hope of humanity, it must continue abundantly in the faith of the Bible.

∽

CALVIN COOLIDGE, JUL. 3, 1925, AT 150TH ANNIVERSARY
OF GEORGE WASHINGTON TAKING COMMAND OF
CONTINENTAL ARMY, CAMBRIDGE, MASSACHUSETTS:

To commemorate this divinely appointed captain...his life and work will forever strengthen our faith in our county and in our country's God...Hardly one...in his own day achieved so much as Washington and left his work so firmly established that posterity, generation after generation, can only increase its tributes to his ability, his wisdom, his patriotism, and his rounded perfection in the character of a Christian citizen...

We have come here because this day a century and half ago, in this place, Washington formally assumed command of the armies of the Colonies. His feet trod this soil. Here was his headquarters. Here was his place of worship...One in his position of leadership, authority, and independent fortune, living as a Virginia gentleman, might easily enough have felt that the troubles of the Massachusetts Bay Colony had small concern for him. High Churchman, conformist in most things, enjoying excellent repute in England and with English officials in America, his influence might logically enough have been thrown to the royalists.

Yet, as early as 1769, he wrote declaring, "Our lordly masters in Great Britain will be satisfied with nothing less than the deprivation of American freedom..." And, inquiring what could be done to avert such a calamity, he added,

"That no man should scruple or hesitate a moment to use arms in defense of so valuable a blessings is clearly my opinion. Yet, arms, I would beg to add, should be the last resource."

✍

CALVIN COOLIDGE, OCT. 6, 1925, AT AMERICAN LEGION CONVENTION, OMAHA, NEBRASKA:

If our country secured any benefit, if it met with any gain, it must have been in moral and spiritual values. It must be not because it made its fortune but because it found its soul...

It is not easy to conceive of anything that would be more unfortunate in a community based on the ideals of which Americans boast than any considerable development of intolerance as regards religion. To a great extent this country owes its beginnings to the determination of our hardy ancestors to maintain complete freedom in religion. Instead of a state church we have decreed that every citizen shall be free to follow the dictates of his own conscience as to his religious beliefs and affiliations...

Divine Providence has not bestowed upon any race a monopoly of patriotism and character...We can not place our main reliance upon material forces. We must reaffirm and reinforce our ancient faith in truth and justice, in charitableness and tolerance. We must make our supreme commitment to the everlasting spiritual forces of life. We must mobilize the conscience of mankind.

✍

CALVIN COOLIDGE, MAY 1, 1926, TO NATIONAL COUNCIL OF THE BOY SCOUTS OF AMERICA, WASHINGTON, D.C:

The boy on becoming a scout binds himself on his honor to do his best, as the oath reads:

"1. To do my duty to God and my country, and to obey the scout law.

2. To help other people at all times.

3. To keep myself physically strong, mentally awake, and morally straight." The twelve articles in these scout laws are not prohibitions, but obligations; affirmative rules of conduct. Members must promise to be trustworthy, loyal, helpful, friendly, courteous, kind, obedient, cheerful, thrifty, brave, clean, and reverent...

What a formula for developing moral and spiritual character!...It would be a perfect world if everyone exemplified these virtues in daily life.

Acting under these principles, remarkable progress has been made. Since 1910, 3,000,000 boys in the United States have been scouts - one out of every seven eligible. Who can estimate the physical, mental, and spiritual force that would have been added to our national life during this period if the other six also had been scouts?...Such service is service to God and to country...The boy may not be merely passive in his allegiance to righteousness. He must be an active force in his home, his church and his community...The last item in the scout "duodecalogue" is impressive. It declares that a scout shall be reverent. "He is reverent toward God," the paragraph reads. "He is faithful in his religious duties, and respects the convictions of others in matters of custom and religion."

In the past I have declared my conviction that our Government rests upon religion; that religion is the source from which we derive our reverence for truth and justice, for equality and liberty, and for the rights of mankind. So wisely and liberally is the Boy Scout movement designed that the various religious denominations have found it a most helpful agency in arousing and maintaining interest in the work of their various societies. This has helped to emphasize in the minds of youth the importance of teaching our boys to respect the religious opinions and social customs of others...

We know too well what fortune overtakes those who attempt to live in opposition to these standards. They become at once rightfully and truly branded as outlaws. However much they may boast of their freedom from all restraints and their disregard of all conventionalities of society, they are immediately the recognized foes of their brethren. Their short existence is lived under greater and greater restrictions, in terror of the law, in flight from arrest, or in imprisonment. Instead of gaining freedom, they become slaves of their own evil doing, realizing the scriptural assertion that they who sin are the servants of sin and that the wages of sin is death.

The Boy Scout movement has been instituted in order that the youth, instead of falling under the domination of habits and actions that lead only to destruction, may come under the discipline of a training that leads to eternal life.

⤚

CALVIN COOLIDGE, JUL. 5, 1926, AT 150TH ANNIVERSARY OF DECLARATION OF INDEPENDENCE, PHILADELPHIA:

Three very definite propositions were set out in its preamble regarding the nature of mankind and therefore of government. These were the doctrine that all men are created equal, that they are endowed with certain inalienable rights, and that therefore the source of just powers of government must be derived from the consent of the governed...

The principles of our declaration had been under discussion in the Colonies for nearly two generations...

In the assertion of the Rev. Thomas Hooker of Connecticut as early as 1638, when he said in a sermon before the General Court that: "The foundation of authority is laid in the free consent of the people." "The choice of public magistrates belongs unto the people by God's own allowance." This doctrine found wide acceptance among the nonconformist clergy who later made up the Congregational Church.

⤚

CALVIN COOLIDGE, JUL. 5, 1926, AT 150TH ANNIVERSARY OF DECLARATION OF INDEPENDENCE, PHILADELPHIA:

The great apostle of this movement was the Rev. John Wise, of Massachusetts. He was one of the leaders of the revolt against the royal governor Andros in 1687, for which he suffered imprisonment...

His works were reprinted in 1772 and have been declared to have been nothing less than a textbook of liberty for our Revolutionary fathers...That these ideas were prevalent in Virginia is further revealed by the Declaration of Rights, which was prepared by George Mason and presented to the general assembly on May 27, 1776.

This document asserted popular sovereignty and inherent natural rights, but confined the doctrine of equality to the assertion that "All men are created equally free and independent." It can scarcely be imagined that Jefferson was unacquainted with what had been done in his own Commonwealth of Virginia when he took up the task of drafting the Declaration of Independence.

But these thoughts can very largely be traced back to what John Wise was writing in 1710. He said, "Every man must be acknowledged equal to every man."

Again, "The end of all good government is to cultivate humanity and promote the happiness of all and the good of every man in all his rights, his life, liberty, estate, honor, and so forth..."

And again, "For as they have a power every man in his natural state, so upon combination they can and do bequeath this power to others and settle it according as their united discretion shall determine." And still again, "Democracy is Christ's government in church and state."

Here was the doctrine of equality, popular sovereignty, and the substance of the theory of inalienable rights clearly asserted by Wise at the opening of the eighteenth century, just as we have the principle of the consent of the governed stated by Hooker as early as 1638.

&

CALVIN COOLIDGE, JUL. 5, 1926, AT 150TH ANNIVERSARY OF DECLARATION OF INDEPENDENCE, PHILADELPHIA:

It is but natural that the first paragraph of the Declaration of Independence should open with a reference to Nature's God and should close in the final paragraphs with an appeal to the Supreme Judge of the world and an assertion of a firm reliance on Divine Providence....

It is no wonder that Samuel Adams could say, "The people seem to recognize this revolution as though it were a decree promulgated from heaven." No one can examine this record and escape the conclusion that in the great outline of its principles the Declaration was the result of the religious teachings of the preceding period. The profound philosophy which Jonathan Edwards applied to theology, the popular preaching of George Whitefield, had aroused the thought and stirred the people of the Colonies in preparation for this great event...

The principles...are found in the texts, the sermons, and the writings of the early colonial clergy who were earnestly undertaking to instruct their congregations in the great mystery of how to live.

They preached equality because they believed in the fatherhood of God and the brotherhood of man. They justified freedom by the text that we are all created in the divine image, all partakers of the divine spirit...

In those days such doctrines would scarcely have been permitted to flourish and spread in any other country....In order that they might have freedom to express these thoughts and opportunity to put them into action, whole congregations with their pastors had migrated to the colonies.

ॐ

CALVIN COOLIDGE, JUL. 5, 1926, AT 150TH ANNIVERSARY OF DECLARATION OF INDEPENDENCE, PHILADELPHIA:

In its main feature the Declaration of Independence is a great spiritual document. It is a declaration not of material but of spiritual conceptions. Equality, liberty, popular sovereignty, the rights of man - these are the elements which we can see and touch.

They are ideals. They have their source and their roots in the religious convictions. Unless the faith of the American in these religious convictions is to endure, the principles of our Declaration will perish. We can not continue to enjoy the result if we neglect and abandon the cause.

ॐ

CALVIN COOLIDGE, JUL. 5, 1926, AT 150TH ANNIVERSARY OF DECLARATION OF INDEPENDENCE, PHILADELPHIA:

We hold that the duly authorized expression of the will of the people has a divine sanction. But even in that we come back to the theory of John Wise that "Democracy is Christ's government..." The ultimate sanction of law rests on the righteous authority of the Almighty...

Before we can understand their conclusions we must go back and review the course which they followed. We must think the thoughts which they thought. Their intellectual life centered around the meeting-house. They were intent upon religious worship...While scantily provided with other literature, there was a wide acquaintance with the Scriptures.

Over a period as great that which measures the existence of our independence they were subject to this discipline not only in their religious life and educational training, but also in their political thought. They were a people who came under the influence of a great spiritual development and acquired a great moral power...

We live in an age of science and of abounding accumulation of material things. These did not create the Declaration. Our Declaration created them. The things of the spirit come first.

Unless we cling to that, all our material prosperity, overwhelming though it may appear, will turn to a barren sceptre in our grasp. If we are to maintain the great heritage which has been bequeathed to us, we must be like-minded as the fathers who created it.

We must not sink into a pagan materialism. We must cultivate the reverence which they had for the things that are holy. We must follow the spiritual and moral leadership which they showed. We must keep replenished, that they may glow with a more compelling flame, the altar fires before which they worshipped.

∽

HERBERT HOOVER

HERBERT HOOVER, MAR. 4, 1929, INAUGURAL:

This occasion is not alone the administration of the most sacred oath which can be assumed by an American citizen. It is a dedication and consecration under God to the highest office in service of our people.

I assume this trust in the humility of knowledge that only through the guidance of Almighty Providence can I hope to discharge its ever-increasing burdens...Knowing what the task means and the responsibility which it involves, I beg your tolerance, your aid, and your cooperation. I ask the help of Almighty God in this service to my country to which you have called me.

⋙

HERBERT HOOVER, MAY 5, 1929, MESSAGE TO THE NATIONAL FEDERATION OF MEN'S BIBLE CLASSES CONVENTION, BALTIMORE, MESSAGE READ BY REPRESENTATIVE WALTER H. NEWTON OF MINNESOTA:

There is no other book so various as the Bible, nor one so full of concentrated wisdom. Whether it be of law, business, morals, or that vision which leads the imagination in the creation of constructive enterprises for the happiness of mankind, he who seeks for guidance in any of these things may look inside its covers and find illumination.

The study of this Book in your Bible classes is a postgraduate course in the richest library of human experience. As a nation we are indebted to the Book of Books for our national ideals and representative institutions. Their preservation rests in adhering to its principles.

◈

HERBERT HOOVER, DEC. 8, 1929, MESSAGE TO GEORGE WILLIAM CARTER, GENERAL SECRETARY, NEW YORK BIBLE SOCIETY, 5 EAST 48TH ST, NEW YORK, READ DURING A SERVICE HELD AT TRINITY LUTHERAN CHURCH IN NEW YORK:

My dear Dr. Carter: Mr. Akerson has handed to me your kind letter of November 29 and the Bible which the Society has been so good as to send me in commemoration of its 120th Anniversary. I am glad to receive it and do appreciate the kindness which prompted this thoughtful gift. Thank you too for your heartening expressions of confidence and approval. Yours faithfully.

◈

HERBERT HOOVER, APR. 27, 1931, AT GRIDIRON CLUB:

If, by the grace of God, we have passed the worst of this storm, the future months will be easy. If we shall be called upon to endure more of this period, we must gird ourselves for even greater effort.

If we can maintain this courage and resolution we shall have written this new chapter in national life in terms to which our whole idealism has aspired. May God grant to us the spirit and strength to carry through to the end.

◈

HERBERT HOOVER, MAY 30, 1931, AT VALLEY FORGE:

If those few thousand men endured that long winter of privation and suffering, humiliated by the despair of their countrymen, and deprived of support save their own indomitable will, yet held their countrymen to the faith, and by that holding held fast the freedom of America, what right have we to be of little faith?

✎

HERBERT HOOVER, OCT. 18, 1931, ADDRESS WHICH BEGAN A NATION-WIDE DRIVE TO AID PRIVATE RELIEF AGENCIES DURING THE GREAT DEPRESSION:

Time and time again the American people have demonstrated a spiritual quality, a capacity for unity of action, of generosity, a certainty of results in time of emergency that have made them great in the annals of the history of all nations. This is the time and this is the occasion when we must arouse that idealism, that spirit...This civilization and this great complex, which we call American life, is builded and can alone survive upon the translation into individual action of that fundamental philosophy announced by the Savior nineteen centuries ago. Part of our national suffering today is from failure to observe these primary yet inexorable laws of human relationship. Modern society can not survive with the defense of Cain, "Am I my brother's keeper?"

✎

HERBERT HOOVER, NOV. 25, 1931, MESSAGE TO MR. GEORGE W. BROWN, GENERAL SECRETARY, AMERICAN BIBLE SOCIETY, BIBLE HOUSE, ASTOR PLACE, NEW YORK CITY, ON UNIVERSAL BIBLE SUNDAY:

My dear Mr. Brown: I am interested to know that December 6th is to be observed as Universal Bible Sunday. Our institutions and common life are grounded in spiritual ideals. I hope that the observation of Bible Sunday will quicken the spiritual impulses of our people and contribute to the spiritual advancement which underlies our stability, service and progress as a nation and as individuals. Yours faithfully.

✎

HERBERT HOOVER, MAY 23, 1932, TO DR. JOHN H. FINLEY, THE NEW YORK TIMES, NEW YORK CITY, MESSAGE READ AT BIBLE SEMINARY'S COMMENCEMENT EXERCISES:

The need in the United States and throughout the world for trained and effective religious leadership must appear to all thoughtful citizens as not less but greater today than in ordinary times.

I am therefore happy to express my sincere wish that the Biblical Seminary in New York have the support for which you and your coworkers are now asking and that it shall continue its interdenominational work of training Bible inspired preachers, teachers, missionaries and other Christian workers. No institution doing the work this Seminary is doing should be allowed to fail, particularly in times like these.

&

HERBERT HOOVER, SEP. 15, 1932, TO THE NATIONAL
DRIVE COMMITTEE FOR VOLUNTARY RELIEF AGENCIES:

Our tasks are definite...that we maintain the spiritual impulses in our people for generous giving and generous service - in the spirit that each is his brother's keeper...Many a family today is carrying a neighbor family over the trough of this depression not alone with material aid but with that encouragement which maintains courage and faith.

&

HERBERT HOOVER, SEP. 19, 1932, TO THE AMERICAN
BIBLE SOCIETY, BIBLE HOUSE, ASTOR PLACE,
NEW YORK CITY, ON UNIVERSAL BIBLE SUNDAY:

My dear Mr. Brown: Universal Bible Sunday once a year brings to all our people simultaneously a concerted stimulus to study the Bible and to ponder its inexhaustible wealth of inspiration and example. The spiritual life is enriched by the annual observance of this day.

&

HERBERT HOOVER, OCT. 31, 1932, IN AN ADDRESS
AT MADISON SQUARE GARDEN IN NEW YORK:

To enter upon a series of deep changes, to embark upon this inchoate new deal which has been propounded in this campaign would be to undermine and destroy our American system...

No man who has not occupied my position in Washington can fully realize the constant battle which must be carried on against incompetence, corruption, tyranny of government expanded into business activities...Free speech does not live many hours after free industry and free commerce die.

&

HERBERT HOOVER, DEC. 25, 1932, TO THE NATION'S CHRISTMAS TREE ASSOCIATION, FRESNO, CALIFORNIA, READ AT ANNUAL CEREMONY IN GENERAL GRANT NATIONAL PARK AT BASE OF THE GENERAL GRANT REDWOOD, WHICH WAS DESIGNATED AS THE NATION'S CHRISTMAS TREE IN 1925:

Your Christmas Service held each year at the foot of a living tree which was alive at the time of the birth of Christ, has now for several years lent an inspiring note to the celebration of Christmas. It should be continued as a further symbol of the unbroken chain of life leading back to this great moment in the spiritual life of mankind.

∾

HERBERT HOOVER, 1934, THE CHALLENGE OF LIBERTY:

While I can make no claim for having introduced the term, "rugged individualism," I should be proud to have invented it. It has been used by American leaders for over a half-century in eulogy of those God-fearing men and women of honesty whose stamina and character and fearless assertion of rights led them to make their own way in life.

∾

HERBERT HOOVER, SEP. 17, 1935, SAN DIEGO, CA:

Our Constitution is not alone the working plan of a great Federation of States under representative government. There is embedded in it also the vital principles of the American system of liberty.

That system is based upon certain inalienable freedoms and protections which in no event the government may infringe and which we call the Bill of Rights. It does not require a lawyer to interpret those provisions.

They are as clear as the Ten Commandments. Among others the freedom of worship, freedom of speech and of the press, the right of peaceable assembly, equality before the law...

In them lies a spiritual right of men. Behind them is the conception which is the highest development of the Christian faith - the conception of individual freedom with brotherhood.

∾

HERBERT HOOVER, 1943, JOINT STATEMENT WITH MRS. CALVIN COOLIDGE, MRS. THEODORE ROOSEVELT, MRS. WILLIAM H. TAFT, MRS. BENJAMIN HARRISON, MRS. GROVER CLEVELAND, ALFRED SMITH, ALFRED LANDON, JAMES M. COX, AND JOHN W. DAVIS:

Menaced by collectivist trends, we must seek revival of our strength in the spiritual foundations which are the bedrock of our republic. Democracy is the outgrowth of the religious conviction of the sacredness of every human life. On the religious side, its highest embodiment is The Bible; on the political side, the Constitution.

⋌

HERBERT HOOVER, APR. 27, 1950, NATIONALLY BROADCAST ADDRESS TO THE AMERICAN NEWSPAPERS PUBLISHERS ASSOCIATION:

What the world needs today is a definite, spiritual mobilization of the nations who believe in God against this tide of Red agnosticism. It needs a moral mobilization against the hideous ideas of the police state and human slavery...I suggest that the United Nations should be reorganized without the Communist nations in it.

If that is impractical, then a definite New United Front should be organized of those peoples who disavow communism, who stand for morals and religion, and who love freedom...It is a proposal based solely upon moral, spiritual and defense foundations. It is a proposal to redeem the concept of the United Nations to the high purpose for which it was created. It is a proposal for moral and spiritual cooperation of Godfearing free nations. And in rejecting an atheistic other world, I am confident that the Almighty God will be with us.

⋌

HERBERT HOOVER, AUG. 10, 1954, RECEPTION ON HIS 80TH BIRTHDAY, WEST BRANCH, IOWA:

I have witnessed the legacy of war in doubting minds, brutality, crime and debased morals. Moreover, I have witnessed on the ground in 20 nations the workings of the philosophy of that antiChrist, Karl Marx. After these long years and from all these experiences, there rises constantly in my mind the forces which make for progress and those which may corrode away the safeguards of freedom in America.

I want to say something about these forces but I shall endeavor to do so, not in the tones of Jeremiah but in the spirit of Saint Paul...

Our Founding Fathers did not invent the priceless boon of individual freedom and respect for the dignity of men. That great gift to mankind sprang from the Creator and not from governments. The Founding Fathers, with superb genius, welded together the safeguards of these freedoms...

Today the Socialist virus and poison gas generated by Karl Marx and Friedrich Engels have spread into every nation on the earth. Their dogma is absolute materialism which defies truth and religious faith. Their poisons are of many sorts. The preservation of the safeguards of liberty makes it imperative that we give heed to their every variety...A nation is strong or weak, it thrives or perishes upon what it believes to be true. If our youth is rightly instructed in the faith of our fathers; in the traditions of our country; in the dignity of each individual man, then our power will be stronger than any weapon of destruction that man can devise.

And now as to this whole gamut of Socialist infections, I say to you...God has blessed us with another wonderful word heritage. The great documents of that heritage are not from Karl Marx. They are from the Bible, the Declaration of Independence and the Constitution of the United States. Within them alone can the safeguards of freedom survive...

These new frontiers give us other blessings. Not only do they expand our living but also they open new opportunities and new areas of adventure and enterprise. They open new vistas of beauty. They unfold the wonders of the atom and the heavens. Daily they prove the reality of an allwise Supreme Giver of Law.

⮜

HERBERT HOOVER, STATEMENT:

The principle thing we can do, if we really want to make the world over again, is to try the use of the word "old" again. It was the "old" things that made this country the great nation it is. There is the old virtue of religious faith. There are the old virtues of integrity and truth. There is the old virtue of incorruptible service and honor in public service.

∾

HERBERT HOOVER, STATEMENT:

Freedom is an open window through which pours the sunlight of the human spirit and of human dignity. With the preservation of these moral and spiritual qualities and with God's grace will come further greatness for our country.

∾

FRANKLIN D. ROOSEVELT

FRANKLIN D. ROOSEVELT, MAR. 4, 1933, 1ST INAUGURAL:

First of all, let me assert my firm belief that the only thing we have to fear is fear itself...In such a spirit on my part and on yours we face our common difficulties. They concern, thank God, only material things...Practices of the unscrupulous money changers stand indicted in the court of public opinion, rejected by the hearts and minds of men...They know only the rules of a generation of self-seekers. They have no vision, and where there is no vision the people perish.(Pr. 29:18)

The money changers have fled from their high seats in the temple of our civilization. We may now restore that temple to the ancient truths...We face arduous days that lie before us in the warm courage of national unity; with the clear consciousness of seeking old and precious moral values...In this dedication of a nation we humbly ask the blessing of God. May He protect each and every one of us! May He guide me in the days to come.

❧

FRANKLIN D. ROOSEVELT, DEC. 6, 1933, ADDRESS TO THE FEDERAL COUNCIL OF CHURCHES OF CHRIST:

If I were asked to state the great objective which Church and State are both demanding for the sake of every man and woman and child in this country, I would say that that great objective is "a more abundant life."

ح

FRANKLIN D. ROOSEVELT, DEC. 24, 1933, CHRISTMAS GREETING TO THE NATION:

This year marks a greater national understanding of the significance in our modern lives of the teachings of Him whose birth we celebrate. To more and more of us the words "Thou shalt love thy neighbor as thyself" have taken on a meaning that is showing itself and proving itself in our purposes and daily lives. May the practice of that high ideal grow in us all in the year to come. I give you and send you one and all, old and young, a Merry Christmas and a truly Happy New Year. And so, for now and for always "God Bless Us Every One."

ح

FRANKLIN D. ROOSEVELT, DEC. 24, 1934, CHRISTMAS EVE:

Let us make the spirit of Christmas of 1934 that of courage and unity...That is, I believe, an important part of what the Maker of Christmas would have it mean. In this sense, the Scriptures admonish us to be strong and of good courage, to fear not, to dwell together in Unity.

ح

FRANKLIN D. ROOSEVELT, OCT. 6, 1935, ON THE 400TH ANNIVERSARY OF THE PRINTING OF THE ENGLISH BIBLE:

When Myles Coverdale, an Augustinian Friar, later the Bishop of Exeter, produced this Book in the common vernacular, we trace not only a measurable increase in the cultural value and influence of this greatest of books, but a quickening in the widespread dissemination of those moral and spiritual precepts that have so greatly affected the progress of Christian civilization. The part that William Tyndale played in this English translation is generally acknowledged by the historian...

To it may be traced the richest and best we have in our literature. Poetry, prose, painting, music and oratory have had in it their guide and inspiration. In it Lincoln found the rounded euphonious phrases for his Gettysburg address. Speaking of its place in his life, he says: "In regard to the great Book, I have only to say, it is the best gift which God has ever given to man."

One cannot study the story of the rise and development of the men and women who have been and continue to be the pathfinders and benefactors of our people and not recognize the outstanding place the Bible has occupied as the guide and inspiration of their thought and practice.

Apart from their professed allegiance to any particular form of Christian doctrine or creedal expression of faith, they have found in it that which has shaped their course and determined their action...Even in periods that have been marked by apostasy and doubt, still men have found here in these sacred pages that which has refreshed and encouraged...

In the formative days of the Republic the directing influence the Bible exercised upon the fathers of the Nation is conspicuously evident. To Washington it contained the sure and certain moral precepts that constituted the basis of his action...It transcended all other books...To his astute mind moral and religious principles were the "indispensable supports" of political prosperity, the "essential pillars of civil society."

Learned as Jefferson was in the best of the ancient philosophers, he turned to the Bible as the source of his higher thinking and reasoning. Speaking of the lofty teachings of the Master, he said: "He pushed His scrutinies into the heart of man; erected His tribunal in the region of his thoughts, and purified the waters at the fountain head." Beyond this he held that the Bible contained the noblest ethical system the world has known...

This Book continues to hold its unchallenged place as the most loved, the most quoted and the most universally read and pondered of all the volumes which our libraries contain...

We cannot read the history of our rise and development as a Nation, without reckoning with the place the Bible has occupied in shaping the advances of the Republic. Its teaching, as has been wisely suggested, is ploughed into the very heart of the race. Where we have been truest and most consistent in obeying its precepts we have attained the greatest measure of contentment and prosperity.

∽

FRANKLIN D. ROOSEVELT, JAN. 20, 1937, 2ND INAUGURAL:

I shall do my utmost to speak their purpose and to do their will, seeking Divine Guidance to help each and every one to give light to them that sit in darkness and to guide our feet into the way of peace.

∼

FRANKLIN D. ROOSEVELT, JAN. 6, 1941, FOUR FREEDOMS:

We look forward to a world founded upon four essential human freedoms. The first in freedom of speech and expression...The second is freedom of every person to worship God in his own way...This nation has placed its destiny in the hands and heads and hearts of its millions of free men and women; and its faith in freedom under the guidance of God.

∼

FRANKLIN D. ROOSEVELT, JAN. 20, 1941, 3RD INAUGURAL:

A nation, like a person, has something deeper, something more permanent, something larger than the sum of all its parts...It is the spirit - the faith of America. It is the product of centuries. It was born in the multitudes of those who came from many lands - some of high degree, but mostly plain people, who sought here, early and late, to find freedom more freely. The democratic aspiration is no mere recent phase of human history. It is human history. It permeated the ancient life of early peoples. It blazed anew in the middle ages. It was written in the Magna Carta.

In the Americas its impact has been irresistible. America has been the New World in all tongues, to all peoples, not because this continent was a new-found land, but because all those who came here believed they could create upon this continent a new life - a life that should be new in freedom. Its vitality was written into our own Mayflower Compact, into the Declaration of Independence, into the Constitution of the United States, into the Gettysburg Address...

If the spirit of America were killed, even though the Nation's body and mind, constricted in an alien world, lived on, the America we know would have perished. That spirit - that faith - speaks to us in our daily lives in ways often unnoticed...We do not retreat. We are not content to stand still. As Americans, we go forward in the service of our country by the will of God.

∼

FRANKLIN D. ROOSEVELT, JAN. 25, 1941, PROLOGUE OF GIDEONS NEW TESTAMENT & BOOK OF PSALMS DISTRIBUTED TO SOLDIERS DURING WORLD WAR II:

To the Armed Forces: As Commander-in-Chief, I take pleasure in commending the reading of the Bible to all who serve in the armed forces of the United States. Throughout the centuries men of many faiths and diverse origins have found in the Sacred Book words of wisdom, counsel and inspiration. It is a fountain of strength and now, as always, an aid in attaining the highest aspirations of the human soul. Very sincerely yours, Franklin D. Roosevelt.

∽

FRANKLIN D. ROOSEVELT, DEC. 8, 1941, NATIONAL ADDRESS:

December 7, 1941 - a date which will live in infamy - the United States of America was suddenly and deliberately attacked by naval and air forces of the Empire of Japan...Our people, our territory and our interests are in grave danger. With confidence in our armed forces, with the unbounding determination of our people, we will gain the inevitable triumph. So help us God.

∽

FRANKLIN D. ROOSEVELT, DEC. 21, 1941, CHRISTMAS EVE:

Sincere and faithful men and women...are asking themselves this Christmas: How can we light our trees? How can we give our gifts? How can we meet and worship with love and with uplifted spirit and heart in a world at war, a world of fighting and suffering and death? How can we pause, even for a day, even for Christmas Day, in our urgent labor of arming a decent humanity against the enemies which beset it? How can we put the world aside, as men and women put the world aside in peaceful years, to rejoice in the birth of Christ?...

Looking into the days to come, I have set aside a day of prayer, and in that Proclamation I have said: "The year 1941 has brought upon our Nation a war of aggression by powers dominated by arrogant rulers whose selfish purpose is to destroy free institutions. They would thereby take from the freedom-loving peoples of the earth the hard-won liberties gained over many centuries. The new year of 1942 calls for the courage...Our strength, as the strength of all men everywhere, is of greater avail as God upholds us.

Therefore, I...do hereby appoint the first day of the year 1942 as a day of prayer, of asking forgiveness for our shortcomings of the past, of consecration to the tasks of the present, of asking God's help in days to come. We need His guidance that this people may be humble in spirit but strong in the conviction of the right; steadfast to endure sacrifice, and brave to achieve a victory of liberty and peace."

Our strongest weapon in this war is that conviction of the dignity and brotherhood of man which Christmas Day signifies...Against enemies who preach the principles of hate and practice them, we set our faith in human love and in God's care for us and all men everywhere...And so I am asking my associate, my old and good friend, to say a word to the people of America, old and young, tonight Winston Churchill, Prime Minister of Great Britain.

ᡗᶗ

FRANKLIN D. ROOSEVELT, JAN. 6, 1942, STATE OF THE UNION:

Our enemies are guided by brutal cynicism, by unholy contempt for the human race. We are inspired by a faith which goes back through all the years to the first chapter of the Book of Genesis - "God created man in His own image." We on our side are striving to be true to that Divine heritage. We are fighting, as our fathers have fought, to uphold the doctrine that all men are equal in the sight of God. Those on the other side are striving to destroy this deep belief and to create a world in their own image, a world of tyranny and cruelty and serfdom.

ᡗᶗ

FRANKLIN D. ROOSEVELT, DEC. 24, 1942, CHRISTMAS EVE:

To you who serve in uniform I also send a message of cheer that you are in the thoughts of your families and friends at home, and that Christmas prayers follow you wherever you may be. To all Americans I say that loving our neighbor as we love ourselves is not enough-that we as a Nation and as individuals will please God best by showing regard for the laws of God. There is no better way of fostering good will toward man than by first fostering good will toward God. If we love Him we will keep His Commandments.

In sending Christmas greetings to the armed forces and merchant sailors of the United Nations we include therein our pride in their bravery on the fighting fronts and on all the seas....

It is significant that tomorrow- Christmas Day- our plants and factories will be stilled. That is not true of the other holidays we have long been accustomed to celebrate. On all other holidays work goes on-gladly-for the winning of the war. So Christmas becomes the only holiday in all the year. I like to think that this is so because Christmas is a holy day. May all it stands for live and grow throughout the years.

∽

FRANKLIN D. ROOSEVELT, JUN. 6, 1944, ADDRESS UPON D-DAY INVASION OF NORMANDY, FRANCE:

Almighty God: Our sons, pride of our nation, this day have set upon a mighty endeavor, a struggle to preserve our Republic, our religion and our civilization, and to set free a suffering humanity. Lead them straight and true; give strength to their arms, stoutness to their hearts, steadfastness in their faith...And for us at home- fathers, mothers, children, wives, sisters and brothers of brave men overseas, whose thoughts and prayers are ever with them- help us, Almighty God, to rededicate ourselves in renewed faith in Thee in this hour of great sacrifice.

∽

FRANKLIN D. ROOSEVELT, DEC. 24, 1944, CHRISTMAS EVE:

It is not easy to say "Merry Christmas" to you, my fellow Americans, in this time of destructive war. Nor can I say "Merry Christmas" lightly tonight to our armed forces at their battle stations all over the world- or to our allies who fight by their side.

Here, at home, we will celebrate this Christmas Day in our traditional American way- because of its deep spiritual meaning to us; because the teachings of Christ are fundamental in our lives; and because we want our youngest generation to grow up knowing the significance of this tradition and the story of the coming of the immortal Prince of Peace and Good Will...

Anxious thoughts will be continually with the millions of our loved ones who are suffering hardships and misery, and who are risking their very lives to preserve for us and for all mankind the fruits of His teachings and the foundations of civilization itself.

The Christmas spirit lives tonight in the bitter cold of the front lines in Europe and in the heat of the jungles and swamps of Burma and the Pacific islands. Even the roar of our bombers and fighters in the air and the guns of our ships at sea will not drown out the messages of Christmas which come to the hearts of our fighting men...

They know the determination of all right-thinking people and Nations, that Christmases such as those that we have known in these years of world tragedy shall not come again to beset the souls of the children of God. This generation has passed through many recent years of deep darkness, watching the spread of the poison of Hitlerism and Fascism in Europe-the growth of imperialism and militarism in Japan-and the final clash of war all over the world.

Then came the dark days of the fall of France, and the ruthless bombing of England, and the desperate battle of the Atlantic, and of Pearl Harbor and Corregidor and Singapore. Since then the prayers of good men and women and children the world over have been answered.

The tide of battle has turned, slowly but inexorably, against those who sought to destroy civilization...We pray that that day may come soon. We pray that until then, God will protect our gallant men and women in the uniforms of the United Nations- that He will receive into His infinite grace those who make their supreme sacrifice in the cause of righteousness, in the cause of love of Him and His teachings.

We pray that with victory will come a new day of peace on earth in which all the Nations of the earth will join together for all time. That is the spirit of Christmas, the holy day.

ക്

FRANKLIN D. ROOSEVELT, JAN. 20, 1945, 4TH INAUGURAL:

As I stand here today, having taken the solemn oath of office in the presence of my fellow countrymen - in the presence of God - I know that it is America's purpose that we shall not fail...The Almighty God has blessed our land in many ways. He has given our people stout hearts and strong arms with which to strike mighty blows for freedom and truth. He has given to our country a faith which has become the hope of all peoples in an anguished world.

So we pray to Him now for the vision to see our way clearly - to see the way that leads to a better life for ourselves and for all our fellow men - to the achievement of His will, to peace on earth. In the presence of God - I know that it is America's purpose that we shall not fail.

HARRY S
TRUMAN

HARRY S TRUMAN, APR. 12, 1945, 1ST ADDRESS,
DELIVERED UPON ASSUMING THE PRESIDENCY
AFTER THE DEATH OF PRESIDENT ROOSEVELT:

At this moment I have in my heart a prayer. As I have assumed my heavy duties, I humbly pray to Almighty God in the words of King Solomon: "Give therefore Thy servant an understanding heart to judge Thy people that I may discern between good and bad; for who is able to judge this Thy so great a people?" I ask only to be a good and faithful servant of my Lord and my people.

٭

HARRY S TRUMAN, JUL. 24, 1945,
MEMORANDUM TO WINSTON CHURCHILL:

The drastic restrictions imposed on the Jewish immigration by the British White Paper of May, 1939, continue to provoke passionate protest from Americans most interested in Palestine and in the Jewish problem. They fervently urge the lifting of these restrictions which deny to Jews, who have been so cruelly uprooted by ruthless Nazi persecutions, entrance into the land which represents for so many of them their only hope of survival.

✍

HARRY S TRUMAN, MAR. 6, 1946, ADDRESS TO A CONFERENCE OF THE FEDERAL COUNCIL OF CHURCHES, DESHLER-WALLICK HOTEL, COLUMBUS, OHIO:

We have just come though a decade in which the forces of evil in various parts of the world have been lined up in a bitter fight to banish from the face of the earth both these ideals - religion and democracy...In that long struggle between these two doctrines, the cause of decency and righteousness has been victorious.

The right of every human being to live in dignity and freedom, the right to worship God in his own way, the right to fix his own relationship to his fellow men and to his Creator - these again have been saved for mankind...Now that we have preserved our freedom of conscience and religion, our right to live by a decent moral and spiritual code of our own choosing, let us make full use of that freedom....

The spiritual welfare of our people of tomorrow is going to depend on the kind of home life which our Nation has today for home life reflects the nation's life. It must conform to an ever-rising standard...Let us determine to carry on in a spirit of tolerance, and understanding for all men and for all nations - in the spirit of God and religious unity....The last five years have produced many awesome discoveries in material things. But it has been truthfully said that the greatest discoveries of the future will be in the realm of the spirit.

There is no problem on this earth tough enough to withstand the flames of genuine renewal of religious faith. And some of the problems of today will yield to nothing less than that kind of revival.

✍

HARRY S TRUMAN, APR. 6, 1946, 598TH NEWS CONFERENCE, SPEAKING TO KEEN TEEN CLUB OF CHICAGO, SPONSORED BY THE CHICAGO DAILY NEWS:

Q. "Mr. President, what part has religion played in your advancement from local official to the highest office in tour land?"

THE PRESIDENT: "Well, a system of morals is necessary

for the welfare of any individual or any nation. The greatest system of morals in the history of the world is that set out in the Sermon on the Mount, which I would advise each of you to study with everything you have."

❦

HARRY S TRUMAN, MAY 11, 1946, AT FORDHAM UNIVERSITY:
I fear we are too much concerned with material things to remember that our real strength lies in spiritual values. I doubt whether there is in this troubled world today, when nations are divided by jealousy and suspicion, a single problem that could not be solved if approached the spirit of the Sermon on the Mount.

❦

HARRY S TRUMAN, 1946, STATEMENT:
If men and nations would but live by the precepts of the ancient prophets and the teachings of the Sermon on the Mount, problems which now seem so difficult would soon disappear...That is a supreme opportunity for the church to continue to fulfill its mission on earth.

The Protestant church, the Catholic church, and the Jewish synagogue - bound together in the American unity of brotherhood - must provide the shock forces to accomplish this moral and spiritual awakening. No other agency can do it. Unless it is done, we are headed for the disaster we would deserve. Oh, for an Isaiah or a St. Paul to reawaken a sick world to its moral responsibilities.

❦

HARRY S TRUMAN, MEMOIRS -YEARS OF TRIAL AND HOPE —VOLUME TWO, PUBLISHED 1956, NOTE TO ASSISTANT:
I surely wish God Almighty would give the Children of Israel an Isaiah, the Christians a St. Paul, and the Sons of Ishmael a peep at the Golden Rule.

❦

HARRY S TRUMAN, DEC. 24, 1946, AT CEREMONY LIGHTING THE NATIONAL CHRISTMAS TREE:
our thoughts and aspirations and the hopes of future years turn to a little town in the hills of Judea where on a winter's night two thousand years ago the prophecy of Isaiah was fulfilled. Shepherds keeping the watch by night over their flock heard the glad tidings of

great joy from the angels of the Lord singing,

"Glory to God in the Highest and on Earth, peace, good will toward men."

The message of Bethlehem best sums up our hopes tonight. If we as a nation, and the other nations of the world, will accept it, the star of faith will guide us into the place of peace as it did the shepherds on that day of Christ's birth long ago. I am sorry to say all is not harmony in the world today. We have found that it is easier for men to die together on the field of battle than it is for them to live together at home in peace.

But those who died have died in vain if in some measure, at least, we shall not preserve for the peace that spiritual unity in which we won the war. The problems facing the United Nations-the world's hope for peace-would overwhelm faint hearts.

But, as we continue to labor for an enduring peace through that great organization, we must remember that the world was not created in a day. We shall find strength and courage at this Christmas time because so brave a beginning has been made. So with faith and courage we shall work to hasten the day when the sword is replaced by the plowshare and nations do not "learn war any more." Selfishness and greed, individual or national, cause most of our troubles.

He whose birth we celebrate tonight was the world's greatest teacher. He said: "Therefore all things whatsoever ye would that men should do to you, do ye even so to them; for this is the law and the prophets." Through all the centuries since He spoke, history has vindicated His teaching.

In this great country of ours has been demonstrated the fundamental unity of Christianity and democracy. Under our heritage of freedom for everyone on equal terms, we also share the responsibilities of government.

Our support of individual freedom-free speech, free schools, free press, and a free conscience-transcends all our differences. Although we may not hope for a New Heaven and a New Earth in our day and generation; we may strive with undaunted faith and courage to achieve in the present some measure of that unity with which the Nation's sons and the sons of our allies went forth to win the war.

We have this glorious land not because of a particular religious faith, not because our ancestors sailed from a particular foreign port.

We have our unique national heritage because of a common aspiration to be free and because of our purpose to achieve for ourselves and for our children the good things of life which the Christ declared He came to give to all mankind. We have made a good start toward peace in the world. Ahead of us lies the larger task of making the peace secure. The progress we have made gives hope that in the coming year we shall reach our goal. May 1947 entitle us to the benediction of the Master:

"Blessed are the peacemakers, for they shall be called the children of God."

Because of what we have achieved for peace, because of all the promise our future holds, I say to all my countrymen: Merry Christmas! Merry Christmas, and may God bless you all!

∾

HARRY S TRUMAN, AUG. 28, 1947, IN AN EXCHANGE OF MESSAGES WITH POPE PIUS XII:

Our common goal is to arouse and invigorate the faith of men to attain eternal values in our own generation - no matter what obstacles exist of may arise in the path...An enduring peace can be built only upon Christian principles. To such a consummation we dedicate all our resources, both spiritual and material, remembering always that "except the Lord build the house, they labor in vain who build it."

∾

HARRY S TRUMAN, SEP. 26, 1947, RADIO ADDRESS:

In our generous impulses we should follow the admonition set forth in St. Matthew's Gospel. Our Lord, bidding us to aid and comfort our stricken neighbor, whoever he may be, spoke words as true today as when He uttered them more than nineteen hundred years ago: "Inasmuch as ye have done it unto one of the least of these my brethren, ye have done it unto me."

∾

HARRY S TRUMAN, DEC. 6, 1947, IN AN ADDRESS GIVEN AT DEDICATION OF EVERGLADES NATIONAL PARK:

For conservation of the human spirit, we need places such as

Everglades National Park where we may be more keenly aware of our Creator's infinitely beautiful, and infinitely bountiful handiwork.

Here we may draw strength and peace of mind from our surroundings. Here we can truly understand what that great Israelite Psalmist meant when he sang: "He maketh me to lie down in green pastures, He leadeth me beside still water; He restoreth my soul."

✦

HARRY S TRUMAN, DEC. 24, 1947, NATIONALLY BROADCAST ADDRESS AT LIGHTING OF THE NATIONAL COMMUNITY CHRISTMAS TREE, WHITE HOUSE LAWN:

My fellow countrymen: We are met on the south lawn of the White House. Above the barren treetops rises the towering shaft of the Washington Monument. The scene is peaceful and tranquil. The shadows deepen and the Holy Night falls gently over the National Capital as we gather around our Christmas tree. Down the ages from the first Christmas through all the years of nineteen centuries, mankind in its weary pilgrimage through a changing world has been cheered and strengthened by the message of Christmas.

The angels sang for joy at the first Christmas in faraway Bethlehem. Their song has echoed through the corridors of time and will continue to sustain the heart of man through eternity. Let us not forget that the first Christmas was a homeless one. A humble man and woman had gone up from Galilee out of the City of Nazareth to Bethlehem. There is a sense of desolation in St. Luke's brief chronicle that Mary "brought forth her firstborn son, wrapped Him in swaddling clothes, and laid Him in a manger; because there was no room for them in the inn." For many of our brethren in Europe and Asia this too will be a homeless Christmas.

There can be little happiness for those who will keep another Christmas in poverty and exile and in separation from their loved ones. As we prepare to celebrate our Christmas this year in a land of plenty, we would be heartless indeed if we were indifferent to the plight of less fortunate peoples overseas.

We must not forget that our Revolutionary fathers also knew a Christmas of suffering and desolation. Washington wrote from Valley Forge 2 days before Christmas in 1777:

"We have this day no less than 2,873 men in camp unfit for duty because they are barefooted and otherwise naked."

We can be thankful that our people have risen today, as did our forefathers in Washington's time, to our obligation and our opportunity. At this point in the world's history, the words of St. Paul have greater significance than ever before. He said: "And now abideth faith, hope, charity, these three; but the greatest of these is charity."

We believe this. We accept it as a basic principle of our lives. The great heart of the American people has been moved to compassion by the needs of those in other lands who are cold and hungry. We have supplied a part of their needs and we shall do more. In this, we are maintaining the American tradition. In extending aid to our less fortunate brothers we are developing in their hearts the return of "hope."

Because of our forts, the people of other lands see the advent of a new day in which they can lead lives free from the harrowing fear of starvation and want. With the return of hope to these peoples will come renewed faith - faith in the dignity of the individual and the brotherhood of man.

The world grows old but the spirit of Christmas is ever young. Happily for all mankind, the spirit of Christmas survives travail and suffering because it fills us with hope of better things to come. Let us then put our trust in the unerring Star which guided the Wise Men to the Manger of Bethlehem.

Let us hearken again to the Angel Choir singing: "Glory to God in the highest, and on earth peace, good will toward men." With hope for the future and with faith in God, I wish all my countrymen a very Merry Christmas.

❧

HARRY S TRUMAN, JAN. 7, 1948, STATE OF THE UNION:

The basic source of our strength is spiritual. For we are a people with a faith. We believe in the dignity of man. We believe that he was created in the image of the Father of us all.

We do not believe that men exist merely to strengthen the state or to be cogs in the economic machines. We do believe that governments are created to serve the people and that the economic systems exist to minister to their wants.

We have a profound devotion to the welfare and rights of the individual as a human being.

✑

HARRY S TRUMAN, JUL. 7, 1948, STATE OF THE UNION:

It is our faith in human dignity that underlies our purposes. It is this faith that keeps us a strong and vital people. This is the hour to rededicate ourselves to the faith in mankind that makes us strong. This is the hour to rededicate ourselves to the faith in God that gives us confidence as we face the challenge of the years ahead.

✑

HARRY S TRUMAN, OCT. 25, 1948, AT CHICAGO STADIUM:

The American people cannot afford to trust their future to men of little vision. The Bible warns us that where there is no vision the people perish...Racial and religious oppression - big business domination - inflation - these forces must be stopped and driven back while there is yet time.

✑

HARRY S TRUMAN, NOV. 29, 1948, TO DR. CHAIM WEIZMANN, PRESIDENT OF THE STATE OF ISRAEL:

I remember well our conversations about the Negeb, to which you referred in your letter. I agree fully with your estimate of the importance of the area to Israel, and I deplore any attempt to take it away from Israel. I had thought that my position would have been clear to all the world, particularly in the light of the specific wording of the Democratic Party platform...In closing, I want to tell you how happy and impressed I have been at the remarkable progress made by the new State of Israel.

✑

HARRY S TRUMAN, DEC. 24, 1948, LIGHTING THE COMMUNITY CHRISTMAS TREE:

For of all the days of the year Christmas is the family day. Christmas began that way. The moving event of the first Christmas was the bringing forth of the first born in the stable in Bethlehem.

There began in humble surroundings the home life of the Holy Family glorified in song and story and in the hearts of men down through the centuries.

The great joys and mysteries of that event have forever sanctified and enriched all home life....The hallowed associations of Christmas draw all hearts toward home. With one accord we receive with joy and reverence the message of the first Christmas: "Glory to God in the highest and on earth peace, good will to men."..

What could be more appropriate than for all of us to dedicate ourselves to the cause of peace on this Holy Night. As a Nation we have a history of a little more than a century and a half. But the religion which came to the world heralded by the song of the Angels has endured for nineteen centuries. It will continue to endure. It remains today the world's best hope for peace if the world will accept its fundamental teaching that all men are brothers.

"God that made the world and all things therein...hath made of one blood all nations of man for to dwell on all the face of the earth." In the spirit of that message from the Acts of the Apostles, I wish all of you a Merry Christmas.

∽

HARRY S TRUMAN, JAN. 20, 1949, INAUGURAL:

In performing the duties of my office, I need the help and the prayers of every one of you...The American people stand firm in the faith which has inspired this Nation from the beginning.

We believe that all men have a right to equal justice under the law and equal opportunity to share in the common good. We believe that all men have the right to freedom of thought and expression.

We believe that all men are created equal because they are created in the image of God. From this faith we will not be moved...

Communism is based on the belief that man is so weak and inadequate that he is unable to govern himself, and therefore requires the rule of strong masters.

Democracy is based on the conviction that man has the moral and intellectual capacity, as well as the inalienable right, to govern himself with reason and justice.

Communism subjects the individual to arrest without lawful cause, punishment without trial, and forced labor as a chattel of the state. It decrees what information he shall receive, what art he shall produce, what leaders he shall follow, and what thoughts he shall think.

Democracy maintains that government is established for the benefit of the individual, and is charged with the responsibility of protecting the rights of the individual and his freedom in the exercise of his abilities...

These differences between communism and democracy do not concern the United States alone. People everywhere are coming to realize that what is involved is material well-being, human dignity, and the right to believe in and worship God...We are aided by all who desire freedom of speech, freedom of religion, and freedom to live their own lives for useful ends.

Our allies are the millions who hunger and thirst after righteousness (Mat. 5:6)...Steadfast in our faith in the Almighty, we will advance toward a world, where man's freedom is secure.

To that end we will devote our strength, our resources, and our firmness of resolve. With God's help the future of mankind will be assured in a world of justice, harmony, and peace. I need the help and the prayers of every one of you...The American people stand firm in the faith which has inspired this Nation from the beginning.

∾

HARRY S TRUMAN, 1949, NOTES ON INAUGURATION IN HIS MEMOIRS-YEARS OF TRIAL & HOPE-VOLUME TWO:

At twelve twenty-three Associate Justice Reed swore Senator Barkley in as Vice-President, and six minutes later I took the oath from Chief Justice Vinson. The words were the same that I had repeated three years and nine months earlier when I had been called so unexpectedly to the White House, but then only a handful of people were with me in the Cabinet Room. I raised my hand; once more I swore faithfully to defend the Constitution of the United States, repeating the short and simple oath, and kissed the Bible. Then I stepped to the rostrum to begin my inaugural address which is traditionally a part of the ceremony.

∾

HARRY S TRUMAN, OCT. 30, 1949, RADIO ADDRESS:

Religion is like freedom. We cannot take it for granted. Man - to be free - must work at it. And man - to be truly religious - must work at that, too. Unless men live by their faith, and practice that faith in their daily lives, religion cannot be a living force in the world today...

Religious faith and religious work must be our reliance as we strive to fulfill our destiny in the world...When the United States was established, its coins bore witness to the American faith in a benevolent deity.

The motto then was "In God We Trust." That is still our motto and we, as a people, still place our firm trust in God.

❧

HARRY S TRUMAN, DEC. 17, 1949, TO POPE PIUS XII:

Your Holiness: The summons to peace on earth, good will toward men has come ringing down the ages, giving direction to the thought and the action of every human being whose life is lived according to God's purpose.

The significance of the divine call, personified in the birth and mission of the Savior, is increasingly visible in the record of history despite the vicissitudes oftentimes encountered on the long path of the centuries. It is found in the progress that man is making toward a better world.

It is found in the humanitarian help given to lighten the burden of suffering wherever it has overtaken men, women and children. It is found in the steady achievement of friendly, mutually helpful relations among most of the world's peoples today, living indeed as Good Neighbors.

It is found in the efforts of these peoples to persuade and encourage the leaders of the few nations not following this path to an enlightened and advancing world order rounded on morality, justice, truth and freedom to permit their peoples to live also as Good Neighbors, and to join with the multitude in striving to build a world wholly and truly at peace.

It is at this Christmastide when, consecrating ourselves afresh to the service of mankind and meditating on the glorious lessons for man taught by the life of the Savior, all men of good will can again feel in their hearts the inward peace that is the Well-Spring of the Good Life. To bring a just, enduring peace among the nations is the great task that beckons still ahead and calls for re-dedication.

Mindful of its Christian heritage, and of the moral tenets that alone can lead to the Good and the True in the lives of the far-flung community of the nations as in the lives of individuals, the United States gladly rededicates its efforts to the creation of a peaceful and advancing world order.

This is my message to you for the most blessed day of the year. Faithfully yours, Harry S Truman.

ఉ

HARRY S TRUMAN, DEC. 24, 1949, UPON LIGHTING THE NATIONAL COMMUNITY CHRISTMAS TREE:

The first Christmas had its beginning in the coming of a Little Child. It remains a child's day, a day of childhood love and of childhood memories. That feeling of love has clung to this day down all the centuries from the first Christmas. There has clustered around Christmas Day the feeling of warmth, of kindness, of innocence, of love-the love of little children-the love for them-the love that was in the heart of the Little Child whose birthday it is.

Through that child love, there came to all mankind the love of a Divine Father and a Blessed Mother so that the love of the Holy Family could be shared by the whole human family. These are some of the thoughts that came to mind as I gave the signal to light our National Christmas Tree in the south grounds of the White House...We must not forget that there are thousands and thousands of families homeless, hopeless, destitute, and torn with despair on this Christmas Eve. For them as for the Holy Family on the first Christmas, there is no room in the inn...

Let us not on this Christmas, in our enjoyment of the abundance with which Providence has endowed us, forget those who, because of the cruelty of war, have no shelter-those multitudes for whom, in the phrase of historic irony, there is no room in the inn....We shall not solve a moral question by dodging it. We can scarcely hope to have a full Christmas if we turn a deaf ear to the suffering of even the least of Christ's little ones. Since returning home, I have been reading again in our family Bible some of the passages which foretold this night. It was that grand old seer Isaiah who prophesied in the Old Testament the sublime event which found fulfillment almost 2,000 years ago.

Just as Isaiah foresaw the coming of Christ, so another battler for the Lord, St. Paul, summed up the law and the prophets in a glorification of love which he exalts even above both faith and hope.

We miss the spirit of Christmas if we consider the Incarnation as an indistinct and doubtful, far-off event unrelated to our present problems. We miss the purpose of Christ's birth if we do not accept it as a living link which joins us together in spirit as children of the ever-living and true God.

In love alone-the love of God and the love of man-will be found the solution of all the ills which afflict the world today. Slowly, sometimes painfully, but always with increasing purpose, emerges the great message of Christianity: only with wisdom comes joy, and with greatness comes love.

In the spirit of the Christ Child-as little children with joy in our hearts and peace in our souls-let us, as a nation, dedicate ourselves anew to the love of our fellowmen.

In such a dedication we shall find the message of the Child of Bethlehem, the real meaning of Christmas.

<6

HARRY S TRUMAN, FEB. 15, 1950, TO ATTORNEY GENERAL'S CONFERENCE ON LAW ENFORCEMENT PROBLEMS, DEPARTMENT OF JUSTICE AUDITORIUM:

The fundamental basis of this nation's laws was given to Moses on the Mount. The fundamental basis of our Bill of Rights comes from the teachings we get from Exodus and St. Matthew, from Isaiah and St. Paul. I don't think we emphasize that enough these days.

If we don't have a proper fundamental moral background, we will finally end up with a totalitarian government which does not believe in rights for anybody except the State!

<6

HARRY S TRUMAN, DEC. 5, 1950, TO MID-CENTURY WHITE HOUSE CONFERENCE ON CHILDREN & YOUTH:

The basis of mental and moral strength for our children lies in spiritual things. It lies first of all in the home.

And next, it lies in the religious and moral influences which are brought to bear on the children. If children have a good home - a home in which they are loved and understood - and if they have good teachers in the first few grades of school, I believe they are well started on the way toward being useful and honorable citizens...

I no not think I am being old fashioned when I say that children ought to have religious training when they are young, and that they will be happier for it and better for it the rest of their lives.

∽

HARRY S TRUMAN, JUN. 17, 1952, ANNUAL NATIONAL DAY OF PRAYER PROCLAMATION:

Whereas from the earliest days of our history our people have been accustomed to turn to Almighty God for help and guidance; and Whereas in times of national crisis when we are striving to strengthen the foundations of peace and security we stand in special need of Divine support; and

Whereas the Congress, by a joint resolution approved on April 17, 1952 (66 Stat. 64), has provided that the President "shall set aside and proclaim a suitable day each year, other than Sunday, as a National Day of Prayer, on which the people of the United States may turn to God in prayer and meditation"; and Whereas I deem it fitting that this Day of Prayer coincide with the anniversary of the adoption of the Declaration of Independence, which published to the world this Nation's "firm reliance on the protection of Divine Providence":

Now, Therefore, I, Harry S Truman, President of the United States of America, do hereby proclaim Friday, July 4, 1952, as a National Day of Prayer, on which all of us, in our churches, in our homes, and in our hearts, may beseech God to grant us wisdom to know the course which we should follow, and strength and patience to pursue that course steadfastly. May we also give thanks to Him for His constant watchfulness over us in every hour of national prosperity and national peril...

Done at the City of Washington this 17th day of June in the year of our Lord nineteen hundred and fifty-two.

∽

HARRY S TRUMAN, DEC. 24, 1952, UPON LIGHTING THE NATIONAL COMMUNITY CHRISTMAS TREE:

My fellow Americans: As we light this National Christmas tree tonight, here on the White House lawn-as all of us light our own Christmas trees in our own homes-we remember another night long ago. Then a Child was born in a stable.

A star hovered over, drawing wise men from afar. Shepherds, in a field, heard angels singing: "Glory to God in the highest, and on earth peace, good will toward men." That was the first Christmas and it was God's great gift to us.

This is a wonderful story. Year after year it brings peace and tranquility to troubled hearts in a troubled world. And tonight the earth seems hushed, as we turn to the old, old story of how "God so loved the world, that He gave His only begotten Son, that whosoever believeth in Him should not perish, but have everlasting life." Tonight, our hearts turn first of all to our brave men and women in Korea. They are fighting and suffering and even dying that we may preserve the chance of peace in the world. The struggle there has been long and bitter.

But it has a hopeful meaning. It has a hopeful meaning because it is the common struggle of many free nations which have joined together to seek a just and lasting peace. We know, all of us, that this is the only way we can bring about peace in the conditions of our time on this earth. Whether we shall succeed depends upon our patience and fortitude. We still have a long road ahead of us before we reach our goal.

We must remain steadfast. And as we go about our business of trying to achieve peace in the world, let us remember always to try to act and live in the spirit of the Prince of Peace. He bore in His heart no hate and no malice-nothing but love for all mankind. We should try as nearly as we can to follow His example. Our efforts to establish law and order in the world are not directed against any nation or any people.

We seek only a universal peace, where all nations shall be free and all peoples shall enjoy their inalienable human rights. We believe that all men are truly the children of God. As we worship at this Christmastide, let us worship in this spirit. As we pray for our loved ones far from home-as we pray for our men and women in Korea, and all our service men and women wherever they are-let us also pray for our enemies.

Let us pray that the spirit of God shall enter their lives and prevail in their lands. Let us pray for a fulfillment of the brotherhood of man. Through Jesus Christ the world will yet be a better and a fairer place.

This faith sustains us today as it has sustained mankind for centuries past.

This is why the Christmas story, with the bright stars shining and the angels singing, moves us to wonder and stirs our hearts to praise. Now, my fellow countrymen, I wish for all of you a Christmas filled with the joy of the Holy Spirit, and many years of future happiness with the peace of God reigning upon this earth.

৶

DWIGHT EISENHOWER

DWIGHT EISENHOWER, JUN. 6, 1944, D-DAY ORDERS:
You are about to embark upon the Great Crusade, toward which we have striven these many months. The eyes of the world are upon you. The hopes and prayers of liberty-loving people everywhere march with you. In company with our brave Allies and brothers-in-arms on other Fronts, you will bring...the elimination of Nazi tyranny over the oppressed peoples of Europe...We will accept nothing less than full Victory! Good luck! And let us all beseech the blessing of Almighty God upon this great and noble undertaking.

᭟

DWIGHT EISENHOWER, DEC. 22, 1944,
ORDERS OF THE DAY, DURING BATTLE OF THE BULGE:
The enemy may give us the chance to turn his great gamble into his worst defeat. So I call upon every man, of all the Allies, to rise now to new heights of courage, of resolution and of effort. Let everyone hold before him a single thought - to destroy the enemy on the ground,

in the air, everywhere - destroy him! United in this determination and with unshakable faith in the cause for which we fight, we will, with God's help, go forward to our greatest victory.

❦

DWIGHT EISENHOWER, JAN. 20, 1953, INAUGURAL, FIRST SUCH ADDRESS TO BE TELEVISED:

My friends, before I begin the expression of those thoughts that I deem appropriate to this moment, would you permit me the privilege of uttering a little private prayer of my own. And I ask that you bow your heads. Almighty God, as we stand here at this moment, my future associates in the Executive Branch of our Government join me in beseeching that Thou will make full and complete our dedication to the service of the people in this throng and their fellow citizens everywhere. Give us, we pray, the power to discern clearly right from wrong and allow all our words and actions to be governed thereby and by the laws of the land. Especially we pray that our concern shall be for all the people regardless of station, race, or calling. May cooperation be permitted and be the mutual aim of those who, under the concepts of our Constitution, hold to differing political faiths; so that all may work for the good of our beloved country and Thy glory. Amen.

❦

DWIGHT EISENHOWER, JAN. 20, 1953, INAUGURAL, FIRST SUCH ADDRESS TO BE TELEVISED:

We are summoned by this honored and historic ceremony to witness more than the act of one citizen swearing his oath of service, in the presence of God. We are called as a people to give testimony in the sight of the world our faith that the future shall belong to the free...

In the swift rush of great events, we find ourselves groping to know the full sense and meaning of these times in which we live. In our quest of understanding, we beseech God's guidance...

We who are free must proclaim anew our faith. This faith in America is the abiding creed of our fathers. It is our faith in the deathless dignity of man, governed by eternal moral and natural laws. This faith defines our full view of life. It establishes beyond debate, those gifts of the Creator that are man's inalienable rights, and that makes all men equal in His sight...

This faith rules our whole way of life. It decrees that we, the people, elect leaders not to rule but to serve...It is because we, all of us, hold to these principles that the political changes accomplished this day do not imply turbulence, upheaval or disorder. Rather this change expresses a purpose of strengthening our dedication and devotion to the precepts of our founding documents, a conscious renewal of faith in our country and in the watchfulness of a Divine Providence.

The enemies of this faith know no god but force, no devotion but it use. They tutor men in treason. They feed upon the hunger of others. Whatever defies them, they torture, especially the truth. Here, then, is joined no argument between slightly differing philosophies.

This conflict strikes directly at the faith of our fathers and the lives of our sons. No principle or treasure that we hold, from the spiritual knowledge of our free schools and churches to the creative magic of free labor and capital, nothing lies safely beyond the reach of this struggle. Freedom is pitted against slavery; lightness against the dark...We feel this moral strength because we know that we are not helpless prisoners of history. We are free men...

These basic precepts are not lofty abstractions, far removed from matters of daily living. They are laws of spiritual strength that generate and define our material strength. Patriotism means equipped forces and a prepared citizenry. Moral stamina means more energy and more productivity. Love of liberty means the guarding of every resource that makes freedom possible - from the sanctity of our families and the wealth of our soil to the genius our scientists...

This is the hope that beckons us onward in this century of trial. This is the work that awaits us all, to be done with bravery, with charity, and with prayer to Almighty God.

∽

DWIGHT EISENHOWER, FEB. 5, 1953, PRAYER BREAKFAST OF INTERNATIONAL CHRISTIAN LEADERSHIP, WASHINGTON:

There is a need we all have in these days and times for some help which comes from outside ourselves as we face the multitude of problems that are part of this confusing situation...Each of us realizes that he has responsibilities that are equal to his privileges and to his rights...Once in a while it might be a good thing for us to turn back to history. Let us study a little bit of what happened at the founding of this Nation. It is not merely the events that led up to the Revolutionary War...Did you ever stop to think, for example, that the first year of that war was fought in order that we might establish our right to be free British citizens, not to be independent. From April 1775 until July 4, 1776, there was no struggle for independence. It was a struggle to make people understand that we were free British citizens...

In the Declaration they acknowledged the need to respect public opinion. They said, "When in the course of human events"-and they went on to say a decent respect for mankind impelled them to declare the decisions which led to the separation. They realized that the good opinion of the whole world was necessary if this venture was to succeed...They went on to try to explain it. What did they say? The very basis of our government is: "We hold that all men are endowed by their Creator" with certain rights.

When we came to that turning point in history, when we intended to establish a government for free men and a Declaration and Constitution to make it last, in order to explain such a system we had to say: "We hold that all men are endowed by their Creator." In one sentence we established that every free government is imbedded soundly in a deeply-felt religious faith or it makes no sense...

If we recall those things...and depend upon a power greater than ourselves, I believe that we begin to draw these problems into focus. As Benjamin Franklin said at one time during the course of the stormy consultation at the Constitutional Convention, because he sensed that the convention was on the point of breaking up: "Gentlemen, I suggest that we have a word of prayer." And strangely enough, after a bit of prayer the problems began to smooth out and the convention moved to the great triumph that we enjoy today-the writing of our Constitution...

Prayer is just simply a necessity, because by prayer I believe we mean an effort to get in touch with the Infinite. We know that even our prayers are imperfect. Even our supplications are imperfect. Of course they are. We are imperfect human beings. But if we can back off from those problems and make the effort, then there is something that ties us all together. We have begun in our grasp of that basis of understanding, which is that all free government is firmly founded in a deeply-felt religious faith...

If we remind ourselves once in a while of this simple basic truth that our forefathers in 1776 understood so well, we can hold up our heads and be certain that we in our time are going to be able to preserve the essentials, to preserve as a free government and pass it on, in our turn, as sound, as strong, as good as ever. That, it seems to me, is the prayer that all of us have today...

∽

DWIGHT EISENHOWER, APR. 12, 1953, TO THE COUNCIL OF THE ORGANIZATION OF AMERICAN STATES:

However real and just be our concern with constructive material development, we must never forget that the strength of America continues ever to be the spirit of America. We are Christian nations, deeply conscious that the foundation of all liberty is religious faith.

∽

DWIGHT EISENHOWER, NOV. 10, 1953, TO THE U.S. INFORMATION AGENCY, DEPARTMENT OF THE INTERIOR:

First you must know what Americanism really is. You have got to know that here a government, of, by, and for free men, is based solidly on some religious concept, for the simple reason that otherwise we cannot prove equality among men....The objective of the cold war is to maintain some kind of arrangement for getting along in this world until enough of all the world's people come to believe with you, with us, that the things for which the Americans stand are those things which enrich human life, which ennoble man because he is an individual created in the image of his God and trying to do his best on this earth.

∽

DWIGHT EISENHOWER, JUL. 9, 1953, TO THE NATIONAL CONFERENCE OF CHRISTIANS & JEWS:

The churches of America are citadels of our faith in individual freedom and human dignity. This faith is the living source of our spiritual strength. And this strength is our matchless armor in our world-wide struggle against the forces of Godless tyranny and oppression.

∽

DWIGHT EISENHOWER, SEP. 10, 1953, ON JEWISH NEW YEAR, FROM LOWRY AIR FORCE BASE, DENVER:

I am happy to extend my warmest greetings to all Americans of Jewish faith on the occasion of the Jewish New Year...The world struggles to find its way toward peace...Patience and good will that have so frequently seen expression in the thousands of years of Jewish life...bring to peoples of good faith everywhere the reassurance...that the citizens of all nations will learn to live together with the understanding and harmony that God-loving people so fervently desire.

∾

DWIGHT EISENHOWER, OCT. 15, 1953, LAYING CORNERSTONE FOR THE ANTHONY WAYNE LIBRARY OF AMERICAN STUDY, DEFIANCE COLLEGE, DEFIANCE, OH:

I am here because of my ultimate faith in education as the hope of the world-Christian religious education, man's free access to knowledge, his right to use it...

At one spot in this town...a stone marks the site of the first French mission on the Maumee River, established more than 300 years ago. At another, the earthworks of Fort Defiance remind us that 160 years ago the forward command post of the American Nation was here. Other landmarks are canal locks and monuments and buildings that recall the mighty expansion of the American economy from an agricultural society to the first place among the world's industrial powers.

In Defiance, whose roots are deep in the American past, it is fitting that I humbly salute the generations of men and women, the builders of Ohio, in this, the sesquicentennial year of their State. They were explorers and trappers and missionaries, traders, and farmers, and teachers, diggers of waterways and skilled operators of an industrial empire.

Above all...they helped construct a way of life-the American way of life, of which the cornerstone is an indestructible faith in man's dignity as a child of God.

∾

DWIGHT EISENHOWER, OCT. 15, 1953, LAYING CORNERSTONE FOR THE ANTHONY WAYNE LIBRARY OF AMERICAN STUDY, DEFIANCE COLLEGE, DEFIANCE, OH:

Our forebears added the community school to the home that was the center of man's life as a family being, and to the church that was the fountain of his faith as a religious being. They were intent on providing an armory of knowledge where Americans might gird themselves for the obligations and the challenges that those Founding Fathers knew would be inescapable in a system of representative government...

In the dedication of this library...we symbolize our continuing faith in man's ability, under God, to govern himself intelligently.

∽

DWIGHT EISENHOWER, OCT. 31, 1953, BROADCAST FOR THE COMMITTEE ON RELIGION IN AMERICAN LIFE:

Each Year the Committee on Religion in American Life reminds us of the importance of faithful church attendance. It urges full support of religious institutions to the end that we may add strength and meaning to the religious virtues - charity, mercy, brother love, and faith in Almighty God. These spiritual concepts are the inspiration of the American way. It was once said, "America is great because America is good - and if America ever ceases to be good, America will cease to be great." By strengthening religious institutions, the Committee on Religion in American Life is helping to keep America good, thus it helps each of us to keep America great.

∽

DWIGHT EISENHOWER, DEC. 14, 1953, OPENING THE WHITE HOUSE CONFERENCE OF MAYORS:

I want to point out something about fighting-about war. Many of you here, of course, have been through the very worst parts of our past war. One great military leader said, "The moral is to the physical in war as three is to one," and I think every soldier who has come after him has believed that he understated the case. The winning of war-the effectiveness in such things-is in the heart, in the determination, in the faith. It is in our beliefs in our country, in our God, everything that goes to make up America.

∽

DWIGHT EISENHOWER, DEC. 24, 1953, UPON LIGHTING THE NATIONAL COMMUNITY CHRISTMAS TREE:

This evening's ceremony, here at the White House, is one of many thousands in America's traditional celebration of the birth, almost 2,000 years ago, of the Prince of Peace. For us, this Christmas is truly a season of good will-and our first peaceful one since 1949...Our hopes are bright even though the world still stands divided in two antagonistic parts. More precisely than in any other way, prayer places freedom and communism in opposition, one to the other. The Communist can find no reserve of strength in prayer because his doctrine of materialism and statism denies the dignity of man and consequently the existence of God.

But in America, George Washington long ago rejected exclusive dependence upon mere materialistic values. In the bitter and critical winter at Valley Forge, when the cause of liberty was so near defeat, his recourse was sincere and earnest prayer. From it he received new hope and new strength of purpose out of which grew the freedom in which we celebrate this Christmas season. As religious faith is the foundation of free government, so is prayer an indispensable part of that faith...Would it not be fitting for each of us to speak in prayer to the Father of all men and women on this earth, of whatever nation, and of every race and creed-to ask that He help us-and teach us-and strengthen us-and receive our thanks. Should we not pray that He help us?

Help us to remember that the founders of this, our country, came first to these shores in search of freedom-freedom of man to walk in dignity; to live without fear; beyond the yoke of tyranny; ever to progress. Help us to cherish freedom, for each of us and for all nations. Might we not pray that He teach us?...Teach us the security of faith. And may we pray that He strengthen us...

Should we not pray that He receive our thanks? For certainly we are grateful for...the opportunity given us to use our strength and our faith to meet the problems of this hour. And on this Christmas Eve, all hearts in America are filled with special thanks to God that the blood of those we love no longer spills on battlefields abroad. May He receive the thanks of each of us for this, His greatest bounty-and our supplication that peace on earth may live with us, always.

ॐ

DWIGHT EISENHOWER, FEB. 1, 1954, TO THE CATHOLIC ORGANIZATIONS FOR FREEING CARDINAL MINDSZENTY:

We in the free world have not forgotten that this is the fifth anniversary of Cardinal Mindszenty's trial and imprisonment by the Communist authorities in Hungary. The unjust nature of the proceedings against Cardinal Mindszenty is, of course, well known to the American people. They regarded the attack upon him as a blow against religious freedom in Hungary and an unprincipled attempt to destroy spiritual and moral influences in that country.

The Communist assault upon religious liberty and leadership in Hungary has failed, however, to turn the Hungarian people from their faith in God. The plight of Cardinal Mindszenty and of other churchmen who have suffered at the hands of the Communists has not been forgotten. Their situation continues deeply to concern the people of Hungary and to evoke the sympathy of the free world. Despite the constraints of person and silence imposed on Cardinal Mindszenty and other church leaders by their persecutors, the spirit of these men has defied confinement by the totalitarian State. It has become, indeed, a symbol of faith and freedom for our times.

∾

DWIGHT EISENHOWER, FEB. 7, 1954, BROADCAST FROM THE WHITE HOUSE FOR THE AMERICAN LEGION BACK-TO-GOD PROGRAM:

As a former soldier, I am delighted that our veterans are sponsoring a movement to increase our awareness of God in our daily lives. In battle, they learned a great truth-that there are no atheists in the foxholes. They know that in time of test and trial, we instinctively turn to God for new courage and peace of mind. All the history of America bears witness to this truth. Out of faith in God, and through faith in themselves as His children, our forefathers designed and built this Republic.

We remember from school days that, aboard a tiny ship of destiny called the Mayflower, self-government on our continent was first conceived by the Pilgrim Fathers. Their immortal compact began with the words, "In the name of God, Amen."

We remember the picture of the Father of our Country, on his knees at Valley Forge seeking divine guidance in the cold gloom of a bitter winter. Thus Washington gained strength to lead to independence a nation dedicated to the belief that each of us is divinely endowed with indestructible rights. We remember, too, that three-fourths of a century later, on the battle-torn field of Gettysburg, and in the silence of many a wartime night, Abraham Lincoln recognized that only under God could this Nation win a new birth of freedom.

And we remember that, only a decade ago, aboard the transport Dorchester, four chaplains of four faiths together willingly sacrificed their lives so that four others might live. In the three centuries that separate the Pilgrims of the Mayflower from the chaplains of the Dorchester, America's freedom, her courage, her strength, and her progress have had their foundation in faith.

Today as then, there is need for positive acts of renewed recognition that faith is our surest strength, our greatest resource. This "Back to God" movement is such a positive act. As we take part in it, I hope that we shall prize this thought: Whatever our individual church, whatever our personal creed, our common faith in God is a common bond among us. In our fundamental faith, we are all one.

Together we thank the Power that has made and preserved us a nation. By the millions, we speak prayers, we sing hymns-and no matter what their words may be, their spirit is the same-"In God is our trust."

❦

DWIGHT EISENHOWER, APR. 22, 1954,
TO DAUGHTERS OF THE AMERICAN REVOLUTION,
63RD CONTINENTAL CONGRESS, CONSTITUTION HALL:

Our Founding Fathers in writing the Declaration of Independence put it in a nutshell when they said, "We hold that all men are endowed by their Creator with certain rights." In that one phrase was created a political system which demands and requires that all men have equality of right before the law, that they are not treated differently merely because of social distinction, of money, of economic standing, indeed of intelligence of intellectual capacity, or anything else.

It acknowledges that man has a soul, and for that reason is equal to every other man, and that is the system, that is the principle-that is the cornerstone of what we call the American system. There are, of course, dozens of auxiliary principles that go along with this one, but rip out this one and you have destroyed America...

Now, how do we apply such a system in a world where there is present one great power complex that stands for the exact opposite?

Remember, in the phrase I quoted to you, "Men are endowed by their Creator." Our system demands the Supreme Being. There is no question about the American system being the translation into the political world of a deeply felt religious faith.

The system that challenges us today is the atheistic. It is self-admitted as an atheistic document. They believe in a materialistic dialectic. In other words, there are no values except material values. It challenges us today in every corner of the globe.

✦

DWIGHT EISENHOWER, MAY 20, 1954, TO THE COMMITTEE FOR ECONOMIC DEVELOPMENT:

Now everybody knows that no security force is any good at all unless it is one of high morale, belief, and conviction. Consequently, the first thing we must do, it seems to me, is to believe in this system of freedom with all our hearts, to realize we are defending, first of all, our great system of freedoms and of rights. Everything we do that seems to impinge upon them, although at times we may think it is necessary in their modification, we must examine carefully and say how far may we go and still not ruin this system.

Where do we establish the line beyond which we must not step, unless we are going to go and lose internally what we so desperately try to defend against externally? I believe all the way through we must in this manner of faith recognize a relationship between free government and a religious faith. I believe that if there is no religious faith whatsoever, then there is little defense you can make of a free system. If men are only animals, why not try to dominate them?

✦

DWIGHT EISENHOWER, MAY 26, 1954, TOASTS TO ETHIOPIAN EMPEROR HAILE SELASSIE, STATE DINNER:

I read once that no individual can really be known to have greatness until he has been tested in adversity. By this test, our guest of honor has established new standards in the world. In 5 years of adversity, with his country overrun but never conquered, he never lost for one single second his dignity. He never lost his faith in himself, in his people, and in his God. I deem it a very great privilege, ladies and gentlemen, to ask you to rise and with me to drink a Toast to His Imperial Majesty, the Emperor of Ethiopia.

∽

DWIGHT EISENHOWER, JUN. 14, 1954, SIGNED THE BILL PLACING "ONE NATION UNDER GOD" IN THE PLEDGE OF ALLEGIANCE, THEN RECITED ON THE U.S. CAPITOL STEPS:

I pledge allegiance to the flag of the United States of America, and to the Republic for which it stands, one nation under God, indivisible, with liberty and justice for all.

∽

DWIGHT EISENHOWER, JUN. 14, 1954, AFTER SIGNING RESOLUTION 243 ADDING "UNDER GOD" TO THE PLEDGE:

From this day forward, the millions of our school children will daily proclaim in every city and town, every village and rural school house, the dedication of our nation and our people to the Almighty. To anyone who truly loves America, nothing could be more inspiring than to contemplate this rededication of our youth, on each school morning, to our country's true meaning...

Over the globe, mankind has been cruelly torn by violence and brutality and, by the millions, deadened in mind and soul by a materialistic philosophy of life. Man everywhere is appalled by the prospect of atomic war. In this somber setting, this law and its effects today have profound meaning. In this way we are reaffirming the transcendence of religious faith in America's heritage and future; in this way we shall constantly strengthen those spiritual weapons which forever will be our country's most powerful resource, in peace or in war.

∽

DWIGHT EISENHOWER, OCT. 24, 1954, MARKING THE 75TH ANNIVERSARY OF THE INCANDESCENT LAMP:

Faith and the American individual. Yes, it is on these two pillars that our future rests. It was Thomas Edison who said: "Be courageous; be as brave as your fathers before you. Have faith. Go forward." Seventy-five years ago this very week, Tom Edison-a humble, typical sort of American-put this credo into action and gave a new light to the world.

It is faith that has made our Nation-has made it, and kept it free. Atheism substitutes men for the supreme creator and this leads inevitably to domination and dictatorship. But we believe-and it is because we believe that God intends all men to be free and equal that we demand free government.

Our Government is servant, not master, our chosen representatives are our equals, not our czars or commissars. We must jealously guard our foundation in faith. For on it rests the ability of the American individual to live and thrive in this blessed land-and to be able to help other less fortunate people to achieve freedom and individual opportunity. These we take for granted, but to others they are often only a wistful dream.

"In God we trust." Often have we heard the words of this wonderful American motto. Let us make sure that familiarity has not made them meaningless for us. We carry the torch of freedom as a sacred trust for all mankind. We do not believe that God intended the light that He created to be put out by men....It can be a confident kind of a prayer too, for God has made us strong and faith has made and kept us free.

∽

DWIGHT EISENHOWER, NOV. 9, 1954, TO CONFERENCE ON THE SPIRITUAL FOUNDATION OF AMERICAN DEMOCRACY:

Dr. Lowry said something about my having certain convictions as to a God in Heaven and an Almighty power. Well, I don't think anyone needs a great deal of credit for believing what seems to me to be obvious...Now it seems to me that this relationship between a spiritual faith, a religious faith, and our form of government is so clearly defined and so obvious that we should really not need to identify a man as unusual because he recognizes it....Let us just come down to modern times since the Reformation. Milton asserted that all men are born equal, because each is born in the image of his God.

Our whole theory of government finally expressed in our Declaration, you will recall, said-and remember the first part of the Preamble of the Declaration was to give the reasons to mankind why we had established such a government: "Man is endowed by his Creator." It did not assert that Americans had certain rights. "Man" is endowed by his Creator-or "All Men"...

So this connection is very, very clear. And no matter what Democracy tries to do in the terms of maximum individual liberty for an individual, in the economic and in the intellectual and every other field, no matter what it tries to do in providing a system of justice, and a system of responsibility-of public servants to all the people-and identifying the people as the source of political power in that government, when you come back to it, there is just one thing: it is a concept, it is a subjective sort of thing, that a man is worthwhile because he was born in the image of his God...

The challenges of today...are of two kinds, one from within...as to the worth-whileness of this form of government...and on the other side we are attacked by the Communists who in their own documents state that capitalism-Democracy-carries within itself the seeds of its own destruction...We are under tremendous attacks...

Fundamentally, Democracy is nothing in the world but a spiritual conviction, a conviction that each of us is enormously valuable because of a certain standing before our own God. Now, any group that binds itself together to awaken all of us to these simple things...is, to my mind, a dedicated, patriotic group that can well take the Bible in one hand and the flag in the other, and march ahead.

⁌

DWIGHT EISENHOWER, FEB. 20, 1955, FOR THE AMERICAN LEGION BACK-TO-GOD PROGRAM:

The Founding Fathers expressed in words for all to read the ideal of Government based upon the dignity of the individual. That ideal previously had existed only in the hearts and minds of men. They produced the timeless documents upon which the Nation is rounded and has grown great. They, recognizing God as the author of individual fights, declared that the purpose of Government is to secure those rights.

To you and to me this ideal of Government is a self-evident truth. But in many lands the State claims to be the author of human rights. The tragedy of that claim runs through all history and, indeed, dominates our own times.

If the State gives rights, it can-and inevitably will-take away those rights. Without God, there could be no American form of Government, nor an American way of life.

Recognition of the Supreme Being is the first-the most basic-expression of Americanism. Thus the Founding Fathers saw it, and thus, with God's help, it will continue to be. It is significant, I believe, that the American Legion-an organization of war veterans-has seen fit to conduct a "Back to God" movement as part of its Americanism program.

Veterans realize, perhaps more clearly than others, the prior place that Almighty God holds in our national life. And they can appreciate, through personal experience, that the really decisive battleground of American freedom is in the hearts and minds of our own people...Each day we must ask that Almighty God will set and keep His protecting hand over us so that we may pass on to those who come after us the heritage of a free people, secure in their God-given rights and in full control of a Government dedicated to the preservation of those rights.

∾

DWIGHT EISENHOWER, JUN. 3, 1955, ON ACCEPTANCE OF PALESTINIAN LAMP OF FREEDOM FROM WILLIAM ROSENWALD, CHAIRMAN OF THE UNITED JEWISH APPEAL:

I am delighted, on behalf of the Allied Forces who, advancing from the west, did so much to crush Nazi tyranny, to accept this beautiful and ancient relic of Jewish civilization. I am certain that those Forces-the American forces and their Allies-were representing only what we would call the heart of freedom, the belief that all people are entitled to life, liberty, and the pursuit of happiness-that where these are denied one man, they are threatened for all.

And so I am sure those Forces felt that in uncovering these camps, relieving the disasters and correcting the terrible conditions under which those people were living, they were not doing it fundamentally and merely because they were Jews, or anybody else. It was a tremendous privilege and a great change from the killing of war to turn your armies to saving human lives and human dignity.

∾

DWIGHT EISENHOWER, AUG. 17, 1955, TO U.S. ARMED SERVICES, CODE OF CONDUCT FOR WAR PRISONERS:

When questioned, should I become a prisoner of war, I am

bound to give only name, rank, service number, and date of birth...I will never forget that I am an American fighting man, responsible for my actions, and dedicated to the principles which made my country free. I will trust in my God and in the United States of America.

∽

DWIGHT EISENHOWER, JAN. 21, 1957, 2ND INAUGURAL:

Before all else, we seek upon our common labor as a nation, the blessings of Almighty God. And the hopes in our hearts fashion the deepest prayers of our whole people...We look upon this shaken earth, and we declare our firm and fixed purpose - the building of a peace with justice in a world where moral law prevails...And so the prayer of our people carries far beyond our own frontiers, to the wide world of our duty and our destiny.

∽

DWIGHT EISENHOWER, SEP. 26, 1957,
ON THE OCCASION OF THE JEWISH HIGH HOLY DAYS:

At the beginning of the Jewish New Year, it is fitting for all to give thanks for the past twelve months and to look to the future with confidence born of the mercy of God. The blessings of life and the freedoms all of us enjoy in this land today are based in no small measure on the Ten Commandments which have been handed down to us by the religious teachers of the Jewish faith. These Commandments of God provide endless opportunities for fruitful service, and they are a stronghold of moral purpose for men everywhere. In this season, as our fellow citizens of the Jewish faith bow their heads in prayer and lift their eyes in hope, we offer them the best wishes of our hearts.

∽

DWIGHT EISENHOWER, APR. 2, 1958, NEWS CONFERENCE:

Just before I walked across the street in the beautiful sunlight and saw this revolution in Washington weather, someone called my attention to a passage in the Bible. It is in the Song of Solomon, second chapter. Read the verses 11 and 12.1 That is my announcement: "For, lo, the winter is past, The rain is over and gone; The flowers appear on the earth; The time of the singing of birds is come, And the voice of the turtle is heard in our land."

∽

DWIGHT EISENHOWER, OCT. 12, 1958, LAYING THE CORNERSTONE FOR THE INTERCHURCH CENTER, NY:

As this cornerstone is placed in the walls of the Interchurch Center, we see in it a special meaning. That cornerstone symbolizes a prime support of our faith-"The Truth" that sets men free. The freedom of a citizen and the freedom of a religious believer are more than intimately related; they are mutually dependent. These two liberties give life to the heart of our Nation.

We are politically free people because each of us is free to express his individual faith. As Washington said in 1793, so we can say today: "We have abundant reason to rejoice that in this land the light of truth and reason has triumphed over the power of bigotry and superstition, and that every person may here worship God according to the dictates of his own heart."

My friends, freedom has been given one definition that has for me a very great appeal, and I believe it has a great appeal for every true American. It is this: freedom is the priceless opportunity for self-discipline. Can you imagine the outrage that would have been expressed by our first President today, had he read in the news dispatches of the bombing of a synagogue?...

I think we would all share in the feeling of horror, that any brigand would want to desecrate the holy place of any religion...If we are believers in the tradition by which we have lived, that freedom of worship is inherent in human liberty, then we will not countenance the desecration of any edifice that symbolizes one of the great faiths.

Freedom of worship is a basic privilege; guaranteed by the Constitution, and it was by deliberate design our Founding Fathers selected the very first article in our Bill of Rights to proclaim the right of each citizen to worship according to his conscience...Our first President spoke gratefully of religious liberty, but he spoke also of the moral requirements which religion places on the shoulders of each citizen, singly and together. Washington believed that national morality could not be maintained without a firm foundation of religious principle.

When a President of the United States takes his oath of office, he places his hand upon the Bible. In that ceremony, the Bible symbolizes the solemn obligations which he takes "to preserve, protect and defend the Constitution of the United States." This, for me, is summed up in the final words of that oath: "So help me God." Clearly, civil and religious liberties are mutually reinforcing.

In this land our churches have always been sturdy defenders of the Constitutional and God-given rights of each citizen. They have sought to protect, to broaden and to sustain the historic laws of justice and truth and honor which are the foundations of our community life. May they always do so. I deeply value the privilege of taking part in this ceremony and of wishing to each of you here present, "Godspeed."

↭

DWIGHT EISENHOWER, ARTICLE PRINTED IN THE EPISCOPAL CHURCHNEWS MAGAZINE:

It was part of the privilege into which I was born that my home was a religious home. My father and mother believed that "the fear of God is the beginning of wisdom."...The history of our country is inseparable from the history of such Godfearing families. In this fact we accept the explanation of the miracle of America...

The founding fathers had to refer to the Creator in order to make their revolutionary experiment make sense; it was because "all men are endowed by their Creator with certain inalienable rights" that men could dare to be free. They wrote their religious faith into our founding documents, stamped their trust in God on the face of our coins and currency, put it boldly at the base of our institutions, and when they drew up their bold Bill of Rights, where did they put freedom to worship? First, in the cornerstone position! That was no accident.

Our forefathers proved that only a people strong in Godliness is a people strong enough to overcome tyranny and make themselves and others free...What is our battle against communism if it is not a fight between antiGod and a belief in the Almighty?

If there was nothing else in my life to prove the existence of an Almighty and Merciful God, the events of the next twenty-four hours did it. This is what I found out about religion: It gives you courage to make the decisions you must make in a crisis, and then the confidence to leave the results to a higher power.

Only by trust in oneself and trust in God can a man carrying responsibility find repose. If each of us in his own mind would dwell upon the simple virtues - integrity, courage, selfconfidence, and unshakable belief in his Bible - would not some of our problems tend to simplify themselves?

✍

DWIGHT EISENHOWER, SEP. 10, 1959, RADIO & TELEVISION REPORT ON EUROPEAN TRIP:

We venerate more widely than any other document, except only the Bible, the American Declaration of Independence. That Declaration was more than a call to national action. It is a voice of conscience establishing clear, enduring values applicable to the lives of all men. It stands enshrined today as a charter of human liberty and dignity. Until these things belong to every living person their pursuit is an unfinished business to occupy our children and generations to follow them...I know that all America prays to the Almighty that this might come to pass.

✍

DWIGHT EISENHOWER, OCT. 2, 1959, ON JEWISH HOLY DAYS:

Greetings to my fellow citizens of Jewish faith as they enter the season of their High Holy Days. The teachings of your ancient belief have long sustained you and strengthened the communities in which you live. By constant repetition-in word and deed-of the commandments of God, you have nourished the noblest principles of mankind. The demands of justice, the plea for mercy, the rights and the responsibilities of each individual; these should be uppermost in our thoughts at home and at work, when we sleep and when we awake.

✍

DWIGHT EISENHOWER, FEB. 24, 1960, TO THE CONGRESS OF BRAZIL, AT TIRADENTES PALACE IN RIO DE JANEIRO:

We pray that all of us will reject cruel tyranny, for tyranny is, in simple essence, the outright denial of the teachings of Christ...

Perhaps inseparable from the decision of freedom or slavery, we face the philosophic issue which today brings fear, misgiving, and mistrust to mankind. In contrast to our adherence to a philosophy of common sonship, of human dignity, and of moral law, millions now live in an environment permeated with a philosophy which denies the existence of God.

That doctrine insists that any means justifies the end sought by the rulers of the state, calls Christianity the "sigh of the oppressed," and, in short, seeks to return mankind to the age-old fatalistic concept of the omnipotent state and omnipotent fate.

&

DWIGHT EISENHOWER, JUN. 1, 1960, ON THE 50TH ANNIVERSARY OF THE BOY SCOUTS OF AMERICA:

I might say that after I finally lose the loving care of the Secret Service, that should I be standing one day on the corner of a busy street and a Boy Scout sees this rather elderly-looking fellow looking a little doubtful, if he offers to take me across the street, he can do it...To my mind, that is the great thing about Scouting. It doesn't make any difference whether they wrap up their bed-rolls just right, or pitch their tent exactly right, or whether they do their cookout and burn the eggs and the bacon not fit to eat.

As long as they have that feeling and that development-if they get the same feeling that we did when we read in our Bibles the Parable of the Good Samaritan and then as time comes along, if they individually and collectively begin to think of their nation in part as a "good Samaritan," doing the decent thing in this world, then I will tell you: Scouting is indeed doing something for all of us that is not only necessary but I would say vital to our vigor as a nation based upon a religious concept.

&

FORMER PRESIDENT DWIGHT EISENHOWER, NOV. 23, 1963, AFTER RECEIVING NEWS OF JOHN F. KENNEDY'S ASSASSINATION, TO PRESIDENT LYNDON B. JOHNSON:

Confidential Notes for the President...I am bold enough to suggest that you call a Joint Session of the Congress to make a speech of not over ten or twelve minutes. I think it might cover the following...That you have come to this office unexpectedly and you accept the decision of the Almighty, who in His inscrutable wisdom has now place you in the position of highest responsibility of this nation.

&

JOHN F. KENNEDY

JOHN F. KENNEDY, JAN. 20, 1961, INAUGURAL:

For I have sworn before you and Almighty God, the same solemn oath our forbears prescribed nearly a century and three quarters ago. The world is very different now. For man holds in his mortal hands the power to abolish all forms of human poverty and all forms of human life. And yet the same revolutionary beliefs for which our forebears fought are still at issue around the globe - The belief that the rights of man come not from the generosity of the state but from the hand of God.

᷍

JOHN F. KENNEDY, JAN. 20, 1961, INAUGURAL:

Let every nation know, whether it wishes us well or ill, that we shall pay any price, bear any burden, meet any hardship, support any friend, oppose any foe, in order to assure the survival and the success of liberty...Let both sides united to heed in all corners of the earth the command of Isaiah - to "undo the heavy burdens and to let the oppressed go free."(Is. 58:6)...Now the trumpet summons us again -

not as a call to bear arms, though arms we need; not as a call to battle, though embattled we are; but a call to bear the burden of a long twilight struggle, year in, and year out, "rejoicing in hope, patient in tribulation"(Romans 12:12) - a struggle against the common enemies of man: tyranny, poverty, disease, and war itself...

The energy, the faith, the devotion which we bring to this endeavor will light our country and all who serve it - and the glow from that fire can truly light the world. And so, my fellow Americans - ask not what your country can do for you - ask what you can do for your country...Let us go forth to lead the land we love, asking His blessing and His help, but knowing that here on earth God's work must truly be our own.

<s

JOHN F. KENNEDY, SEP. 28, 1961, NATIONAL DAY OF PRAYER PROCLAMATION:

Our founding fathers came to these shores trusting in God, and in reliance upon His grace. They charted the course of free institutions under a government deriving its powers from the consent of the people. In the General Congress assembled they appealed the rectitude of their intentions to the Supreme Judge of the world, and "with firm reliance on the protection of Divine Providence" they mutually pledged their lives, their fortunes, and their most sacred honor.

During the deliberations in the Constitutional Convention they were called to daily prayers, with the reminder in sacred Scripture it is written that "except the Lord build the house, they labor in vain that build It," and they were warned that without the concurring aid of Providence they would succeed in the political building "no better than the builders of Babel." In every succeeding generation the people of this country have emulated their fathers in defending their liberties with their fortunes and their lives.

Conscious of our continuing need to bring our actions under the searching light of Divine Judgment, the Congress of the United States by joint resolution approved on the seventeenth day of April 1952 provided that "The President shall set aside and proclaim a suitable day each year, other than a Sunday, as a National Day of Prayer, on which the people of the United States may turn to God in prayer and meditation at churches, in groups, and as individuals."...

Recognizing our own shortcomings may we be granted forgiveness and cleansing, that God shall bless us and be gracious unto us, and cause His face to shine upon us as we stand everyone of us on this day in His Presence.

∽

JOHN F. KENNEDY, 1960, INTRODUCTION TO 16-VOLUME AMERICAN HERITAGE NEW ILLUSTRATED HISTORY OF THE UNITED STATES:

There is little that is more important for an American citizen to know than the history and traditions of his country. Without such knowledge, he stands uncertain and defenseless before the world, knowing neither where he has come from or where he is going. With such knowledge, he is no longer alone but draws a strength far greater than his own from the cumulative experience of the past and the cumulative vision of the future...

History is the means by which a nation established its sense of identity and purpose. The future arises out to the past, and a country's history is a statement of the values and hopes which, having forged what has gone before, will now forecast what is to come.

∽

JOHN F. KENNEDY, FEB. 9, 1961, 9th ANNUAL PRESIDENTIAL PRAYER BREAKFAST, MAYFLOWER HOTEL:

While they came from a wide variety of religious backgrounds and held a wide variety of religious beliefs, each of our Presidents in his own way has placed a special trust in God. Those who were strongest intellectually were also strongest spiritually.

∽

JOHN F. KENNEDY, STATEMENT:

Human brotherhood is not just a goal it is a condition on which our way of life depends. The question for our time is not whether all men are brothers. That question has been answered by the God who placed us on Earth together. The question is whether we have the strength and will to make the brotherhood of man the guiding principle of our daily lives.

∽

JOHN F. KENNEDY, JAN. 31, 1961, GREETING PRESIDENT QUADROS OF BRAZIL ON HIS INAUGURATION:

Once in every twenty years presidential inaugurations in your country and mine occur within days of each other. This year of 1961 is signalized by the happy coincidence. At this time, each of us assumes challenging duties for which he has been freely chosen by his fellow citizens. To each of us is entrusted the heavy responsibility of guiding the affairs of a democratic nation founded on Christian ideals.

∽

JOHN F. KENNEDY, FEB. 9, 1961, 9TH ANNUAL PRESIDENTIAL PRAYER BREAKFAST:

Let us go forth to lead this land that we love, joining in the prayer of General George Washington in 1783, "that God would...be pleased to dispose us all to do justice, to love mercy, and to demean ourselves with...the characteristics of the Divine Author of our blessed religion, without an humble imitation of whose example we can never hope to be a happy nation." The guiding principle and prayer of this Nation has been, is now, and ever shall be "In God We Trust."

∽

JOHN F. KENNEDY, OCT. 28, 1961, PROCLAMATION 3438, NATIONAL THANKSGIVING DAY:

The Pilgrims, after a year of hardship and peril, humbly and reverently set aside a special day upon which to give thanks to God...I ask the head of each family to recount to his children the story of the first New England Thanksgiving, thus to impress upon future generations the heritage of this nation born in toil, in danger, in purpose, and in the conviction that right and justice and freedom can through man's efforts persevere and come to fruition with the blessing of God.

∽

JOHN F. KENNEDY, NOV. 16, 1961, AT UNIVERSITY OF WASHINGTON:

This nation was then torn by war. This territory had only the simplest elements of civilization...But a university was one of their earliest thoughts, and they summed it up in the motto that they adopted: "Let there be light." What more can be said today regarding all the dark and tangled problems we face than: Let there be light.

❧

JOHN F. KENNEDY, NOV. 21, 1961, NATIONAL CONFERENCE OF CHRISTIANS AND JEWS, WHITE HOUSE:

It has always seemed to me that when we all - regardless of our particular religious convictions - draw our guidance and inspiration, and really, in a sense, moral direction, from the same general area, the Bible, the Old and the New Testaments, we have every reason to believe that our various religious denominations should live together in the closest harmony...The basic presumption of the moral law, the existence of God, man's relationship to Him - there is generally consensus on those questions.

❧

JOHN F. KENNEDY, MAR. 1, 1962, 10TH ANNUAL PRESIDENTIAL PRAYER BREAKFAST:

There is a quotation from Lincoln which I think is particularly applicable today. He said, "I believe there is a God. I see the storm coming, and I believe He has a hand in it. If He has a part and a place for me, I believe that I am ready." We see the storm coming, and we believe He has a hand in it; and if He has a place and a part for us, I believe that we are ready.

❧

JOHN F. KENNEDY, DEC. 17, 1962, LIGHTING THE NATIONAL COMMUNITY CHRISTMAS TREE:

With the lighting of this tree, which is an old ceremony in Washington and one which has been among the most important responsibilities of a good many Presidents of the United States, we initiate, in a formal way, the Christmas Season. We mark the festival of Christmas which is the most sacred and hopeful day in our civilization. For nearly 2,000 years the message of Christmas, the message of peace and good will towards all men, has been the guiding star of our endeavors...I had a meeting...which included some of our representatives from far off countries in Africa and Asia. They were returning to their posts for the Christmas holidays. Talking with them...I was struck by the fact that in the far off continents Moslems, Hindus, Buddhists, as well as Christians, pause from their labors on the 25th day of December to celebrate the birthday of the Prince of Peace.

There could be no more striking proof that Christmas is truly the universal holiday of all men. It is the day when all of us dedicate our thoughts to others; when all are reminded that mercy and compassion are the enduring virtues; when all show, by small deeds and large and by acts, that it is more blessed to give than to receive. It is the day when we remind ourselves that man can and must live in peace with his neighbors and that it is the peacemakers who are truly blessed. In this year of 1962 we greet each other at Christmas with some special sense of the blessings of peace.

This has been a year of peril when the peace has been sorely threatened. But it has been a year when peril was faced and when reason ruled. As a result, we may talk, at this Christmas, just a little bit more confidently of peace on earth, good will to men. As a result, the hopes of the American people are perhaps a little higher. We have much yet to do. We still need to ask that God bless everyone.

∽

JOHN F. KENNEDY, JUL. 11, 1963,
RADIO & TELEVISION ADDRESS TO THE NATION:

It ought to be possible, in short, for every American to enjoy the privileges of being American without regard to his race or his color...We are confronted primarily with a moral issue. It is as old as the Scriptures and is as clear as the American Constitution...We face, therefore, a moral crisis as a country and as a people.

∽

JOHN F. KENNEDY, NOV. 22, 1963, UNDELIVERED TEXT OF PLANNED SPEECH TO BE DELIVERED AT DALLAS TRADE MART THE DAY HE WAS ASSASSINATED:

We in this country, in this generation, are - by destiny rather than choice - the watchmen on the walls of world freedom. We ask, therefore, that we may achieve in our time and for all time the ancient vision of peace on earth, goodwill toward men. That must always be our goal - and the righteousness of our cause must always underlie our strength. For as was written long ago, "Except the Lord keep the city, the watchman waketh but in vain."

∽

LYNDON B. JOHNSON

LYNDON B. JOHNSON, NOV. 22, 1963, TO THE PRESS AS HE DISEMBARKED THE AIR FORCE ONE, ANDREWS AIR FORCE BASE OUTSIDE WASHINGTON D.C:

This is a sad time for all people. We have suffered a loss that cannot be weighed. For me, it is a deep personal tragedy. I know that the world shares the sorrow that Mrs. Kennedy and her family bear. I will do my best. That is all I can do. I ask for your help - and God's.

✥

LYNDON B. JOHNSON, NOV. 27, 1963, 1ST FORMAL ADDRESS BEFORE A JOINT SESSION OF CONGRESS, WITH MEMBERS OF SUPREME COURT AND CABINET, DELIVERED UPON ASSUMING THE PRESIDENCY AFTER THE DEATH OF PRESIDENT KENNEDY:

Let us here highly resolve that John Fitzgerald Kennedy did not live - or die - in vain. And on this Thanksgiving Eve, as we gather together to ask the Lord's blessings and give Him our thanks, let us unite in those familiar and cherished words: America, America, God shed His grace on thee, And crown thy good, With brotherhood, From sea to shining sea.

∽

LADY BIRD JOHNSON, MAY 14, 1964, NOTE TO HER HUSBAND, PRESIDENT LYNDON B. JOHNSON, PRIOR TO HIS 1964 PRESIDENTIAL CAMPAIGN:

If you win, let's do the best we can for 3 years and 3 or 4 months and then, the Lord letting us live that long, announce in February or March of 1968 that you are not a candidate for re-election.

∽

LYNDON B. JOHNSON, AUG. 25, 1964, THOUGHTS PENNED CONCERNING CAMPAIGNING FOR PRESIDENT:

In the time given me, I did my best. On that fateful day last year I accepted the responsibilities of the Presidency, asking God's guidance and the help of all of the people. For nine months I've carried on as effectively as I could.

∽

LYNDON B. JOHNSON, JAN. 20, 1965, INAUGURAL:

Under this covenant of justice, liberty, and union we have become a nation-prosperous, great, and mighty. And we have kept our freedom. But we have no promise from God that our greatness will endure. We have been allowed by Him to seek greatness with the sweat of our hands and the strength of our spirit...If we fail now, we shall have forgotten in abundance what we learned in hardship: that democracy rests on faith, that freedom asks more than it gives, and that the judgement of God is harshest on those who are most favored....For myself, I ask only in the words of an ancient leader: "Give me now wisdom and knowledge, that I may go out and come in before this people: for who can judge this thy people, that is so great?"

∽

LYNDON B. JOHNSON, 1965, COMMENT ON HIS DESIRE FOR THE WATER QUALITY ACT TO BE PASSED:

I wanted, as I once expressed it, to leave to future generations "a glimpse of the world as God really made it," not as it looked when we got through with it.

LYNDON B. JOHNSON, JUN. 23, 1967,
AT PRESIDENT'S CLUB DINNER IN LOS ANGELES:

I think you know me well enough to recognize that that is my way of doing things - "Come now," as Isaiah said, "and let us reason together."...that is the way I think we must finally achieve peace. Those who do not smell the powder or hear the blast of cannon, who enjoy the luxury and freedom of free speech and the right to exercise it most freely at times really do not understand the burdens that our Marines are carrying there tonight, who are dying for their country...

But they can't be and still retain our national honor. They can't be and still preserve our freedom. They can't be and still protect our system...Sometimes I think of that Biblical injunction, when I see them advising their fellow citizens to negotiate and saying we want peace and all of those things. I try to look with understanding and charity upon them, and in the words of that Biblical admonition, "God, forgive them for they know not really what they do." I can just say this to you: There is no human being in this world who wants to avoid war more than I do. There is no human being in this world who wants peace in Vietnam or in the Middle East more than I do. When they tell me to negotiate, I say, "Amen."

LYNDON B. JOHNSON, SEP. 1966, IN SUPPORT OF
MODEL CITIES ACT, PASSED BY CONGRESS:

Every family in America deserves a decent home, whether a farmhouse or a city apartment, rented or owned, modest or splendid. What matters is that the home be a place for a family to live in health and grow in dignity. I have been criticized for such statements by people who think I raised hopes that can never be fulfilled, but I believe in the wisdom of the Bible - "Where there is no vision, the people perish."

LYNDON B. JOHNSON, NOV. 2, 1966, IN DULLES AIRPORT
AFTER ASIAN/ PACIFIC TOUR, RECALLING A PRAYER
OFFERED TEN DAYS EARLIER AT SUNDAY SERVICE
THEY ATTENDED IN CATHEDRAL CHURCH OF ST.
JAMES, TOWNSVILLE, NORTHERN AUSTRALIA:

O God, Who has bound us together in the bundle of life, give us grace to understand how our lives depend upon the courage, the industry, the honesty, and the integrity of our fellow men; that we may be mindful of their needs and grateful for their faithfulness, and faithful in our responsibilities to them.

❦

LYNDON B. JOHNSON, MAR. 31, 1968, NOTES CONCERNING HIS SONS-IN-LAW WRITTEN AFTER ATTENDING ST. DOMINIC'S CHURCH, WASHINGTON D.C:

They were so very young, and they had such promising and happy lives ahead of them, if they were lucky. Pat already had his orders for Vietnam. In a matter of days, by his own insistence, he would be with Chuck Robb in action in Vietnam. The good Lord had blessed us with two brave sons-in-law, and no man could have been prouder of them than I. Now, for a year or more, their wives would wait and pray, as other wives across America would, for their husbands to return to them and their babies.

❦

LYNDON B. JOHNSON, MAR. 31, 1968, ADDRESS BROADCAST FROM THE OVAL OFFICE:

In a moment of tragedy and trauma, the duties of this office fell upon me. I asked then for "your help and God's" that we might continue America on its course, binding up our wounds....With America's sons in the field far away, with America's future under challenge right here at home, with our hopes and the world's hopes for peace in the balance every day, I do not believe that I should devote an hour or a day of my time to any personal partisan causes or to any duties other than the awesome duties of this office - the Presidency of your country. Accordingly, I shall not seek, and I will not accept, the nomination of my party for another term as your President.

But let men everywhere know, however, that a strong, a confident, and a vigilant America stands ready tonight to seek an honorable peace - and stands ready tonight to defend an honored cause - whatever the price, whatever the burden, whatever the sacrifice that duty may require. Thank you for listening. Good night and God bless all of you.

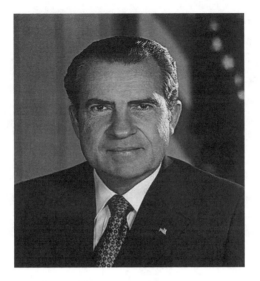

RICHARD M. NIXON

RICHARD NIXON, OCT. 1, 1955, AS VICE-PRESIDENT
CALLING TO ORDER A MEETING OF
THE NATIONAL SECURITY COUNCIL FOLLOWING
PRESIDENT EISENHOWER'S HEART ATTACK.

Gentlemen, as we all know, it is a custom of the Cabinet to open with a silent prayer. While this has not been the practice of the Security Council, may I propose a moment of silent prayer of thanksgiving for the marvelous record of recovery the President has made up to this hour.

⋘

RICHARD NIXON, JAN. 20, 1969, FIRST INAUGURAL:

Standing in this same place a third of a century ago, Franklin Delano Roosevelt addressed a nation ravaged by depression and gripped in fear. He could say in surveying the Nation's troubles: "They concern, thank God, only material things."...No man can be fully free while his neighbor is not. To go forward at all is to go forward together. This means black and white together as one nation, not two. The laws have caught up with our conscience. What remains is to give life to what is in the law: to insure at last that as all are born equal in dignity before God, all are born equal in dignity before man.

✤

RICHARD NIXON, JAN. 20, 1969, FIRST INAUGURAL:

I have taken an oath in the presence of God and my countrymen to uphold and defend the Constitution of the United States. To that oath I now add this sacred commitment: I shall consecrate my Office, my energies, and all the wisdom I can summon to the cause of peace among nations. Let this message be heard by strong and weak alike: The peace we seek - the peace we seek to win - is not victory over any other people but the peace that comes "with healing in its wings."

✤

RICHARD NIXON, JAN. 20, 1969, FIRST INAUGURAL:

Only a few short weeks ago we shared the glory of man's first sight of the world as God sees it, as a single sphere reflecting light in the darkness. As the Apollo astronauts flew over the moon's gray surface on Christmas Eve, they spoke to us of the beauty of earth - and in that voice so clear across the lunar distance, we heard them invoke God's blessing on its goodness. Let us go forward, firm in our faith, steadfast in our purpose, cautious of the dangers, but sustained by our confidence in the will of God.

✤

RICHARD NIXON, JUL. 16, 1969,
ON LAUNCH OF APOLLO 11 FROM CAPE KENNEDY:

Apollo 11 is on its way to the moon. It carries three brave astronauts; it also carries the hopes and prayers of hundreds of millions of people...That moment when man first sets foot on a body other than earth will stand through the centuries as one supreme in human experience...I call upon all of our people...to join in prayer for the successful conclusion of Apollo 11's mission.

✤

RICHARD NIXON, JUL. 29, 1969, SPEAKING
TO APOLLO 11 ASTRONAUTS ON THE MOON:

This certainly has to be the most historic telephone call ever made from the White House...The heavens have become a part of man's world...For one priceless moment in the whole history of man all the people on this earth are truly one...one in our prayers that you will return safely to earth.

❧

RICHARD NIXON, JUL. 24, 1969, GREETING APOLLO 11 ASTRONAUTS ON THE U.S.S. HORNET:

The millions who are seeing us on television now...feel as I do, that...our prayers have been answered...I think it would be very appropriate if Chaplain Piirto, the Chaplain of this ship, were to offer a prayer of thanksgiving.

❧

RICHARD NIXON, APR. 19, 1970, AT KAWAIAHAO CHURCH, OLDEST CHURCH IN HAWAII, ON RETURN OF APOLLO 13:

When we learned of the safe return of our astronauts, I asked that the Nation observe a National Day of Prayer and Thanksgiving today...This event reminded us that in these days of growing materialism, deep down there is still a great religious faith in this Nation...I think more people prayed last week than perhaps have prayed in many years in this country...We pray for the assistance of God when...faced with...great potential tragedy.

❧

RICHARD NIXON, AT KAWAIAHAO CHURCH, BUILT 1836-1842, KNOWN AS WESTMINISTER ABBEY OF HAWAII:

Reverend Akaka...I wanted to attend...this great church, with all of its history that is here...having in mind the fact that today...you will be commemorating the 150th anniversary of Christianity in...these islands.

❧

RICHARD NIXON, JAN., 20, 1973, SECOND INAUGURAL:

We have the chance today to do more than ever before in our history to make life better in America -to ensure better education, better health, better housing, better transportation, a cleaner environment - to restore respect for law, to make our communities more livable - and to insure the God-given right of every American to full and equal opportunity...We shall answer to God, to history, and to our conscience for the way in which we use these years.

᪥

RICHARD NIXON, JAN., 20, 1973, SECOND INAUGURAL:

Today, I ask your prayers that in the years ahead I may have God's help in making decisions that are right for America, and I pray for your help so that together we may be worthy of our challenge...Let us go forward from here confident in hope, strong in our faith in one another, sustained by our faith in God who created us, and striving always to serve His purpose.

᪥

RICHARD NIXON, AUG. 8, 1974, TELEVISED ADDRESS ANNOUNCING HIS RESIGNATION:

As President, I must put the interest of America first. America needs a full-time President and a full-time Congress, particularly at this time with problems we face at home and abroad...To have served in this office is to have felt a very personal sense of kinship with each and every American. In leaving it, I do so with this prayer: May God's grace be with you in all the days ahead.

᪥

RICHARD NIXON, AUG. 8, 1974, PRIVATE FAREWELL TO CABINET, THE WHITE HOUSE STAFF AND FRIENDS:

Mistakes, yes. But for personal gain, never. You did what you believed in. Sometimes right, sometimes wrong...Nobody will ever write a book, probably, about my mother. Well, I guess all of you would say this about you mother - my mother was a saint. And I think of her, two boys dying to tuberculosis, nursing four others in order that she could take care of my older brother for 3 years in Arizona, and seeing each of them die, and when they died, it was like one of her own.

Yes, she will have no books written about her, but she was a saint...Always remember others may hate you, but those who hate you don't win unless you hate them, and then you destroy yourself...I can only say to each and every one of you, we come from many faiths...but really the same God...you will be in our hearts and you will be in our prayers.

᪥

GERALD
FORD

GERALD FORD, AUG. 9, 1974, UPON ASSUMING THE
PRESIDENCY AFTER PRESIDENT NIXON'S RESIGNATION:

I am acutely aware that you have not elected me as your
President by your ballots, and so I ask you to confirm me as your
President with your prayers. And I hope that such prayers will also be
the first of many...Our Constitution works; our great Republic is a
Government of laws and not of men. Here the people rule. But
there is a Higher Power, by whatever name we honor Him, who
ordains not only righteousness but love, not only justice but mercy.

ॐ

GERALD FORD, AUG. 9, 1974, ADDRESS
DELIVERED UPON ASSUMING THE PRESIDENCY:

As we bind up the internal wounds...let us restore the Golden
Rule to our political process, and let brotherly love purge our hearts of
suspicion and of hate. In the beginning, I asked you to pray for me.
Before closing, I ask again your prayers, for Richard Nixon and his
family. May our former President, who brought peace to millions, find

it for himself. May God bless and comfort his wonderful wife and daughters, whose love and loyalty will forever be a shining legacy to all who bear the lonely burdens of the White House...I now solemnly reaffirm my promise I made to you last December 6; to uphold the Constitution, to do what is right as God gives me to see the right, and to do the very best I can for America. God helping me, I will not let you down.

❦

GERALD FORD, AUG. 12, 1974,
1ST ADDRESS TO CONGRESS:

I am not here to make an Inaugural Address. The Nation needs action, not words. Nor will this be a formal report of the State of the Union. God willing, I will have at least three more chances to do that...I do not want a honeymoon with you. I want a good marriage.

❦

GERALD FORD, SEP. 8, 1974, PARDON DECISION:

To procrastinate, to agonize, and to wait for a more favorable turn of events that may never come or more compelling external pressures that may as well be wrong as right, is itself a decision of sorts and a weak and potentially dangerous course for a President to follow. I have promised to uphold the Constitution, to do what is right as God gives me to see the right, and to do the very best that I can for America. I have asked your help and your prayers, not only when I became President but many times since.

The Constitution is the supreme law of our land and it governs our actions as citizens. Only the laws of God, which govern our consciences, are superior to it. As we are a Nation under God, so I am sworn to uphold our laws with the help of God. And I have sought such guidance and searched my own conscience with special diligence to determine the right thing for me to do...I do believe, with all my heart and mind and spirit, that I, not as President, but as a humble servant of God, will receive justice without mercy if I fail to show mercy.

❦

GERALD FORD, DEC. 5, 1974,
NATIONAL DAY OF PRAYER PROCLAMATION:

Without God there could be no American form of government, nor an American way of life. Recognition of the Supreme Being is the first - the most basic - expression of Americanism. Thus the founding fathers of America saw it, and thus with God's help, it will continue to be.

❦

GERALD FORD, DEC. 18, 1975, NATIONALLY BROADCAST MESSAGE AT 22ND ANNUAL PAGENT OF PEACE CEREMONIES, ELLIPSE OF THE WHITE HOUSE:

As we gather here before our Nation's Christmas tree, symbolic of the communion of Americans at Christmastime, we remind ourselves of the eternal truths by which we live. We celebrate the virtues of the human spirit - faith in God and love of one another, and the guiding principles of America - liberty and justice for all. In our 200 years, we Americans have always honored the spiritual testament of 2,000 years ago. We embrace the spirit of the Prince of Peace so that we might find peace in our own hearts and in our own land, and hopefully in the world as well...As we enter America's third century, let us make sure we carry with us our abiding faith in the ultimate triumph of peace on Earth and the living example of good will to all men and women...With the help of God, America's third century will be our proud legacy to so many generations yet to come.

❦

GERALD FORD, DEC. 24, 1975, CHRISTMAS MESSAGE TO THE NATION:

Merry Christmas! These two words conjure up all of the good feelings that mankind has ever held for itself and its Creator: reverence, tenderness, humility, generosity, tolerance-love. These are the stars we try to follow...The spirit of Christmas is ageless, irresistible and knows no barriers. It reaches out to add a glow to the humblest of homes and the stateliest of mansions. It catches up saint and sinner alike in its warm embrace. It is the season to be jolly-but to be silent and prayerful as well. I know this will be a particularly happy Christmas for me...

I celebrate it by joining with all of our citizens in observing a Christmas when Americans can honor the Prince of Peace in a nation at peace...May God's blessings be with you all.

∽

GERALD FORD, DEC. 16, 1976, CHRISTMAS ADDRESS, 23RD ANNUAL PAGENT OF PEACE CEREMONIES, WHITE HOUSE ELLIPSE:

The message of Christmas has not changed over the course of 20 centuries. Peace on Earth, good will towards men-that message is as inspiring today as it was when it was first proclaimed to the shepherds near Bethlehem. It was first proclaimed, as we all know, then. In 1976 America has been blessed with peace and a significant restoration of domestic harmony.

But true peace is more than an absence of battle. It is also the absence of prejudice and the triumph of understanding. Brotherhood among all peoples must be the solid cornerstone of lasting peace. It has been a sustaining force for our Nation, and it remains a guiding light for our future. The celebration of the birth of Jesus is observed on every continent. The customs and traditions are not always the same, but feelings that are generated between friends and family members are equally strong and equally warm..God bless you.

∽

JIMMY CARTER

JIMMY CARTER, MAR. 16, 1976, INTERVIEW WITH
ROBERT L. TURNER DURING PRESIDENTIAL CAMPAIGN:
We believe that the first time we're born, as children, it's human
life given to us; and when we accept Jesus as our Savior, it's a new life.
That's what "born again" means.

⤚

JIMMY CARTER, JUL. 15, 1976, DEMOCRATIC ACCEPTANCE
SPEECH, MADISON SQUARE GARDEN, NEW YORK CITY:
We feel that moral decay has weakened our country...It is now
a time for healing. We want to have faith again!...We will pray for peace
and we will work for peace...

Ours was the first nation to dedicate itself so clearly to basic
moral and philosophical principles:

That all people are created equal and endowed with inalienable
rights to life, liberty, and the pursuit of happiness; and that the power
of government is derived from the consent of the governed.

⤚

JIMMY CARTER, JAN. 20, 1977, INAUGURAL:

Here before me is the Bible used in the inauguration of our first President in 1789, and I have just taken the oath of office on the Bible my mother gave me just a few years ago, opened to the timeless admonition from the ancient prophet Micah: "He hath showed thee, O man, what is good; and what does the Lord require of thee, but to do justly, and to love mercy, and to walk humbly with thy God"

∾

JIMMY CARTER, JAN. 20, 1977, INAUGURAL:

Ours was the first society openly to define itself in terms of both spirituality and of human liberty. It is that unique self-definition which has given us an exceptional appeal, but it also imposes on us a special obligation, to take on those moral duties...

I join in the hope that when my time as your President has ended, people might say this about our Nation: that we had remembered the words of Micah and renewed our search for humility, mercy, and justice.

∾

JIMMY CARTER, DEC. 15, 1977, AT CHRISTMAS PAGENT OF PEACE CEREMONIES ON WHITE HOUSE ELLIPSE:

For more than 50 years, since Calvin Coolidge lived in the White House, every single President has been over to join in the lighting of the National Christmas Tree.

This also commemorates a continuity of beliefs - belief in one another, belief in our Nation, belief in principles like honesty and justice and freedom, and our religious beliefs, above all. Ours is a nation of peace, and I thank God that our Nation is at peace....

A few months ago, I designated DEC. 15, today, as a day of prayer. And I hope that all of you in this great audience and all who watch and listen on television, radio, will make a special promise to yourselves during this holiday season to pray for guidance in our lives, purposes, guidance for the wisdom and commitment and honesty of public officials and other leaders, guidance that we can see our Nation realize its great potential and the vision that formed it 200 years ago, and guidance that we will fulfill our deepest moral and religious commitments....God has blessed us in this country.

Well, in closing, let me say that Christmas has a special meaning for those of us who are Christians, those of us who believe in Christ, those of us who know that almost 2,000 years ago, the Son of Peace was born to give us a vision of perfection, a vision of humility, a vision of unselfishness, a vision of compassion, a vision of love.

❧

JIMMY CARTER, DEC. 18, 1978, CHRISTMAS MESSAGE:

Rosalynn and I send our warmest wishes to our fellow citizens who celebrate the birth of Christ and who rejoice with us in the coming of the peace He symbolizes. We welcome this opportunity to offer our thanks to those who have given us their encouragement and prayers. We also join in this Season's traditional expression of appreciation to God for His blessings in the past year. And we ask for His continuing guidance and protection as we face the challenges of 1979. We hope that the months ahead will be good to each of you and to our country.

❧

JIMMY CARTER, KEEPING THE FAITH -
MEMOIRS OF A PRESIDENT, PUBLISHED 1982:

I was particularly impressed when the officers and enlisted leaders of the armed forces visited...More than any other group, they were likely to make some reference to their prayers for us or to say, "God be with you." Somehow, this emphasis on their religious faith gave me a good feeling. I experienced a sense of brotherhood with them, and remembered from my own eleven years in the Navy that it was members of the military services who most wanted to maintain peace based on a strong America.

❧

JIMMY CARTER, KEEPING THE FAITH -
MEMOIRS OF A PRESIDENT, PUBLISHED 1982:

My most vivid impression of the Presidency remains the loneliness in which the most difficult decisions had to be made...I prayed a lot - more than ever before in my life - asking God to give me a clear mind, sound judgement, and wisdom in dealing with affairs that could affect the lives of so many people in our own country and around the world. Although I cannot claim that my decisions were always the best ones, prayer was a great help to me.

❧

JIMMY CARTER, KEEPING THE FAITH - MEMOIRS OF A PRESIDENT, PUBLISHED 1982:

The Judeo-Christian ethic and study of the Bible were bonds between Jews and Christians which had always been part of my life. I also believed very deeply that the Jews who had survived the Holocaust deserved their own nation, and that they had a right to live in peace among their neighbors. I considered this homeland for the Jews to be compatible with the teachings of the Bible, hence ordained by God. These moral and religious beliefs made my commitment to the security of Israel unshakable.

❧

JIMMY CARTER, 1997, SOURCES OF STRENGTH - MEDITATIONS ON SCRIPTURE FOR A LIVING FAITH:

God doesn't want us to hide our weaknesses...Remember the end of the story of the bleeding woman: Jesus sought her out in the crowd, told her "Your faith has healed you," and urged her, "Go in peace." Because she'd found within herself the courage to reach out to Jesus in her need, she was renewed and made whole, not only in body but in spirit, forgiven and freed from her sins, her subterfuge, and her shame. Christ is ready to do the same for us.

❧

JIMMY CARTER, 1997, SOURCES OF STRENGTH - MEDITATIONS ON SCRIPTURE FOR A LIVING FAITH:

Niebuhr urged Bonhoeffer to remain in America, for his own safety. Bonhoeffer refused. He felt he had to be among the other Christians who he knew were being persecuted in Germany. So he returned home...He preached publicly against Nazism, racism, and anti-Semitism...was finally arrested and imprisoned, and...executed...He died a disciple and a martyr...The same Holy Spirit that energized and encouraged the first disciples, and that gave Dietrich Bonhoeffer the strength to stand up against Nazi tyranny, is available to us.

❧

RONALD REAGAN

RONALD REAGAN, 1978,
LETTER TO A CALIFORNIA PASTOR ABOUT CHRIST:

Either he was what he said he was or he was the world's greatest liar. It is impossible for me to believe a liar or charlatan could have had the effect on mankind that he has had for 2000 years. We could ask, would even the greatest of liars carry his lie through the crucifixion, when a simple confession would have saved him? ...Did he allow us the choice you say that you and others have made, to believe in his teaching but reject his statements about his own identity?

∾

RONALD REAGAN, JAN. 20, 1981, 1ST INAUGURAL:

Your dreams, your hopes, your goals are going to be the dreams, the hopes, and the goals of this administration, so help me God...I am told that tens of thousands of prayer meetings are being held on this day, and for that I am deeply grateful. We are a nation under God, and I believe God intended for us to be free. It would be fitting and good, I think, if on each Inauguration Day in future years it should be declared a day of prayer...The crisis we are facing today...does require, however...to believe that together, with God's help, we can and will resolve the problems which now confront us. And after all, why shouldn't we believe that? We are Americans. God bless you.

৵

RONALD REAGAN, FEB. 5, 1981,
AT NATIONAL PRAYER BREAKFAST

An unknown author wrote of a dream and in the dream was walking down the beach beside the Lord. As they walked, above him in the sky was reflected each stage and experience of his life. Reaching the end of the beach, and of his life, he turned back, looked down the beach, and saw the two sets of footprints in the sand...

He looked again and realized that every once in a while there was one set of footprints. And each time there was only one set of footprints, it was when the experience reflected in the sky was one of despair, of desolation, of great trial or grief in his life...

He turned to the Lord and said, "You said that if I would walk with you, you would always be beside me and take my hand. Why did you desert me? Why are you not there in my times of greatest need?" And the Lord said, "My child, I did not leave you. Where you see only one set of footprints, it was there that I carried you."...

Abraham Lincoln once said, "I would be the most foolish person on this footstool earth if I believed for one moment that I could perform the duties assigned to me without the help of one who is wiser than all." I know that in the days to come and the years ahead there are going to be many times when there will only be one set of footprints in my life. If I did not believe that, I could not face the days ahead.

৵

RONALD REAGAN, MAR. 19, 1981,
NATIONAL DAY OF PRAYER PROCLAMATION:

Our Nation's motto - "In God We Trust" - was not chosen lightly. It reflects a basic recognition that there is a divine authority in the universe to which this nation owes homage. Throughout   our history, Americans have put their faith in God, and no one can doubt that we have been blessed for it. The earliest settlers of this land came in search of religious freedom.

Landing on a desolate shoreline, they established a spiritual foundation that has served us ever since. It was the hard work of our people, the freedom they enjoyed and their faith in God that built this country and made it the envy of the world. In all of our great cities and towns evidence of the faith of our people is found: Houses of worship of every denomination are among the oldest structures. While never willing to bow to a tyrant, our forefathers were always willing to get to their knees before God. When catastrophe threatened, they turned to God for deliverance. When the harvest was bountiful, the first thought was thanksgiving to God.

∽

RONALD REAGAN, MAR. 19, 1981, NATIONAL DAY OF PRAYER PROCLAMATION:

Prayer is today as powerful a force in our nation as it has ever been. We as a nation should never forget this source of strength. And while recognizing that the freedom to choose a Godly path is the essence of liberty, as a nation we cannot but hope that more of our citizens would, through prayer, come into a closer relationship with their Maker. Recognizing our great heritage, the Congress, by Joint Resolution approved April 17, 1952, has called upon the president to set aside a suitable day each year as a National Day of Prayer.

Now, therefore, I, Ronald Reagan, President of the United States of America, do hereby proclaim Thursday, May 7, 1981, National Day of Prayer. On that day I ask all who believe to join me in giving thanks to Almighty God for the blessings He has bestowed on this land and the protection He affords us as a people. Let us as a nation join together before God, fully aware of the trials that lie ahead and the need, yes, the necessity, for divine guidance. With unshakable faith in God and the liberty which is heritage, we as a free nation will surely survive and prosper.

∽

RONALD REAGAN, MAY 17, 1981, COMMENCEMENT EXERCISES OF THE UNIVERSITY OF NOTRE DAME:

It is time for the world to know our intellectual an spiritual values are rooted in the source of all strength, a belief in a Supreme Being, and a law higher than our own.

✧

RONALD REAGAN, SEP. 28, 1981, MEETING OF INTERNATIONAL ASSOCIATION OF CHIEFS OF POLICE:

Only our deep moral values and our strong social institutions can hold back the jungle and restrain the darker impulses of human nature.

✧

RONALD REAGAN, JAN. 19, 1982, NEWS CONFERENCE:

I have been one who believes that abortion is the taking of a human life...The fact that they could not resolve the issue of when life begins was a finding in and of itself. If we don't know, then shouldn't we morally opt on the side of life? If you came upon an immobile body and you yourself could not determine whether it was dead or alive, I think that you would decide to consider it alive until somebody could prove it was dead. You wouldn't get a shovel and start covering it up. And I think we should do the same thing with regard to abortion.

✧

RONALD REAGAN, FEB. 4, 1982, AT ANNUAL NATIONAL PRAYER BREAKFAST:

I've always believed that we were, each of us, put here for a reason, that there is a plan, somehow a divine plan for all of us. I know now that whatever days are left to me belong to Him...I also believe this blessed land was set apart in a very special way, a country created by men and women who came here not in search of gold, but in search of God. They would be free people, living under the law with faith in their Maker and their future. Sometimes it seems we've strayed from that noble beginning, from our conviction that standards of right and wrong do exist and must be lived up to. God, the source of our knowledge, has been expelled from the classroom.

He gives us His greatest blessing - life - and yet many would condone the taking of innocent life. We expect Him to protect us in a crisis, but turn away from Him too often to our day-to-day living. I wonder if He isn't waiting for us to wake up...We have God's promise that what we give will be given back many times over, so let us go forth from here and rekindle the fire of our faith...We are told in II Timothy that when our work is done, we can say, "We have fought the good fight. We have finished the race. We have kept the faith."

≪

RONALD REAGAN, FEB. 9, 1982,
NATIONAL RELIGIOUS BROADCASTERS CONVENTION:

Its been written that the most sublime figure in American history was George Washington on his knees in the snow at Valley Forge. He personified a people who knew that it was not enough to depend on their own courage and goodness, that they must seek help from God - their Father and Preserver. Where did we begin to lose sight of that noble beginning, of our convictions that standards of right and wrong do exist and must be lived up to?

Do we really think that we can have it both ways, that God will protect us in a time of crisis even as we turn away from Him in our day-to-day life?...The Book of St. John tells us, "For God so loved the world that He gave His only begotten Son that whosoever believeth in Him should not perish but have everlasting life."

We have God's promise that what we give will be given back many times over. And we also have His promise that we could take to heart with regard to our country - "That if my people who are called by my name humble themselves and pray and seek my face and turn from their wicked ways, then will I hear from heaven and will forgive their sins and heal their land."...To preserve our blessed land, we must look to God...Rebuilding America begins with restoring family strength and preserving family values.

≪

RONALD REAGAN, FEB. 12, 1982,
NATIONAL DAY OF PRAYER PROCLAMATION:

Through the storms of Revolution, Civil War, and the great World Wars, as well as during the times of disillusionment and disarray, the nation has turned to God in prayer for deliverance. We thank Him for answering our call, for, surely, He has. As a nation, we have been richly blessed with His love and generosity.

≪

RONALD REAGAN, FEB. 26, 1982, CONSERVATIVE
POLITICAL ACTION CONFERENCE DINNER:

We must with calmness and resolve help the vast majority of our fellow Americans understand that the more than one and one-half million abortions performed in America in 1980 amount to a great moral evil, and assault on the sacredness of human life...Let us go forward, determined to serve selflessly a vision of man with God, government for people, and humanity at peace.

∾

RONALD REAGAN, MAR. 15, 1982, ADDRESS TO THE ALABAMA STATE LEGISLATURE:

To those who cite the First Amendment as reason for excluding God from more and more of our institutions and every-day life, may I just say: The First Amendment of the Constitution was not written to protect the people of this country from religious values; it was written to protect religious values from government tyranny.

∾

RONALD REAGAN, MAY 10, 1982, IN AN ADMINISTRATIVE BRIEFING WITH EDITORS FROM THE MIDWEST:

The First Amendment is to protect not government from religion, but religion from government tyranny...The polls show that it is overwhelming, the percentage of people who want prayer restored...We refer to ours as a country under God. It says "In God We Trust" on our coins. They open the Congress sessions with a chaplain. I've never been sure whether he prays for the Congress or for the nation.

∾

RONALD REAGAN, MAY 17, 1982, PROPOSED CONSTITUTIONAL AMENDMENT FOR PRAYER IN SCHOOLS:

The public expression through prayer of our faith in God is a fundamental part of our American heritage and a privilege which should not be excluded by law from any American school, public or private. One hundred fifty years ago, Alexis de Tocqueville found that all Americans believed that religious faith was indispensable to the maintenance of their republican institutions. Today, I join with the people of this nation in acknowledging this basic truth, that our liberty springs from and depends upon an abiding faith in God.

∾

RONALD REAGAN, SEP. 9, 1982, AT ALFRED M. LANDON LECTURE SERIES ON PUBLIC ISSUES:

I know now what I'm about to say will be very controversial, but I also believe that God's greatest gift is human life and that we have a sacred duty to protect the innocent human life of an unborn child...I think the American people are hungry for a spiritual revival. More and more of us are beginning to sense that we can't have it both ways. We can't expect God to protect us in a crisis and just leave Him over there on the shelf in our day-to-day living. I wonder if sometimes He isn't waiting for us to wake up, He isn't maybe running out of patience.

∽

RONALD REAGAN, SEP. 18, 1982, RADIO ADDRESS:

At every crucial turning point in our history Americans have faced and overcome great odds, strengthened by spiritual faith. The Plymouth settlers triumphed over hunger, disease, and a cruel Northern wilderness because, in the words of William Bradford, "They knew they were Pilgrims, so they committed themselves to the will of God and resolved to proceed."

George Washington knelt in prayer at Valley Forge and in the darkest days of our struggle for independence said that "the fate of unborn millions will now depend, under God, on the courage and conduct of this army."

Thomas Jefferson, perhaps the wisest of our founding fathers, had no doubt about the source from which our cause was derived. "The God who gave us life," he declared, "gave us liberty."

And nearly a century later, in the midst of a tragic and at times seemingly hopeless Civil War, Abraham Lincoln vowed that "this nation, under God, shall have a new birth of freedom." It's said that prayer can move mountains.

Well, it's certainly moved the hearts and minds of Americans in their times of trial and helped them to achieve a society that, for all its imperfections, is still the envy of the world and the last, best hope of mankind.

∽

RONALD REAGAN, SEP. 18, 1982, RADIO ADDRESS:

Just as prayer has helped us as a nation, it helps us as individuals. In nearly all our lives, there are moments when our prayers and the prayers of our friends and loved ones help to see us through and keep

[us] on the right path. In fact, prayer is one of the few things in the world that hurts no one and sustains the spirit of millions.

The founding fathers felt this so strongly that they enshrined the principle of freedom of religion in the First Amendment of the Constitution. The purpose of that amendment was to protect religion from the interference of government and to guarantee, in its own words, "the free exercise of religion."

Yet today we're told that to protect that First Amendment, we must suppress prayer and expel God from our children's classrooms. In one case, a court has ruled against the right of children to say grace in their own school cafeteria before they had lunch. A group of children who sought, on their initiative and with their parents' approval, to begin the school day with a one-minute prayer meditation have been forbidden to do so. And some students who wanted to join in prayer or religious study on school property, even outside of regular class hours, have been banned from doing so.

A few people have been objected to prayers being said in Congress. That's just plain wrong. The Constitution was never meant to prevent people from praying; its declared purpose was to protect their freedom to pray. The time has come for this Congress to give a majority of American families what they want for their children - the firm assurance that children can hold voluntary prayers in their schools just as the Congress, itself, begins each of its daily sessions with an opening prayer.

∽

RONALD REAGAN, SEP. 18, 1982, RADIO ADDRESS:

I proposed to the Congress a measure that declares once and for all that nothing in the Constitution prohibits prayer in public schools or institutions. It also states that no person shall be required by government to participate in prayer who does not want to. So, everyone's rights - believers and nonbelievers alike - are protected by our voluntary prayer measure. I'm sorry to say that so far the Congress has failed to vote on the issue of school prayer.

∽

RONALD REAGAN, OCT. 4, 1982, SIGNED JOINT RESOLUTION OF 97TH CONGRESS, PUBLIC LAW 97-280:

Now, Therefore, be it Resolved by the Senate and House of Representatives of the United States of America in Congress assembled, That the President is authorized and requested to designate 1983 as a national "Year of the Bible" in recognition of both the formative influence the Bible has been for our Nation, and our national need to study and apply the teachings of the Holy Scriptures.

※

RONALD REAGAN, JAN. 27, 1983, NATIONAL DAY OF PRAYER PROCLAMATION:

Abraham Lincoln said, "Intoxicated with unbroken success, we have become too self-sufficient to feel the necessity of redeeming and preserving grace, too proud to pray to the God that made us." Revived as an annual observance by Congress in 1952, the National Day of Prayer has become a great unifying force for our citizens...This common expression of reverence heals and brings us together as a nation, and we pray it may one day bring renewed respect for God to all peoples of the world.

※

RONALD REAGAN, JAN. 31, 1983, ANNUAL CONVENTION OF NATIONAL RELIGIOUS BROADCASTERS:

When American reach out for values of faith, family, and caring for the needy, they're saying, "We want the Word of God. We want to face the future with the Bible." We're blessed to have its words of strength, comfort, and truth. I'm accused of being simplistic at times with some of the problems that confront us. But I've often wondered: Within the covers of that single Book are all the answers to all the problems that face us today, if we'd only look there.

"The grass withereth, the flower fadeth, but the word of our God shall stand forever." It's my firm belief that the enduring values, as I say, presented in its pages have a great meaning for each of us and for our nation. The Bible can touch our hearts, order our minds, refresh our souls.

※

RONALD REAGAN, JAN. 31, 1983, ANNUAL CONVENTION OF NATIONAL RELIGIOUS BROADCASTERS:

Now, I realize it's fashionable in some circles to believe that no one in government should...encourage others to read the Bible...

We're told that will violate the constitutional separation of church and state established by the founding fathers in the First Amendment. Well, it might interest those critics to know that none other than the father of our country, George Washington, kissed the Bible at his inauguration.

And he also said words to the effect that there could be no real morality in a society without religion. John Adams called it "the best book in the world," and Ben Franklin said, "...the longer I live, the more convincing proofs I see of this truth, that God governs in the affairs of men...without His concurring aid, we shall succeed in this political building no better than the builders of Babel; we shall be divided by our little, partial, local interests, our projects will be confounded, and we ourselves shall become a reproach, a bye-word down to future ages."...

All of us, as Protestants, Catholics, and Jews, have a special responsibility to remember our fellow believers who are being persecuted in other lands. We're all children of Abraham. We're children of the same God.

◈

RONALD REAGAN, AUG. 1, 1983, ANNUAL MEETING OF THE AMERICAN BAR ASSOCIATION, ATLANTA, GEORGIA:

It's not good enough to have equal access to our law; we must also have equal access to the higher law - the law of God. George Washington warned that morality could not prevail in exclusion of religious principles. And Jefferson asked, "Can the liberties of a nation be thought secure, when we've removed their only firm basis, a conviction in the minds of people that these liberties are the gifts of God?" We must preserve the noble promise of the American dream for every man, woman, and child in this land. And make no mistake, we can preserve it, and we will.

That promise was not created by America. It was given to America as a gift from a loving God - a gift proudly recognized by the language of liberty in the world's greatest charters of freedom: our Declaration of Independence, the Constitution, and the Bill of Rights...The explicit promise in the Declaration that we're endowed by our Creator with certain inalienable rights was meant for all of us. It wasn't meant to be limited or perverted by special privilege or by double standards...Trusting in God and helping one another, we can and will preserve the dream of America, the last best hope of man on earth.

∽

RONALD REAGAN, JAN. 21, 1985, 2ND INAUGURAL:

God bless you and welcome back...I wonder if we could all join in a moment of silent prayer...This is...the 50th time that we the people have celebrated this historic occasion. When the first President, George Washington, placed his hand upon the Bible, he stood less than a single day's journey by horseback from raw, untamed wilderness. So much has changed. And yet we stand together as we did two centuries ago...One people under God determined that our future shall be worthy of our past.

∽

RONALD REAGAN, AUG. 23, 1984, AT ECUMENICAL
PRAYER BREAKFAST, REUNION ARENA, DALLAS, TX,
FOLLOWING ENACTMENT OF 1984 EQUAL ACCESS BILL:

In 1962, the Supreme Court in the New York prayer case banned the...saying of prayers. In 1963, the Court banned the reading of the Bible in our public schools. From that point on, the courts pushed the meaning of the ruling ever outward, so that now our children are not allowed voluntary prayer.

We even had to pass a law - pass a special law in the Congress just a few weeks ago - to allow student prayer groups the same access to school rooms after classes that a Young Marxist Society, for example, would already enjoy with no opposition...

The 1962 decision opened the way to a flood of similar suits. Once religion had been made vulnerable, a series of assaults were made in one court after another, on one issue after another. Cases were started to argue against tax-exempt status for churches. Suits were brought to abolish the words "Under God" from the Pledge of Allegiance, and to remove "In God We Trust" from public documents and from our currency.

Without God there is no virtue because there is no prompting of the conscience...without God there is a coarsening of the society; without God democracy will not and cannot long endure...

America needs God more than God needs America. If we ever forget that we are One Nation Under God, then we will be a Nation gone under.

∽

RONALD REAGAN, DEC. 19, 1988,
MESSAGE ON THE OBSERVANCE OF CHRISTMAS:

The themes of Christmas and of coming home for the holidays have long been intertwined in song and story. There is a profound irony and lesson in this, because Christmas celebrates the coming of a Savior Who was born without a home. There was no room at the inn for the Holy Family. Weary of travel, a young Mary close to childbirth and her carpenter husband Joseph found but the rude shelter of a stable.

There was born the King of Kings, the Prince of Peace-an event on which all history would turn. Jesus would again be without a home, and more than once; on the flight to Egypt and during His public ministry, when He said, "The foxes have holes, and the birds of the air have nests; but the Son of man hath no where to lay his head."

From His very infancy, on, our Redeemer was reminding us that from then on we would never lack a home in Him. Like the shepherds to whom the angel of the Lord appeared on the first Christmas Day, we could always say, "Let us now go even unto Bethlehem, and see this thing which is come to pass, which the Lord hath made known unto us."

As we come home with gladness to family and friends this Christmas, let us also remember our neighbors who cannot go home themselves.

Our compassion and concern this Christmas and all year long will mean much to the hospitalized, the homeless, the convalescent, the orphaned-and will surely lead us on our way to the joy and peace of Bethlehem and the Christ Child Who bids us come. For it is only in finding and living the eternal meaning of the Nativity that we can be truly happy, truly at peace, truly home. Merry Christmas, and God bless you!

∽

GEORGE H.W. BUSH

GEORGE H.W. BUSH, JAN. 20, 1989, INAUGURAL:

I have just repeated word for word the oath taken by George Washington 200 years ago, and the Bible on which I place my hand is the Bible on which he place his...My first act as President is a prayer. I ask you to bow your heads...Heavenly Father, we bow our heads and thank You for Your love. Accept our thanks for the peace that yields this day and the shared faith that makes its continuance likely. Make us strong to do Your work, willing to heed and hear Your will, and write on our hearts these words: "Use power to help people." For we are given power not to advance our own purposes, nor to make a great show in the world, nor a name. There is but one just use of power, and it is to serve people. Help us to remember it, Lord. Amen.

❧

GEORGE H.W. BUSH, JAN. 20, 1989, INAUGURAL:

We as a society must rise up united and express our intolerance. The most obvious now is drugs. And when that first cocaine was smuggled in on a ship, it may as well have been a deadly bacteria, so much has it hurt the body, the soul of our country...Our challenges are great, but our will is greater. And if our flaws are endless, God's love is truly boundless...God bless you and God bless the United States of America.

∽

GEORGE H.W. BUSH, FEB. 26, 1989, PRAYER SERVICE, CHONGMENWEN CHRISTIAN CHURCH, BEIJING, CHINA:

Pastor Kan and Pastor Shi and Pastor Yin, thank you, and thank this congregation for your generosity...It is a special pleasure for Barbara and me to return to this special place of worship. We have so many fond memories of our time in Beijing...The building is different, but the church itself is the same; the spirit is the same. Our family has always felt that church is the place to seek guidance and seek strength and peace...This church, in a sense, was our home away from home...Today we came up with 20 motorcars in a motorcade, and I used to come to church on my bicycle, my Flying Pigeon. But it doesn't matter how you come to church; the important thing is that the feeling is the same, the feeling of being in the spirit of Jesus Christ. And, yes, our daughter, Dorothy, now the mother of two children, was baptized in this church; and that gives us a special feeling of identity and warmth.

∽

GEORGE H.W. BUSH, MAR. 22, 1989, MEETING WITH AMISH & MENNONITE LEADERS IN LANCASTER, PA:

Barbara and I went to China...in 1974...And we had wondered about the family in China-Communist country, totalitarian-and the common perception was that there had been an erosion of the strength of family. We knew that there had been a banning-almost entire banning on practicing and teaching Christianity. That was a given...Our daughter was christened in a church service where there was maybe 10 or 12 Westerners and 5 or 6 faithful Chinese who were permitted in what used to be the YMCA to have this Sunday service, mainly for diplomats...In 1989 I went back there as President of the United States. The church had moved even. Now it was in what they call a hutong, an alley. But it moved into an even bigger building. There was close to 1,000 people in it. The choir had vestments. They were able to have hymn books. And the Bible was read from. And the message that I got from all of this is not that there's freedom of worship in China yet-there's not-but that it is moving....faith can't be crushed by a state doctrine.

৵

GEORGE H.W. BUSH, MAR. 28, 1989, Q&A WITH STUDENTS, LIBRARY, JAMES MADISON HIGHSCHOOL, VIENNA, VA:

A lot of people wonder and talk about...the Thousand Points of Light?...You going out and helping some kid that may be tempted to use narcotics. Somebody else mentioned her church group doing something. There's a second point of light. And you can go on and on and on. It's the Red Cross; it's day care centers of a voluntary nature; it is the Boy Scouts; it is Christian Athletes. It is almost anything you can think of that comes under the heading of voluntarism.

৵

GEORGE H.W. BUSH, JUN. 20, 1989, CEREMONY FOR PRESIDENTIAL SCHOLARS AWARDS, WHITE HOUSE:

I'm reminded of how once, marking an examination paper written shortly before Christmas, the noted scholar teaching at Yale, William Lyons Phelps, came across this note: "God only knows the answer to this question. Merry Christmas!" Phelps returned the paper with the annotation: "God gets an A. You get an F. Happy New Year!"

৵

GEORGE H.W. BUSH, AUG. 15, 1989, 20TH NEWS CONFERENCE, BRIEFING ROOM, WHITE HOUSE:

Q. "What is the United States doing, if anything, to try and stop the destruction of Beirut? Is it a fear that if the Syrians succeed in driving the Christians out, that will seriously set back any progress that's been made on settling the West Bank and Gaza problem?"

PRESIDENT: "We're in a very complicated situation in the Lebanon...I am literally heartbroken...I've been to the Lebanon when I was in business, and I recall it as the peaceful oasis in a then-troubled Middle East, and I saw Christians living peacefully with the Moslems. And someday again, I'd like to think that the Lebanon can be restored to that."

৵

GEORGE H.W. BUSH, FEB. 22, 1990, DECLARING 1990 THE INTERNATIONAL YEAR OF BIBLE READING:

Among the great books produced throughout the history of

mankind, the Bible has been prized above all others by generations of men and women around the world - by people of every age, every race, and every walk of life. The Bible has had a critical impact upon the development of Western civilization. Western literature, art, and music are filled with images and ideas that can be traced to its pages. More important, our moral tradition has been shaped by the laws and teachings it contains. It was a biblical view of man - one affirming the dignity and worth of the human person, made in the Image of our Creator - that inspired the principles upon which the United States in founded. President Jackson called the Bible "the Rock on which our Republic rests" because he knew that it shaped the Founding Fathers' concept of individual liberty and their vision of a free and just society.

∽

GEORGE H.W. BUSH, FEB. 22, 1990, YEAR OF BIBLE READING:

The Bible has not only influenced the development of our Nation's values and institutions but also enriched the daily lives of millions of men and women who have looked to it for comfort, hope, and guidance. On the American frontier, the Bible was often the only book a family owned. For those pioneers living far from any church or school, it served both as a source of religious instruction and as the primary text from which children learned to read. The historic speeches of Abraham Lincoln and Dr. Martin Luther King, Jr., provide compelling evidence of the role Scripture played in shaping the struggle against slavery and discrimination...The Bible continues to give courage and direction to those who seek truth and righteousness. In recognizing its enduring value, we recall the words of the prophet Isaiah, who declared, "The grass withereth, the flower fadeth; but the word of our God shall stand forever." Containing revelations of God's intervention in human history, the Bible offers moving testimony to His love for mankind.

∽

GEORGE H.W. BUSH, FEB. 22, 1990, YEAR OF BIBLE READING:

Treasuring the Bible as a source of knowledge and inspiration. President Abraham Lincoln call this Great Book "the best gift God has given to man." President Lincoln believed that the Bible not only reveals the infinite goodness of our Creator, but also reminds us of our worth as individuals and our responsibilities toward one another.

President Woodrow Wilson likewise recognized the importance of the Bible to its readers. "The Bible is the word of life," he once said. Describing its contents, he added:

"You will find it full of real men and women not only but also of the things you have wondered about and been troubled about all your life, as men have been always; and the more you will read it the more it will become plain to you what things are worth while and what are not, what things make men happy - loyalty, right dealing, speaking the truth...and the things that are guaranteed to make men unhappy - selfishness, cowardice, greed, and everything that is low and mean. When you have read the Bible you will know that it is the Word of God, because you will have found it the key to your own heart, your own happiness, and your own duty."

President Wilson believed that the Bible helps its readers find answers to the mysteries and sorrows that often trouble the souls of men. Cherished for centuries by men and women around the world, the Bible's value is timeless. Its significance transcends the boundaries between nations and languages because it carries a universal message to every human heart.

ᕽ

GEORGE H.W. BUSH, FEB. 22, 1990, YEAR OF BIBLE READING:

This year numerous individuals and associations around the world will join in a campaign to encourage voluntary study of the Bible. Their efforts are worthy of recognition and support. In acknowledgment of the inestimable value and timeless appeal of the Bible, the Congress, by Senate Joint Resolution 164, has designated the year 1990 as the "International Year of Bible Reading" and has authorized and requested the President to issue a proclamation in observance of this year. NOW, THEREFORE, I, GEORGE BUSH, President of the United States of America, do hereby proclaim the year 1990 as the International Year of Bible Reading. I invite all Americans to discover the great inspiration and knowledge that can be obtained through thoughtful reading of the Bible. IN WITNESS WHEREOF, I have hereunto set my hand this twenty-second day of February, in the year of our Lord nineteen hundred and ninety.

ᕽ

GEORGE H.W. BUSH, APR. 17, 1990, ON RALPH ABERNATHY:
In recalling Ralph Abernathy's life, we inevitably recall the great campaigns for civil rights for black Americans in which he played such a signal part. From his father's farm in Alabama, he joined the ministry and became pastor of the First Baptist Church in Montgomery. Responding to Rosa Parks' refusal to sit in the back of a segregated bus, he and the Rev. Dr. Martin Luther King, Jr., began the Montgomery Improvement Association to ensure the success of the boycott which led in turn to the desegregation of buses in that city. Later, he and Dr. King organized the Southern Christian Leadership Conference...Rev. Abernathy was committed to the principle of nonviolence. As he said, "Violence is the weapon of the weak, and nonviolence is the weapon of the strong."

୬

GEORGE H.W. BUSH, MAY 3, 1990, NATIONAL DAY OF PRAYER:
The great faith that led our Nation's Founding Fathers to pursue this bold experience in self-government has sustained us in uncertain and perilous times; it has given us strength and inspiration to this very day. Like them, we do very well to recall our "firm reliance on the protection of Divine Providence," to give thanks for the freedom and prosperity this Nation enjoys, and to pray for continued help and guidance from our wise and loving Creator.

୬

GEORGE H.W. BUSH, 1990, THANKSGIVING PROCLAMATION:
The historic observance of a day of thanksgiving at Plymouth, in 1621, was one of many occasions on which our ancestors paused to acknowledge their dependence on the mercy and favor of Divine Providence...Our "errand in the wilderness," begun more than 350 years ago, is not yet complete...We seek lasting solutions to the problems facing our nation and pray for a society "with liberty and justice for all,"...I call upon the American people to...gather together in homes and places of worship on that day of thanks to affirm by their prayers and their gratitude the many blessings God has bestowed upon us.

୬

GEORGE H.W. BUSH, JUN. 6, 1991, SOUTHERN BAPTIST CONVENTION, GEORGIA WORLD CONGRESS CENTER:
American values are ascendant around the world. Look at

Eastern Europe and the Soviet Union: there, places of worship long stood silent and subdued, forced underground by the iron fist of the state. But now...reclaimed by the people, joyfully emerging to proclaim their faith anew. In Africa and Asia and Latin America, your ministries flourish and spread the word of God around the world. And even in the heat of the Persian Gulf, nearly 200 Southern Baptist chaplains reported that well over 1,000 conversions among the service men and women of Operation Desert Storm had taken place, and some solemnified with poncho-lined holes in the sand serving as makeshift baptistries. Southern Baptists have been doing quiet but crucial work, engaging in countless acts of kindness and compassion, spreading the word of God...You prove that the flower of faith can bloom anywhere; that no matter how hard the journey, no matter how humble a surroundings, God's love provides.

∽

GEORGE H.W. BUSH, JUN. 6, 1991, SOUTHERN BAPTIST CONV:
During the Gulf crisis...this nation found guidance and comfort in prayer...Your prayers sustained us...I want to thank you all and ask that you keep those in the decision-making process in your prayers...For me, prayer has always been important, but quite personal. You know us Episcopalians. And like a lot of people, I've worried a little bit about shedding tears in public or the emotion of it. But as Barbara and I prayed at Camp David before the air war began, we were thinking about those young men and women overseas. And I had the tears start down the cheeks...I no longer worried how it looked to others....I think that, like a lot of others who had positions or responsibility in sending someone else's kid to war, we realize that in prayer what mattered is how it might have seemed to God...After all the months of praying and asking for God's guidance, I thought it important to thank God for sustaining our nation through this crisis. And that led to three National Days of Thanksgiving and Prayer, which I really believed strengthened our wonderful nation.

∽

GEORGE H.W. BUSH, JUN. 6, 1991, SOUTHERN BAPTIST CONV.:
We Americans have weakened the two fundamental pillars supporting our society, our families and our faith...A recent survey, 40 percent of Americans named "faith in God" the most important part of their lives. Only 2 percent selected "a job that pays well."

In this bicentennial year of the Bill of Rights, we would do well to pause and reflect on...our society's roots in religion. The Founding Fathers thought long and carefully about the role of religion and government in our society. And it's no accident that among all of the freedoms guaranteed by the first amendment-freedoms of speech, of the press, of assembly, of petition-the first was the freedom of religion.

∽

GEORGE H.W. BUSH, JUN. 6, 1991, SOUTHERN BAPTIST CONV.:

A little girl named Monette Rethford, out in Norman, Oklahoma, is now getting national attention. A fifth-grader in public elementary school, Monette liked to read her Bible under a shade tree during recess. No teachers involved, no disruption of the school activities. Just Monette and then, from time to time, a handful of friends who joined her voluntarily to share their faith and discuss how it touched their daily lives. Yet school officials told Monette that her prayer group was illegal on school property, an "unlawful assembly." They forgot that the first amendment was written to protect people against religious intrusions by the state, not to protect the state from voluntary religious activities by the people. I would add this: that the day a child's quiet, voluntary group during recess becomes an "unlawful assembly," something's wrong...I call on the United States Congress to pass a constitutional amendment permitting voluntary prayer back into our nation's schools...Let's put people first and allow them the freedom to follow their faith.

∽

GEORGE H.W. BUSH, JUN. 6, 1991, SOUTHERN BAPTIST CONV.:

We are, as ever, "One nation under God."...A Kurdish family, Mikail and Safiya Dosky...escaped from Iraq over a decade ago. During their perilous journey across the Iranian border, they became separated from their 2-year-old daughter, Gilawish...After settling in America, Mikail, the father, kept trying to get his daughter out of Iraq...A few weeks ago, the dad, Mikail, got a phone call from an American helicopter pilot in Turkey, one of our heroes. This pilot had been flying supplies to save the lives of these Kurdish refugees when he got a note from Gilawish...now 18 years old-asking him to call her parents in America. He did, and Mikail's friends at the First Baptist Church in Alexandria, Virginia, helped him get to Turkey and bring his daughter back. And after thousands of miles, thousands of days, and thousands of dollars, Mikail and Gilawish arrived in America Tuesday night - where years of sorrow were washed away with tears of joy.

What a testament to the power of faith and hope and love, all of which God provides in abundance...I understand what Lincoln talked about when he said many times he went to his knees as President of the United States. And as the Psalmist wrote, "God is our refuge and strength, a very present help in trouble." God's light leads us forward. And today, as always, let us pray for His continued guidance and His grace.

∽

GEORGE H.W. BUSH, DEC. 11, 1991, CHRISTMAS MESSAGE:

At Christmas, we celebrate the promise of salvation that God gave to mankind almost 2,000 years ago. The birth of Christ changed the course of history, and His life changed the soul of man. Christ taught that giving is the greatest of all aspirations and that the redemptive power of love and sacrifice is stronger than any force of arms. It is testimony to the wisdom and the truth of these teachings that they have not only endured but also flourished over two millennia. Blessed with an unparalleled degree of freedom and security, generations of Americans have been able to celebrate Christmas with open joy...The triumph of democratic ideals and the lessening of global tensions give us added reason for celebration this Christmas season, and as the world community draws closer together, the wisdom of Christ's counsel to "love thy neighbor as thyself" grows clearer.

By His words and by His example, Christ has called us to share our many blessings with others...There are countless ways that we can extend to others the same love and mercy that God showed humankind when He gave us His only Son. During this holy season...let us look to the selfless spirit of giving that Jesus embodied as inspiration in our own lives-giving thanks for what God has done for us and abiding by Christ's teaching to do for others as we would do for ourselves.

∽

GEORGE H.W. BUSH, 1992, NATIONAL DAY OF PRAYER:

Whatever our individual religious convictions may be, each of us is invited to join in this National Day of Prayer...Each of us can echo this timeless prayer of Solomon, the ancient king who prayed for, and received, the gift of wisdom: "The Lord our God be with us, as He was with our fathers; may He not leave us or forsake us; so that He may incline our hearts to Him, to walk in all His ways...that all the peoples of the earth may know that the Lord is God; there is no other."

༄

GEORGE H.W. BUSH, DEC. 8, 1992, ON CHRISTMAS:

During the Christmas season, millions of people around the world gather with family and friends...to recall the events that took place in Bethlehem almost 2,000 years ago. As we celebrate the birth of Jesus Christ, whose life offers us a model of dignity, compassion, and justice, we renew our commitment to peace and understanding throughout the world. Through His words and example, Christ made clear the redemptive value of giving of oneself for others, and His life proved that love and sacrifice can make a profound difference in the world. Over the years, many Americans have made sacrifices in order to promote freedom and human rights around the globe...All have enriched humankind and affirmed the importance of our Judeo-Christian heritage in shaping our government and values. This Christmas we are especially grateful for the expansion of democracy and hope throughout the former Soviet Union, Eastern Europe, and elsewhere.

༄

GEORGE BUSH, DEC. 10, 1992, LIGHTING CHRISTMAS TREE:

It's especially wonderful to see the children. This is their holiday, an entire season dedicated to the impact of one child on the world...We must love one another in order to achieve peace...Let us also say a special prayer for our Armed Forces who are doing their duty, vindicating the values of America and the spirit of Christmas in this far-off land...God bless you all, and God bless our great country.

༄

GEORGE H.W. BUSH, SEP. 28, 2001, TO TOM BROKAW, NBC NIGHTLY NEWS, AFTER 911, REGARDING HIS SON, GEORGE:

This thing about faith - I mean this is real for him...Here's a man that's read the Bible through twice, and it's not to make it holier-than-thou or not to make a political point. It's something that is in his heart. And we see it all the time.

༄

BILL
CLINTON

BILL CLINTON, JAN. 20, 1993, 1ST INAUGURAL:

When our Founders boldly declared America's Independence to the world and our purposes to the Almighty, they knew that America, to endure, would have to change...At the edge of the 21st century, let us begin with energy and hope, with faith and discipline, and let us work until our work is done. The Scripture says, "And let us not be weary in well-doing, for in due season, we shall reap, if we faint not."...With God's help, we must answer the call. Thank you and God bless you.

∞

BILL CLINTON, FEB. 4, 1993, NATIONAL PRAYER BREAKFAST:

The first time I ever saw Billy Graham...he came in the 1950's, in the heat of all our racial trouble, to Arkansas to have a crusade. And the white citizens council tried to get him, because of the tensions of the moment, to agree to segregate his crusade...He said, "If I have to do that, I'm not coming." And I remember I got a Sunday school teacher in my church-and I was about 11 years old-to take me 50 miles to Little Rock so I could hear a man preach who was trying to live by what he said.

And then I remember, for a good while thereafter, trying to send a little bit of my allowance to the Billy Graham crusade because of the impression he made on me.

᙮

BILL CLINTON, FEB. 4, 1993, NATIONAL PRAYER BREAKFAST:

We come here to seek the help and guidance of our Lord, putting aside our differences, as men and women who freely acknowledge that we don't have all the answers...We need faith as a source of strength. "The assurance of things hoped for, the conviction of things unseen," the Scripture says...We need our faith as a source of hope because it teaches us that each of us is capable of redemption...We need our faith as a source of challenge because if we read the Scriptures carefully, it teaches us that all of us must try...to live out the admonition of President Kennedy that here on Earth God's work must truly be our own...We need our faith...as a source of humility, to remember that, as Bishop Sheen said, we are all sinners. St. Paul once said in an incredibly moving Scripture in the Bible, "The very thing which I would not do, that I do, and that which I would, that I do not." And even more, not only because we do wrong but because we don't always know what is right. In funerals and weddings and other important ceremonies, you often hear that wonderful verse from Corinthians cited: "Now abideth faith, hope, and love, but the greatest of these is love."

᙮

BILL CLINTON, FEB. 4, 1993, NATIONAL PRAYER BREAKFAST:

"Now I see through a glass, darkly...now I know only in part." None of us know all that we need to know to do what we need to do. I have always been touched by the living example of Jesus Christ and moved particularly by all the religious leaders of His day who were suspicious of Him and always trying to trap Him because He was so at ease with the hurting and the hungry and the lonely and, yes, the sinners. And in one of those marvelous attempts to trick Christ, He was asked, "What is the greatest Commandment?" And He answered, quoting Moses, "You shall love the Lord, your God, with all your heart and with all your soul and with all your mind." And then He added, as we should add, "This is the great and foremost Commandment. And the second is like it: You shall love your neighbor as yourself."...I took the oath of office as President. You know the last four words..."so help me God."...Deep down inside I wanted to say it the way I was thinking it, which was, "So, help me, God."

∞

BILL CLINTON, APR. 3, 1993,
RADIO ADDRESS, BENSON HOTEL, PORTLAND:

There's much wisdom in these words from the Scriptures, "Come, let us reason together."

∞

BILL CLINTON, APR. 22, 1993, VOLUNTEER CEREMONY:

Just a few moments ago, I was over at the dedication of the Holocaust Museum. And we recognized, of course, the great losses of the Jewish people, of the Gypsies, and others who were systematically exterminated by the Nazis. But we also recognize...those who put their lives at risk to try to save large numbers of the Jews...The most popular speaker at the event was a woman who put her life at risk to shield Jews from almost certain death and, in the process, found a person who became her husband. The Scriptures say that in giving we will receive.

∞

BILL CLINTON, MAY 5, 1993, WELCOMING MILITARY
PERSONNEL RETURNING FROM SOMALIA:

You sometimes were subjected to abuse and forced to dodge rocks and even bullets...But you pressed on with what you set out to do, and you were successful. You have served in the best tradition of the Armed Forces of the United States, and you have made the American people very, very proud...In the words of the Scriptures: "Blessed are the peacemakers."

∞

BILL CLINTON, MAY 12, 1993, AT COOPER UNION FOR
ADVANCEMENT OF SCIENCE & ART, NEW YORK CITY:

The human condition in the end changes by faith. And faith cannot be held in your hand. The Scripture that I carry to my place of worship every Sunday says, "Faith is the assurance of things hoped for, the conviction of things unseen." But make no mistake about it, it is by far the most powerful force that can ever be mustered in the cause of change...We are seeing too much cynicism and too little faith...

Mr. Lincoln closed his Cooper Union speech with the following words: "Let us have faith that right makes might, and in that faith, let us to the end dare to do our duty as we understand it."

∽

BILL CLINTON, MAY 29, 1993, AT U.S. MILITARY ACADEMY COMMENCEMENT, WEST POINT, NY:

Two centuries ago at this bend in the Hudson River, America's first defenders stretched a chain across the river to prevent British ships from dividing and conquering our new Nation. Today we add 1,003 new links to that unbroken chain of America's defenders, 1,003 new and solid segments in the Long Gray Line, a line that stretches back 191 years through your ranks and as far into the future as the Lord lets the United States of America exist....and give other people the opportunity to live as you have lived, to fulfill your God-given capacities.

∽

BILL CLINTON, MAY 31, 1993, MEMORIAL DAY CEREMONY:

The inscription on the Tomb of the Unknown Soldier says that he is "Known only to God." But that is only partly true. While the soldier's name is known only to God, we know a lot about him. We know he served his country, honored his community, and died for the cause of freedom...

From these, our honored dead, we draw strength and inspiration to carry on in our time the tasks of defending and preserving freedom...In the presence of those buried all around us, we ask the support of all Americans in the aid and blessing of God Almighty.

∽

BILL CLINTON, JUN. 29, 1993, ON INDEPENDENCE DAY:

On Independence Day, we celebrate the birth of the first and greatest democracy of the modem era. The ideals embodied by the Declaration of Independence have served as...an inspiration for people around the world. This document delineated the very idea of America, that individual rights are derived not from the generosity of the government, but from the hand of the Almighty. The Founders forever abandoned their allegiance to the old European notions of caste and instead dedicated themselves to the belief that all people are created equal.

∽

BILL CLINTON, AUG. 12, 1993, REMARKS AFTER MEETING
POPE JOHN PAUL II AT REGIS UNIVERSITY, DENVER:

I, like every other person who has ever met him, was profoundly impressed by the depth of His Holiness' conviction, the depth of his faith, and the depth of his commitment to continue on his mission. I very much welcome the Vatican's commitment to human rights, including religious freedom for all. I welcome the progress that is being made in forging relationships and closer ties between the Vatican and Israel...Let me just say once again how very grateful I am to the Holy Father for coming to World Youth Day here in Denver and for the Catholic Church's decision to bring World Youth Day to the United States... The Holy Father presented me with a Bible. And so, I close with a verse from it that I think characterizes his work and I hope in due time will characterize the work that we are doing here, the exhortation in St. Paul's letter to the Galatians, "Let us not grow weary while doing good, for in due season we shall reap if we do not lose heart."

≪

BILL CLINTON, AUG. 30, 1993, INTERFAITH BREAKFAST:

I bought a book on vacation called "The Culture of Disbelief" by Stephen Carter, a professor at our old alma mater, Hillary's and mine, at the Yale Law School. He is himself a committed Christian, very dedicated to the religious freedoms of all people of faith, of any faith, in the United States. And the subtitle of the book is "How American Law and Politics Trivialize Religious Devotion." And I would urge you all to read it from whatever political as well as religious spectrum you have because at least it lays a lot of these issues out that I am trying to grapple with. Sometimes I think the environment in which we operate is entirely too secular. The fact that we have freedom of religion doesn't mean we need to try to have freedom from religion. It doesn't mean that those of us who have faith shouldn't frankly admit that we are animated by the faith, that we try to live by it, and that it does affect what we feel, what we think, and what we do.

≪

BILL CLINTON, SEP. 9, 1993, ON ROSH HASHANA:

The days between Rosh Hashana and Yom Kippur are the most solemn of the Hebrew calendar. But in the midst of heartfelt repentance and prayer, it is the promise of life-the rich possibility of realizing our most compelling dreams-that inspires the soul and lifts the spirit. The ancient customs that are handed down to each new generation in this season are reminders of life's enduring sweetness and its perpetual renewal. The Jewish people celebrate Rosh Hashana above all as a time to rejoice in God for giving us life, for sustaining us, and for again enabling us to reach this season.

✦

BILL CLINTON, SEP. 13, 1993, INTERVIEW AFTER ISRAELI-PALESTINIAN DECLARATION OF PRINCIPLES CEREMONY:
The sound we heard today, once again, as in ancient Jericho, was of trumpets toppling walls, the walls of anger and suspicion between Israeli and Palestinian, between Arab and Jew. This time, praise God, the trumpets heard were not the destruction of that city but its new beginning. Now let each of us here today return to our portion of that effort...guided by the wisdom of the Almighty.

✦

**BILL CLINTON, SEP. 21, 1993, SIGNING
THE NATIONAL & COMMUNITY SERVICE TRUST ACT:**
There are millions of Americans who are not really free today because they cannot reach down inside them and bring out what was put there by the Almighty...The young people of America will preserve the freedom of America for themselves and for all those of their generations by assuming the responsibility to rebuild the American family.

✦

**BILL CLINTON, SEP. 27, 1993, TO 48TH SESSION,
U.N. GENERAL ASSEMBLY, NEW YORK CITY:**
Let us work with new energy to protect the world's people from torture and repression...Human rights are not something conditional, founded by culture, but rather something universal granted by God.

✦

**BILL CLINTON, SEP. 30, 1993, ON RETIREMENT OF
GENERAL COLIN POWELL, FT. MYER, ARLINGTON, VA:**
Thomas Jefferson wrote, "The Creator has not thought proper to mark those in the forehead who are of stuff to make good generals." The Creator has not thought proper to mark them by the color of their

skin or the station of their birth or the place they were born. Thank God for the United States that that is so....General Powell, I am reminded of the words of another young valiant warrior, spoken when, like you, he was finishing one journey...John Bunyan wrote in Pilgrim's Progress of the warrior valiant at the end of his life, as he prepared to present himself to the Almighty, "My sword I give to him that shall succeed me in my pilgrimage and my courage and skill to him that can get them. My marks and scars I carry with me to be a witness for me, to Him who shall be rewarder."

✄

BILL CLINTON, OCT. 23, 1993, ON 200TH ANNIVERSARY OF CAPITOL & REINSTALLATION OF STATUE OF FREEDOM:

The hope still endures that in this country every man and woman without regard to race or religion or station in life would have the freedom to live up to the fullest of his or her God-given potential... that every citizen would get from Government not a guarantee but the promise of an opportunity...to have an equal chance, for the most humble and the most well born, to do what God meant for them to be able to do.

✄

BILL CLINTON, OCT. 23, 1993, B'NAI B'RITH 150TH ANNIVERSARY HAVDALAH, JEFFERSON MEMORIAL:

Jefferson...asked that on his tombstone it be printed only that he was the author of the Declaration of Independence, the founder of the University of Virginia, and perhaps most of all, the author of the Statute of Virginia for Religious Freedom...Jefferson understood that in the end, the deepest power of all in human affairs, the power of ideas and ideals. In words inscribed just up these steps on this memorial, he said, "Almighty God hath created the mind free..." That simple premise on which our first amendment is based is, I believe, the major reason why here in America more people believe in God, more people go to church or synagogue, more people put religion at the center of their lives than in any other advanced society on Earth.

✄

BILL CLINTON, NOV. 13, 1993, CONVOCATION OF CHURCH OF GOD IN CHRIST, MEMPHIS:

It will be my great honor to sign the restoration of religious freedoms act, a bill supported widely by people across all religions and political philosophies to put back the real meaning of the Constitution, to give you and every other American the freedom to do what is most important in your life, to worship God as your spirit leads you...Where there are no families, where there is no order, where there is no hope...who will be there to give structure, discipline, and love to these children? You must do that...Scripture say's, you are the salt of the Earth and the light of the world, that if your light shines before men they will give glow to the Father in heaven.

&

BILL CLINTON, NOV. 16, 1993, RELIGIOUS FREEDOM RESTORATION ACT:

It is interesting...what a broad coalition of Americans came together to make this bill a reality...a 97-to-3 vote in the United States Senate and...adopted on a voice vote in the House. I'm told that, as many of the people in the coalition worked together across ideological and religious lines, some new friendships were formed and some new trust was established, which shows, I suppose, that the power of God is such that even in the legislative process miracles can happen.

&

BILL CLINTON, NOV. 18, 1993, RADIO ADDRESS:

Our families will be gathering together for Thanksgiving to offer our gratitude to God for life's blessings. For all our difficulties, we live in a moment of peace and promise that would have gladdened the hearts of generations that came before us and justified their faith in the future.

&

BILL CLINTON, NOV. 27, 1993, RADIO ADDRESS:

My family celebrated Thanksgiving as most American families did. We gathered around a table filled with the bounty of our great country, and we thanked the Lord for all we have and all we can hope for.

&

BILL CLINTON, DEC. 7, 1993, HANUKKAH MESSAGE:

Hanukkah...the Festival of Lights, a joyous holiday that commemorates a miracle, is a fitting time to give thanks for the blessings of the past year...Hanukkah serves as a reminder that faith and perseverance can sustain us against the most difficult odds...The strong beliefs and confidence that brought victory to the Maccabees and eight days of light to the Temple can guide us as we face the momentous challenges of our times. The eternal lesson of Hanukkah-that faith gives us the strength to work miracles and find light in times of darkness-inspires all of us to strive toward a brighter future.

❧

BILL CLINTON, DEC. 9, 1993, LIGHTING CHRISTMAS TREE:

We are joined by simple and universal convictions: a shared faith, a shared joy, a shared commitment now to follow the directions of our faith, to love our neighbors as ourselves...That is something that would be perfectly consistent with the faith and the life we celebrate tonight, something we could take out of this Christmas season that would be the greatest gift we could ever give...God bless you all.

❧

BILL CLINTON, DEC. 22, 1993, ON GRANTS FOR HOMELESS:

What we're trying to do is take people who are battered and bruised and broken, but who still have a lot of God's grace left in them, and find a way to bring all that back to the surface and put their own lives back more in their control. I hope this new approach works...If it does, we will have given the American people a good Christmas present.

❧

BILL CLINTON, DEC. 25, 1993, RADIO ADDRESS:

Today Christians celebrate God's love for humanity made real in the birth of Christ in a manger almost 2,000 years ago. The humble circumstances of His birth, the example of His life, the power of His teachings inspire us to love and to care for our fellow men and women. On this day we should be especially grateful that here in America we all have the freedom to worship God in our own way, for our faith is purest when it is the offering of a free and joyous spirit....We can see the image of God reflected in our fellow men and women, whatever their creed or color.

❧

BILL CLINTON, DEC. 25, 1993, ON NORMAN VINCENT PEALE:

Dr. Peale was an optimist who believed that whatever the antagonisms and complexities of modern life brought us, that anyone could prevail by approaching life with a simple sense of faith. And he served us by instilling that optimism in every Christian and every other person who came in contact with his writings or his hopeful soul...

There is some poetry in his passing on a day when the world celebrates the birth of Christ, an idea that was central to Dr. Peale's message.

∽

BILL CLINTON, DEC. 15, 1994, CHRISTMAS MESSAGE:

The timeless story of a baby born in a manger amid humble surroundings is the fulfillment of a promise, an affirmation of faith. Jesus' birth demonstrates the infinite love of God. We celebrate the gift of His life, and Christmas softens our hearts and rekindles in us a sincere desire to reach out to others in peace and friendship. As we rejoice in the miracle of Christmas, we reflect on the Holy Family and draw strength from their example of faith. We are reminded that the bonds between parent and child, between husband and wife, and between neighbor and stranger are opportunities to answer Jesus' call to love one another, and we are reminded that one day we will be asked whether we lived out His love in ways that treated all of our brothers and sisters-even the least of them-as we would have treated Him. In holy Bethlehem and throughout the Middle East, ancient enemies are putting aside their differences and coming together in goodwill...We can all share in the fulfillment of the Christmas promise.

∽

BILL CLINTON, JUL. 12, 1995, JAMES MADISON HIGH SCHOOL:

The First Amendment does not require students to leave their religion at the schoolhouse door...It is especially important that parents feel confident that their children can practice religion...We need to make it easier and more acceptable for people to express and to celebrate their faith...If students can wear T-shirts advertising sports teams, rock groups or politicians, they can also wear T-shirts that promote religion...Religion is too important to our history and our heritage for us to keep it out of our schools...

Nothing in the First Amendment converts our public schools into religion-free zones or requires all religious expression to be left behind at the schoolhouse door...Government's schools also may not discriminate against private religious expression during the school day.

∽

BILL CLINTON, JAN. 20, 1997, 2ND INAUGURAL:

Our rich texture of racial, religious and political diversity will be a Godsend in the 21st Century...Like a prophet of old, he told of his dream, that one day America would rise up and treat all its citizens as equals before the law and in the heart. Martin Luther King's dream was the American Dream...From the height of this place and the summit of this century, let us go forth. May God strengthen our hands for the good work ahead - and always, always bless our America.

∽

BILL CLINTON, FEB. 4, 1997, STATE OF THE UNION:

One of the country's best-known pastors, Reverend Robert Schuller, suggested that I read Isaiah 58:12..."Thou shalt raise up the foundations of many generations, and thou shalt be called the repairer of the breach, the restorer of the paths to dwell in." I placed my hand on that verse when I took the oath of office, on behalf of all American, for no matter what our differences in our faiths, our backgrounds, our politics, we must all be repairers of the breach...We may not share a common past, but we surely do share a common future. Building one America is our most important mission, the foundation for many generations of every other strength we must build for this new century....My fellow Americans, we have work to do. Let us seize those days and the century. Thank you. God bless you. And God bless America.

∽

BILL CLINTON, DEC. 20, 1997, HANUKKAH MESSAGE:

The age-old struggle for religious freedom is not yet over. From the days of the ancient Maccabees down to our present time, tyrants have sought to deny people the free expression of their faith and the right to live according to their own conscience and convictions. Hanukkah symbolizes the heroic struggle of all who seek to defeat such oppression and the miracles that come to those full of faith and courage. This holiday holds special meaning for us in America, where freedom of religion is one of the cornerstones of our democracy...The coming year will mark the 50th anniversary of the State of Israel, where the story of the first Hanukkah took place so many centuries ago. As families come together in prayer for the eight nights of Hanukkah, to reaffirm their hope in God and their gratitude for his faithfulness to his people, may the candles of the menorah light our way to a true and lasting peace for the people of the Middle East.

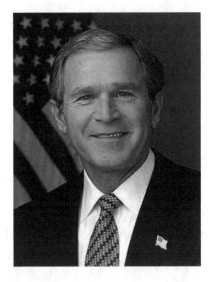

GEORGE W. BUSH

GEORGE W. BUSH, JAN., 20, 2001, 1ST INAUGURAL:

I will work to build a single nation of justice and opportunity. I know this is within our reach, because we are guided by a power larger than ourselves, Who creates us equal in His image...Compassion is the work of a nation, not just a government. And some needs and hurts are so deep they will only respond to a mentor's touch or a pastor's prayer. Church and charity, synagogue and mosque, lend our communities their humanity, and they will have an honored place in our plans and laws...I can pledge our nation to a goal: When we see that wounded traveler on the road to Jericho, we will not pass to the other side...As a saint of our times has said, every day we are called to do small things with great love.

∽

GEORGE W. BUSH, JAN., 20, 2001, 1ST INAUGURAL:

After the Declaration of Independence was signed, Virginia statesman John Page wrote to Thomas Jefferson: "We know the Race is not to the swift nor the Battle to the Strong. Do you not think an

Angel rides in the Whirlwind and directs this Storm?" Much time has passed since Jefferson arrived for his inaugural. The years and changes accumulate. But the themes of this day he would know: our nation's grand story of courage, and its simple dream of dignity.

We are not this story's Author, Who fills time and eternity with His purpose. Yet His purpose is achieved in our duty; and duty is fulfilled in service to one another...This work continues. This story goes on...And an angel still rides in the whirlwind and directs this storm. God bless you, and God bless America.

～

GEORGE BUSH, MAY 3, 2001, AMERICAN JEWISH COMMITTEE:
Our...deep American commitment to freedom of religion...was expressed early and eloquently by our first President, George Washington, in his famous letter to the Touro synagogue in Newport, Rhode Island..."The Government of the United States," he said, "which gives to bigotry no sanction, to persecution no assistance, requires only that they who live under its protection, should demean themselves as good citizens."

～

GEORGE BUSH, MAY 3, 2001, AMERICAN JEWISH COMMITTEE:
We view with special concern the intensifying attacks on religious freedom in China...The Chinese government continues to display an unreasonable and unworthy suspicion of freedom of conscience. The Chinese government restricts independent religious expression. We hear alarming reports of the detention of worshippers and religious leaders. Churches and mosques have been vandalized or demolished...religious practices in Tibet have long been the target of especially harsh and unjust persecution. And most recently, adherents of the Falun Gong spiritual movement...China aspires to national strength and greatness. But these acts of persecution are acts of...weakness. This persecution is...unworthy of all that China should become...

No one is a better witness to the transience of tyranny than the children of Abraham. Forty centuries ago, the Jewish people were entrusted with a truth more enduring than any power of man. In the words of the prophet Isaiah: "This shall be My covenant with them, said the Lord: My spirit which is upon you, and the words which I have placed in your mouth, shall not be absent from your mouth, nor from the mouth of your children, nor from the mouth of your children's children - said the Lord - from now on, for all time."

It is not an accident that freedom of religion is one of the central freedoms in our Bill of Rights. It is the first freedom of the human soul - the right to speak the words that God places in our mouths.

⊸

GEORGE W. BUSH, JUL. 3, 2001, INDEPENDENCE DAY:

Two hundred and twenty-five years ago, the signers of the Declaration of Independence boldly asserted that all are "created equal, that they are endowed by their Creator with certain unalienable Rights, that among these are Life, Liberty, and the pursuit of Happiness." With these words, the Signers announced the birth of a new Nation and put forth a vision of liberty and democracy that would forever alter history.

⊸

GEORGE W. BUSH, SEP. 11, 2001, NATIONAL ADDRESS:

Freedom itself was attacked this morning by a faceless coward, and freedom will be defended...Thousands of lives were suddenly ended by evil, despicable acts of terror. Pictures of planes flying into buildings, fires burning, huge structures collapsing have filled us with disbelief, terrible sadness and a quiet, unyielding anger...America was targeted...because we're the brightest beacon for freedom and opportunity in the world...I ask for your prayers for all those who grieve...And I pray they will be comforted by a power greater than any of us spoken through the ages in Psalm 23: "Even though I walk through the valley of the shadow of death, I fear no evil for you are with me."

⊸

GEORGE W. BUSH, SEP. 13, 2001, NATIONAL DAY OF PRAYER:

September 11, 2001, terrorists attacked America in a series of despicable acts of war. They hijacked four passenger jets, crashed two of them into the World Trade Center's twin towers and a third into the Headquarters of the U.S. Department of Defense at the Pentagon, causing great loss of life and tremendous damage. The fourth plane crashed in the Pennsylvania countryside...All our hearts have been seared by the sudden and sense-less taking of innocent lives. We pray for healing and for the strength to serve and encourage one another in hope and faith. Scripture says: "Blessed are those who mourn for they shall be comforted." I call on every American family and the family of America to observe a National Day of Prayer and Remembrance...In the face of all this evil, we remain strong and united, One Nation under God."

∽

GEORGE W. BUSH, SEP. 14, 2001, NATIONAL DAY OF PRAYER:
We come before God to pray for the missing and the dead, and for those who love them...our country was attacked with deliberate and massive cruelty...Our purpose as a nation is firm. Yet our wounds as a people are recent and unhealed, and lead us to pray. In many of our prayers this week, there is a searching...At St. Patrick's Cathedral in New York a woman said, "I prayed to God to give us a sign that He is still here."...God's signs are not always the ones we look for. We learn in tragedy that his purposes are not always our own. Yet the prayers of private suffering, whether in our homes or in this great cathedral, are known and heard, and understood...Prayers that yield our will to a will greater than our own.

∽

GEORGE W. BUSH, SEP. 14, 2001, NATIONAL DAY OF PRAYER:
This world He created is of moral design. On this national day of prayer and remembrance, we ask almighty God to watch over our nation, and grant us patience and resolve in all that is to come. We pray that He will comfort and console those who now walk in sorrow. We thank Him for each life we now must mourn, and the promise of a life to come. As we have been assured, neither death nor life, nor angels nor principalities nor powers, nor things present nor things to come, nor height nor depth, can separate us from God's love. May He bless the souls of the departed. May He comfort our own. And may He always guide our country. God bless America.

∽

GEORGE W. BUSH, SEP. 20, 2001, TO CONGRESS:
America was touched...to see Republicans and Democrats joined together on the steps of this Capitol singing "God Bless America."...America will never forget the sounds of our national anthem playing at Buckingham Palace, on the streets of Paris and at Berlin's Brandenburg Gate. We will not forget South Korean children gathering to pray outside our embassy in Seoul...The terrorists practice a fringe form of Islamic extremism...The terrorists' directive commands

them to kill Christians and Jews, to kill all Americans and make no distinctions among military and civilians, including women and children.

∾

GEORGE W. BUSH, SEP. 20, 2001, TO CONGRESS:

Afghanistan's people have been brutalized, many are starving and many have fled. Women are not allowed to attend school. You can be jailed for owning a television. Religion can be practiced only as their leaders dictate. A man can be jailed in Afghanistan if his beard is not long enough...Those who commit evil in the name of Allah blaspheme the name of Allah...Our enemy is a radical network of terrorists...They hate...our freedom of religion, our freedom of speech, our freedom to vote and assemble...They want to drive Israel out of the Middle East. They want to drive Christians and Jews out of vast regions of Asia and Africa...We're not deceived by their pretenses to piety...They are the heirs of all the murderous ideologies...sacrificing human life to serve their radical visions, by abandoning every value except the will to power, they follow in the path of fascism, Nazism and totalitarianism...Freedom and fear, justice and cruelty, have always been at war, and we know that God is not neutral between them...In all that lies before us, may God grant us wisdom and may he watch over the United States of America.

∾

GEORGE W. BUSH, NOV. 10, 2001, TO UNITED NATIONS:

In the Second World War, we learned there is no isolation from evil...That evil has returned...A few miles from here, many thousands still lie in a tomb of rubble...The suffering of September the 11th was inflicted on people of many faiths and many nations...The terrorists call their cause holy, yet they fund it with drug-dealing. They encourage murder and suicide...They dare to ask God's blessing as they set out to kill innocent men, women and children. But the God of Isaac and Ishmael would never answer such a prayer. And a murderer is not a martyr. He is just a murderer.

∾

GEORGE W. BUSH, NOV. 10, 2001, TO UNITED NATIONS:

Civilization itself...is threatened...The terrorists are increasingly isolated by their own hatred and extremism. They cannot hide behind Islam. The Taliban are now learning this lesson...Together they promote terror abroad and impose a reign of terror on the Afghan people. Women are executed in Kabul's soccer stadium. They can be beaten for wearing socks that are too thin. Men are jailed for missing prayer meetings. The United States, supported by many nations, is bringing justice to the terrorists in Afghanistan...We know that evil is real, but good will prevail against it...We have a chance to write the story of our times, a story of courage defeating cruelty and light overcoming darkness.

ᴥ

GEORGE W. BUSH, DEC. 6, 2001, CHRISTMAS MESSAGE

We will light the National Christmas Tree, a tradition Americans have been celebrating since 1923...Sixty years ago, less than three weeks after the attack on Pearl Harbor, Prime Minister Winston Churchill made an appearance with President Franklin Roosevelt to light the tree. Now, once again, we celebrate Christmas in a time of testing, with American troops far from home...It is worth recalling the words from a beautiful Christmas hymn-in the third verse of "Oh Holy Night" we sing, "His law is love, and His gospel is peace. Chains He shall break, for the slave is our brother. And in His name all oppression shall cease."

America seeks peace, and believes in justice. We fight only when necessary. We fight so that oppression may cease. And even in the midst of war, we pray for peace on Earth and goodwill to men.

ᴥ

GEORGE W. BUSH, DEC. 10, 2001, LIGHTING OF MENORAH:

Tonight, for the first time in American history, the Hanukkah menorah will be lit at the White House residence...The magnificent menorah before us was crafted over a century ago in the city of Lvov...The Jews of Lvov fell victim to the horror of the Nazi Holocaust, but their great menorah survived. And as God promised Abraham, the people of Israel still live. This has been a year of much sadness in the United States, and for our friends in Israel...But as we watch the lighting of this second candle of Hanukkah, we're reminded of the ancient story of Israel's courage and of the power of faith to make the darkness bright. We can see the heroic spirit of the Maccabees lives on in Israel today, and we trust that a better day is coming, when this Festival of Freedom will be celebrated in a world free from terror.

ᴥ

GEORGE W. BUSH, JAN. 15, 2002, RELIGIOUS FREEDOM DAY:

Religious freedom is a cornerstone of our Republic...Many of those who first settled in America, such as Pilgrims, came for the freedom of worship and belief that this new land promised. And when the British Colonies became the United States, our Founders constitutionally limited our Federal Government's capacity to interfere with religious belief...

Many miles from home, American service men and women have risked their lives in our efforts to drive the Taliban regime from power, ending an era of brutal oppression, including religious oppression. At home...in quiet prayers offered to God...Americans have shown a deep love for others...I urge all Americans to observe this day by asking for the blessing and protection of Almighty God for our Nation.

∽

GEORGE W. BUSH, JAN. 29, 2002, STATE OF THE UNION:

Evil is real, and it must be opposed. Beyond all differences of race or creed, we are one country, mourning together and facing danger together...Many have discovered again that even in tragedy-especially in tragedy-God is near. In a single instant, we realized that this will be a decisive decade in the history of liberty, that we've been called to a unique role in human events...Our enemies send other people's children on missions of suicide and murder. They embrace tyranny and death as a cause and a creed. We stand for a different choice, made long ago, on the day of our founding...We choose freedom and the dignity of every life...We have known freedom's price. We have shown freedom's power...We will see freedom's victory...May God bless.

∽

GEORGE W. BUSH, APR. 10, 2002, BANNING HUMAN CLONING:

All of us here today believe in the promise of modern medicine...and...of ethical medicine. As we seek to improve human life, we must always preserve human dignity. And therefore, we must prevent human cloning by stopping it before it starts...Advances in biomedical technology must never come at the expense of human conscience. As we seek what is possible, we must always ask what is right, and we must not forget that even the most noble ends do not justify any means...Life is a creation, not a commodity.

Our children are gifts to be loved and protected, not products to be designed and manufactured...All human cloning is wrong.

⋙

GEORGE W. BUSH, AUG. 6, 2002, SIGNING
BORN-ALIVE INFANTS PROTECTION ACT H.R. 2175:
The history of our country is the story of...a promise of life and liberty...and protection for the ignored and the weak...We extend the promise and protection to the most vulnerable members of our society...Every infant born alive-including an infant who survives an abortion procedure-is considered a person under federal law...The Born Alive Infants Protection Act establishes a principle in America law and American conscience: there is no right to destroy a child who has been born alive. A child who is born has intrinsic worth and must have the full protection of our laws...Unborn children are members of the human family...They reflect our image, and they are created in God's own image.

⋙

GEORGE W. BUSH, SEP. 4, 2002, PATRIOT DAY, 2002:
On this first observance of Patriot Day, we remember and honor those who perished in the terrorist attacks of September 11, 2001. We will not forget the events of that terrible morning nor will we forget how Americans responded in New York City, at the Pentagon, and in the skies over Pennsylvania-with heroism and selflessness; with compassion and courage; and with prayer and hope.

⋙

GEORGE W. BUSH, SEP. 6-8, 2002, NATIONAL PRAYER:
We remember the tragic events of September 11, 2001, and the thousands of innocent lives lost on that day...I ask all Americans to join together in cities, communities, neighborhoods, and places of worship to honor those who were lost, to pray for those who grieve, and to give thanks for God's enduring blessings on our land...The words of the Psalms brought comfort to many. We trust God always to be our refuge and our strength, an ever-present help in time of trouble. Believing that One greater than ourselves watches over our lives and over this Nation, we continue to place our trust in Him...I ask you to join me during these Days of Prayer and Remembrance in praying for God's continued protection and for the strength to overcome great evil with even greater good.

❧

GEORGE W. BUSH, NOV. 22, 2002, THANKSGIVING:

In celebration of Thanksgiving Day 1902, President Theodore Roosevelt wrote, "Rarely has any people enjoyed greater prosperity than we are now enjoying. For this we render heartfelt and solemn thanks to the Giver of Good; and we seek to praise Him - not by words only - but by deeds, by the way in which we do our duty to ourselves and to our fellow men." ...As the Pilgrims did almost four centuries ago, we gratefully give thanks...We also thank God for the blessings of freedom and prosperity; and, with gratitude and humility, we acknowledge the importance of faith in our lives.

❧

GEORGE W. BUSH, NOV. 26, 2002, HANUKKAH MESSAGE:

For eight days and nights, Hanukkah commemorates the rededication of the Holy Temple in Jerusalem and the ancient story of Israel's courageous faith. In a victorious struggle against their oppressors, the Maccabees heroically overcame enormous odds to liberate the ancient kingdom of Israel. Hanukkah reminds us that faith can give us the strength to overcome oppression. Today, the spirit of the Maccabees continues to live and thrive among the Jewish people and in the State of Israel.

During the eight days of Hanukkah, Jews throughout the world gather with family and friends to rejoice and celebrate. Each night, they light a branch of the menorah to commemorate the miracle of the lamp that, with only enough oil for one day, burned in the ancient Temple for eight days. The festival of lights culminates on the eighth night when all the candles burn in unity, symbolizing the eternal light of the Temple and the long-standing struggle of the Jewish people against adversity. Americans join in thanking God for our blessings and renew our commitment to the values of faith, family, and community.

❧

GEORGE W. BUSH, DEC. 4, 2002, AT MENORAH LIGHTING:

This holiday marks the victory of Jewish patriots over oppression more than two millennia ago...Each year, Hanukkah brings a message of hope - that light will overcome darkness, that goodness will overcome evil, and that faith can accomplish miracles...The spirit of those early patriots lives in the lives of the state of Israel and throughout the Jewish community, and among all brave people who fight violence and terror. We pray that this season of light will also be a season of peace for the Jewish people...I also want to thank Congregation Rodeph Shalom in Philadelphia for the use of this beautiful menorah. Founded in 1795, Rodeph Shalom was the first Ashkenazic congregation established in the Western Hemisphere.

※

GEORGE W. BUSH, DEC. 5, 2002, CHRISTMAS TREE LIGHTING:
God's love is found in humble places, and God's peace is offered to all of us....For nearly 80 years, in times of calm and in times of challenge, Americans have gathered for this ceremony. The simple story we remember during this season speaks to every generation. It is the story of a quiet birth in a little town, on the margins of an indifferent empire. Yet that single event set the direction of history and still changes millions of lives. For over two millennia, Christmas has carried the message that God is with us - and, because He's with us, we can always live in hope...The men and women in the military, many of whom will spend this Christmas at posts far from home...stand between Americans and grave danger. They serve in the cause of peace and freedom.

※

GEORGE W. BUSH, DEC. 20, 2002, CHRISTMAS MESSAGE:
During Christmas, we gather with family and friends to celebrate the birth of our Savior, Jesus Christ. As God's only Son, Jesus came to Earth and gave His life so that we may live. His actions and His words remind us that service to others is central to our lives and that sacrifice and unconditional love must guide us and inspire us to lead lives of compassion, mercy, and justice...As we share love and enjoy the traditions of this holiday, we are also grateful for the men and women of our Armed Forces who are working to defend freedom, secure our homeland, and advance peace and safety around the world. This Christmas, may we give thanks for the blessings God has granted to our Nation.

※

GEORGE W. BUSH, JAN. 28, 2003, STATE OF THE UNION:
There's power, wonder-working power, in the goodness and idealism and faith of the American people...doing the work of compassion

every day-visiting prisoners, providing shelter for battered women, bringing companionship to lonely seniors...Our nation is blessed with recovery programs that do amazing work. One of them is...the Healing Place Church in Baton Rouge, Louisiana. A man in the program said, "God does miracles in people's lives, and you never think it could be you."

∽

GEORGE W. BUSH, JAN. 28, 2003, STATE OF THE UNION:

I ask you to protect infants at the very hour of their birth and end the practice of partial-birth abortion. And because no human life should be started or ended as the object of an experiment, I ask you to set a high standard for humanity, and pass a law against all human cloning....Our founders dedicated this country to the cause of human dignity, the rights of every person, and the possibilities of every life. This conviction leads us into the world to help the afflicted, and defend the peace, and confound the designs of evil men.

∽

GEORGE W. BUSH, JAN. 28, 2003, STATE OF THE UNION:

The liberty we prize is not America's gift to the world, it is God's gift to humanity. We Americans have faith in ourselves, but not in ourselves alone...Placing our confidence in the loving God behind all of life, and all of history. May He guide us now. And may God continue to bless the United States of America.

∽

GEORGE W. BUSH, FEB. 1, 2003, ON SPACE SHUTTLE TRAGEDY:

The Columbia is lost; there are no survivors...These astronauts knew the dangers, and they faced them willingly, knowing they had a high and noble purpose in life...In the skies today we saw destruction and tragedy. Yet farther than we can see there is comfort and hope. In the words of the prophet Isaiah, "Lift your eyes and look to the heavens. Who created all these? He who brings out the starry hosts one by one and calls them each by name. Because of His great power and mighty strength, not one of them is missing." The same Creator who names the stars also knows the names of the seven souls we mourn today. The crew of the shuttle Columbia did not return safely to Earth; yet we can pray that all are safely home...May God continue to bless America.

∽

GEORGE W. BUSH, FEB. 7, 2003, PRAYER BREAKFAST:
Admiral Clark, whatever prayer you used for eloquence, worked...I'm particularly grateful to Lisa Beamer...I appreciate her example of faith made stronger in trial. In the worst moments of her life, Lisa has been a model of grace -her own, and the grace of God...Since we met last year, millions of Americans have been led to prayer...Many, including me, have been on bended knee...

Faith gives the assurance that our lives and our history have a moral design...Once we have recognized God's image in ourselves, we must recognize it in every human being...Faith shows us the reality of good, and the reality of evil...It is always, and everywhere, wrong to target and kill the innocent...to be cruel and hateful, to enslave and oppress. It is always, and everywhere, right to be kind and just, to protect the lives of others, and to lay down your life for a friend...Faith shows us the way to self-giving, to love our neighbor as we would want to be loved ourselves...

For half a century now, the National Prayer Breakfast has been a symbol of the vital place of faith in the life of our nation...Tremendous challenges await this nation, and there will be hardships ahead. Faith will not make our path easy, but it will give us strength for the journey...May God bless you, and may God continue to bless America.

ન્જ

GEORGE W. BUSH, APR. 17, 2003, EASTER MESSAGE:
Easter is the most important event of the Christian faith, when people around the world join together with family and friends to celebrate the Resurrection of Jesus Christ, the Son of God and the hope of life to come. For Christians, the life and death of Jesus are the ultimate expressions of love, and the supreme demonstrations of God's mercy, faithfulness, and redemption. Since Christ's miraculous Resurrection on Easter, more than 2,000 years ago, Christians have expressed joy and gratitude for this wondrous sacrifice and for God's promise of freedom for the oppressed, healing for the brokenhearted, and salvation...During this holy time, may Christ's example of love and sacrifice compel us towards justice and compassion.

ન્જ